GREEK RHETORICAL ORIGINS OF CHRISTIAN FAITH

Greek Rhetorical Origins of Christian Faith

An Inquiry

JAMES L. KINNEAVY

New York Oxford
OXFORD UNIVERSITY PRESS
1987

Oxford University Press

Oxford New York Toronto
Delhi Bombay Calcutta Madras Karachi
Petaling Jaya Singapore Hong Kong Tokyo
Nairobi Dar es Salaam Cape Town
Melbourne Auckland

and associated companies in
Beirut Berlin Ibadan Nicosia

Published by Oxford University Press, Inc.,
200 Madison Avenue, New York, New York 10016

Library of Congress Cataloging-in-Publication Data
Kinneavy, James L.
Greek rhetorical origins of Christian faith.
Bibliography: p. Includes index.
1. Faith—History of doctrines—Early church, ca. 30–600.
2. Pistis (The Greek word) 3. Bible. N.T.—Criticism,
interpretation, etc. 4. Rhetoric, Ancient. I. Title.
BT771.2.K53 1987 234'.2 85-15266
ISBN 0-19-503735-9

Grateful acknowledgment to the publishers for permission to reprint from the following:
The New English Bible, © The Delegates of the Oxford University Press
and The Syndics of the Cambridge University Press 1961, 1970; and
Theological Dictionary of the New Testament, Vol. I, IV, VI, Berhard Kittel,
Gerhard Friedrich, editors, copyright © 1968 by Wm. B. Eerdmans Pub. Co.

1 3 5 7 9 8 6 4 2

Printed in the United States of America
on acid-free paper

To Father William Joseph Rooney,
who first taught me rhetoric

Acknowledgments

Barth, Karl. *Church Dogmatics*. Trans. G. T. Thomson. Edinburgh: T. & T. Clark, 1936. I, IV

Buber, Martin. *Two Types of Faith*. Trans. Norman P. Goldhawk, M.A. London: Macmillan, 1951.

Bultmann, Rudolf. "Pisteūo." *Theological Dictionary of the New Testament (TDNT)*. Ed. Gerhard Kittel. Ed. and trans. in English, Geoffrey Bromiley. Grand Rapids, Mich.: William B. Eerdmans, 1964–1976. VI.

Daube, David. "Rabbinic Methods of Interpretation and Hellenistic Rhetoric." *Hebrew Union College Annual*, 22 (1940): 239–264.

Hengel, Martin. *Judaism and Hellenism: Studies in Their Encounter in Palestine During the Early Hellenistic Period*. Trans. John Bowden. Philadelphia: Fortress Press, 1974. I, II.

Jacobs, Louis. *Faith*. London: Valentine, Mitchell, 1968.

Jones, A. H. M. *The Greek City from Alexander to Justinian*. Oxford: Clarendon Press, 1940.

Kennedy, George. *The Art of Rhetoric in the Roman World*. Princeton, N.J.: Princeton University Press, 1972.

Marrou, Henri I. *Histoire de l'éducation dans l'antiquité*. 6th ed. Rev. and enlarged. Paris: Editions du Seuil, 1965.

———. *A History of Education in Antiquity*. Trans. George Lamb. London: Sheed and Ward, 1956.

Pélékidis, Chrysis. *Histoire de l'éphébie attique des origines à 31 ans avant Jesus*. Paris: Editions E. de Boccard, 1962.
Rengstorf, Karl Heinrich. "Didaskō." *TDNTS*. II.
Schürer, Emil. *The History of the Jewish People in the Age of Jesus (175 B.C. to A.D. 135)*. English version rev. and ed. Geza Vermes, Fergus Millar, and Matthew Black; original trans. John MacPherson. Edinburgh: T. & T. Clark, 1979. I, II.
Tcherikover, Victor. *Hellenistic Civilization and the Jews*. Trans. S. Applebaum. Philadelphia: Jewish Publication Society of America, 1959.
Williamson, Ronald. *Philo and the Epistle to the Hebrews*. Leiden: E. J. Brill, 1970.

Contents

Illustrations

GREEK RHETORICAL ORIGINS OF CHRISTIAN FAITH

CHAPTER I

An Old Thesis and a New Hypothesis

A Strange Juxtaposition

The juxtaposition of "Greek rhetoric" and "Christian faith" may seem a trifle bizarre, maybe even irreverent—the two notions appear somewhat distant. Yet if we remember that rhetoric is the art of persuasion and that the Greek word for persuasion was *pistis* and that the Christian word for faith was also *pistis,* the embodiment of both meanings in the same word suggests that the two notions may not be too far apart. Indeed, in Liddell and Scott, the first meaning of *pistis* conjoins the two concepts: "trust in others, *faith* . . . generally *persuasion* of a thing, confidence, assurance."[1] And both meanings persisted from the seventh and sixth centuries B.C. through the times of classical and Hellenistic Greek and into the period of the church fathers. In other words, a user of Greek in the first century A.D. would ordinarily be aware of the two meanings of the word. But for the typical Christian today, born in a family that for generations may have adhered to, say Catholicism or Lutheranism, there is usually no sense of persuasion in his or her concept of faith. Ordinarily only converts today experience the persuasive notion of faith, because they have to change beliefs.

Yet no scholar, as far as I am aware, has seriously viewed rhetoric as a possible origin, source, or analogue of the Christian concept of faith. Indeed, as we shall see, most authorities agree that it is difficult to posit any definitive source for some of the major features of the Christian notion of faith. It is not Jewish, and it is not Greek, nor does it derive from the mystery religions of the time. This is what I call the old thesis, and I will examine it in the next section of this chapter. Indeed, the origin of faith is clearly a part of what Harnack "rightly called the great historical riddle of the beginnings of Christianity."[2]

It is my contention, on the contrary, that many of the major features of the concept of persuasion, as embodied in Greek rhetoric of the Hellenistic period, are semantically quite close to the Christian notion of faith. I contend further that the writers of the New Testament were, in all probability, aware of these rapprochements. And, finally, I contend that a majority of the texts in the New Testament that mention *pistis* as faith can be read with a rhetorical interpretation. This is my new hypothesis. Why it is new and has not been proposed before will be briefly explained in the third section of this chapter. Why the hypotheses may make a small contribution toward the partial solution of the riddle of Harnack is the subject of the rest of the book.

A FEW DISCLAIMERS

Frank Kermode remarked at the outset of his study of narrative in Mark that he was an outsider and a secular in the field.[3] I would like to make a similar disclaimer. I am not a professional theologian, nor have I had the linguistic background that such a profession implies—like Shakespeare, I have small Latin and less Greek. However, I have some interest in historical rhetoric as well as in its relevance to the rise and spread of Christianity.

This study is, in the main, a rhetorical study. I am attempting to apply to a set of religious texts the rhetorical techniques that are currently being applied to other types of texts—political, literary, commercial, educational, and so on. I believe, frankly, that both religion and rhetoric should benefit from such an study. Before we get into the semantic, historical, and analytical details of the study, however, let us look at the old thesis a little more carefully. Then let me suggest why my new hypothesis is novel.

The Old Thesis

REPUDIATION OF OLD TESTAMENT ORIGINS

Most Christian and some Jewish authorities agree that, although some elements of the Christian notion can be seen in the Old Testament, what is called faith in the Old Testament and what is called faith in the New Testament are quite different concepts. Nearly all the authorities agree on some similaritites and on one difference, but they do emphasize other facets also. Let us survey a few of these analyses.

D. M. Baillie's *Faith in God and Its Christian Consummation*, published in 1927, is one of the recognized classics in this area. The structure of his chapter on sources is quite similar to many others. After an introductory section, he examines the Old Testament, then classical Greek sources, and later rabbinical and Hellenistic sources, and he concludes that the Christian notion did not come from either Jewish or Greek analogues. He posits a hypothetical reader coming to the Old Testament from the New Testament and expecting to find faith "mentioned on almost every page."[4]

> But what he would really find is—to put it roughly and broadly—that the Old Testament never mentions faith at all. That is to say, it contains no word which can quite fairly be so translated. Even the English reader will soon make that discovery. In the Authorized Version he will find the word "faith" only twice, and a little investigation will reveal the fact that in both cases the real meaning is probably "good faith" in the sense of "faithfulness."[5]

After considering both cases, Baillie continues thus:

> It does not seem likely that faith, in the sense of belief or trust in God, is intended. The Hebrew noun here used, and its cognate nouns, never seem in the Old Testament to have that meaning, nor is there (Semitic scholars tell us) any other Hebrew noun by which that meaning could be expressed.[6]

He surveys some of the important statements on faith in the Old Testament (particularly in relation to Abraham), in Isaiah, and in the Psalms. He finds a strong refrain of faith viewed as trust in God. But the combination of trust with belief he does not find.[7] Trust he calls the moral element of faith, and belief he calls the intellectual element, and he particularly does not find this second element in the Old Testament.[8] The distinction of at least these two elements in faith is one that we will see repeatedly in the sequel. The melding of the two into one concept of faith Baillie does not find in the Old Testament. Because this is characteristic of faith in the New Testament, he concludes, "It is not in the Old Testament, but in the New, that we read of *faith* [*his italics*]."[9]

It is, therefore, somewhat surprising that the New Testament writers have both a common word and a fairly common notion:

> What we have to notice is the remarkable outcropping of this idea in *all* parts of the New Testament alike. That body of early Christian literature doubtless reflects different types of Christianity as well as different temperaments. But the deeper one goes into it, the more one is impressed by its deeper unity [*his italics*].[10]

The title of William Henry Paine Hatch's work, *The Pauline Idea of Faith in Its Relation to Jewish and Hellenistic Religion* (1917), admirably reflects his book's structure and thesis. A chapter on Jewish influence and a chapter on Greek influence both reveal no ancestry for the full Christian idea. In between, Hatch devotes a chapter to Paul's concept of faith.

Like Baillie, whom he influenced, Hatch traces the notion of trust in the Old Testament.[11] Unlike Baillie, however, he restricts Jesus' notion of faith to the idea of trust.[12] The change came after Jesus, he maintains:

> When we pass from Jesus to the community of believers which was formed in Jerusalem after his death and resurrection, we are at once conscious that *pistis* is no longer simple trust in God; for the idea of conviction or belief now predominates over that of trust in both the substantive *pistis* and the verb *pisteuein.*[13]

The belief centered on the Resurrection, the messiahship of Jesus, and His speedy return to inaugurate the Kingdom of God.[14] Thus, Hatch concludes this chapter with "the faith of the Christians centered in Jesus as Lord and Messiah, and it was primarily intellectual in character.[15]

Hatch returns at several instances in his discussion of Paul to the complex character of faith—to its intellectual, emotional, volitional, and ethical facets.[16]

The distinction between belief and trust, as made by Baillie and Hatch, is continued by a much more contemporary author, Edward D. O'Connor, a Catholic who in 1961 wrote *Faith in the Synoptic Gospels: A Problem in the Correlation of Scripture and Theology*. He finds in the distinction the historical difference between Catholics and Protestants, with the former emphasizing the intellectual assent and the latter stressing the volitional and emotional aspects of faith.[17] The emphases are now blurring, he contends.[18] Like Baillie and Hatch, he says that "The faith spoken of in the Hebrew Old Testament consisted essentially of trust in Yahweh."[19] He traces this usage in the Old Testament and even in some uncharacteristic passages in the New Testament.[20] The remainder of his book is a careful attempt to show the relationship of the two elements of intellectual belief and emotional trust in the Synoptic Gospels. O'Connor obviously sees much more of the intellectual element in the Synoptics than did Hatch.

This same disjunction is upheld in a quite different context by Louis Jacobs, whose analysis of Jewish faith in 1968, *Faith*, maintains that the intellectual element was only added to Jewish faith in the Middle Ages. He distinguishes between belief *that*, which is "primarily a matter of the intellect," and belief *in*, which is "primarily a matter of the moral will:[21]

> As for the Biblical authors so for the Rabbis *emunah* is "belief *in* . . . ," never "belief *that*. . . . "George Foot Moore, after surveying the references to faith in early Rabbinic literature, rightly says: "In conclusion it may not be superfluous to remark that the words for faith in the literature and thought of this age are not used in the concrete sense of creed, beliefs entertained—or to be entertained—about God."[22]

Jacobs contends that it would never have occurred to the Biblical authors or the early rabbis to attempt to prove God's existence. Even in the early Middle Ages, when the notion of Jewish faith was beginning to change, there was resistance to the new element:

> When the famous Jewish mediaeval philosopher, Moses Maimonides (1135–1204), understood the first of the Ten Commandments as a command to believe that there is a God he was severely criticized on the ground that such a command is logically absurd. If belief is present no command is necessary. If it is absent, there is no one to do the commanding. But, apart from this, there cannot be a command to believe that there is a God because "belief *that* . . ."cannot be commanded.[23]

Eventually, in the Middle Ages, belief *that* became the dominant element in the Jewish notion of faith.

> For "faith" (*emunah*) has now become identified with the belief *that* there is a God. The tensions of faith were shifted from the moral and volitional to the cognitive. . . .
>
> More and more in this peroid *bittanon* ("trust"), used in both Bible and Talmud as a synonym for *emunah* ("faith"), came to be used on its own to denote the trusting aspect of faith, with *emunah* reserved for the new meaning of "belief *that* . . . ."[24]

It is clear that Jacobs supports the position of Baillie, Hatch, and O'Connor: The intellectual element of faith was not a critical element of the concept in the Old Testament. Two other scholars confirm this position, but their analyses are considerably more complex in that both move beyond the dualism we have been considering up until now. Both occur in the *Theological Dictionary of the New Testament* in the article on *pistis* and related terms. Bultmann wrote most of the article, but the most thorough analysis of the Old Testament concept of faith was written by A. Weiser.[25]

Weiser begins his section of the article in this way:

> If very generally faith is regarded as man's relation and attitude to God, the OT statements regarding it are not of primary importance. For the most part anthropological interest is here secondary to the theocentric one. As the OT understands it, faith is always man's reaction to God's primary action.[26]

Nevertheless, Weiser analyzes in careful detail human reactive responses; they constitute the individual's relation to God. These relations Weiser epitomizes in two emotions.

> A consideration of faith in the OT cannot overlook the astonishing fact that two basically different and even contradictory

> groups of meaning are used for man's relation to God, namely, fear on the one side and trust on the other. They were felt to be contradictory right up to the later period, and yet they were close, and even shaded into one another, so that fear of God could often be quite simply an expression for faith.[27]

It is obvious that with fear and trust we are in the realm of the emotional, not the predominantly rational. In this sense, Weiser's exceptionally perceptive analysis can be viewed as a support for the disjunction we have been considering—belief *that* and belief *in,* to use the terminology of Jacobs. Nevertheless, Weiser qualifies the distinction and introduces other elements.

For reasons that are not clear, Weiser chooses, in his analysis, to limit himself to the references of trust although he states, "Fear and trust are used more or less equally for the relationship to God (about 150 times each)."[28] In the trust references, Weiser focuses on those having to do with hope (*emunah*). This is the word that is translated as *pisteuein* (in different forms) in the Septuagint. It means "to say Amen with all of the consequences for both sub[ject] and obj[ject]." It means taking cognizance of a matter and accepting it as true and being aware of a relation to the matter. Thus, it can come to mean the individual's total relation to God. As such, it can emphasize knowledge or feeling or will, depending on the situation.[29]

Of all the trust words, those related to the root *emunah* eventually absorbed the other trust words and became the central concept in the Hebrew concept of faith, according to Weiser.[30] He analyzes the other stems relating to security, shelter and refuge, and expectation, particularly in Isaiah.[31] He also shows the deepening centrality of hope and the convergence of the several roots linguistically, historically, and theologically.[32]

Rudolf Bultmann's article on *pistis* in the *Theological Dictionary of the New Testament* is certainly a major statement on the nature of faith, and we will return to it many times. He first points to some important continuing motifs from the Old Testament and Judaism in the Christian concept: belief in God's word, obedience, trust, hope, and faithfulness.[33] Nonetheless, he concludes that *pisteuō* itself is not a religious term in the Septuagint.[34]

Specifically Christian notes added to the Old Testament concept of faith are belief in the Christian message; belief in the salvation wrought by Christ; a personal relationship to Christ; the sense of believing as a conversion or an adherence; and, on occasion, a metaphoric substitution of the things believed for belief as such.[35] Particularly important is the new emphasis on the Word of God.

> The Word of God, however, has taken on a different character. . . . It is no longer related to God's work in the sense that on the basis of this work it demands faithfulness and obedience, or promises God's work in the future. It is now related to God's deed in the sense that this deed is disclosed only in the Word.
>
> In the OT the righteous (in faithfulness and obedience) believe in God on the basis of His acts. They do not need to believe the acts themselves, since these are plain to see in the history of His people. . . . In the NT, however, it is precisely God's act which has to be believed. For what is plain to see is the life of Jesus which He lived on earth in servant-form, and which ended on the *stauros* [cross]. It is not evident that the folly of the cross is the divine wisdom, that the crucified Jesus is the risen and ascended Lord, that what happened to Him is the divine act of salvation. This has to be brought to light in the Word of proclamation. Hence one may even say that God's act is His Word, so that John—making this deduction—can describe Jesus as the Logos, the Word. On this basis *pisteuein tō logō tou theou* becomes *pisteuein eis Christon* [to believe the word of God becomes to believe in Christ].[36]

To many of these aspects of faith, especially to the notions of conversion, of the content of faith, and of the emphasis on the word rather than the act, we shall return. It is clear, however, that Bultmann, while recognizing some elements of faith as coming from the Old Testament, sees critical distinctions between these and New Testament faith. He, therefore, confirms the general opinion that some aspects of the Christian notion of faith did not originate in the Old Testament.

In particular, *pistis* and *pisteuein* in the Old Testament are not religious terms and do not correspond to the New Testament *faith* and *to believe* in any full sense at all. *Pistis* in the Old Testament is not usually even analyzed because a quick look at any concordance of the Septuagint shows that there are only 29 instances in it translated from the Hebrew (the others are in books of Greek language origin written by Hebrews but not incorporated into the Hebrew Old Testament canon).[37] Of the 29, 21 relate to the sense of loyalty, truth, and honesty, and of these only 3 have any religious connection at all, and these 3 have nothing to do with faith. It is noteworthy, for instance, that none of these occurrences is translated "faith" in the Oxford translation, *The New English Bible with the Apocrypha* (see note 37). Six others come from the same root in Hebrew, one meaning "faithful, true, secure." Only one of these is translated "faith" in the Oxford translation (Prov. 3: 3): "Let your good faith and loyalty never fail." The others all come from separate Hebrew originals and have nothing to do with faith. It is clear that *pistis* in the Septuagint is not related to the Christian concept.

In contrast to *pistis,* the verb *pisteuein* has been thoroughly analyzed by both Weiser and Bultmann. We have already seen the results of their analysis. Bultmann's conclusion is that "pisteuein . . . was not felt to be a religious term" in the Septuagint.[38] Weiser's analysis focuses, as we have seen, on the centrality of the verbs of hope. These are relevant to, but not at all equivalent to, the New Testament notion of faith.

REPUDIATION OF GREEK ORIGINS

There is a certain symmetry in the consideration of the Greek versus the Hebrew origins of the notion of faith. Whereas the Hebrews did not have a word, they certainly had some of the important concepts that were to go into the Christian notion. The Greeks, on the contrary, had the word but not, maintain most of the authorities, the component concepts. Consequently, the attempt on the part of the scholars who repudiate a Greek origin is to deny any significant religious sense to the notion of *pistis* in literary, philosophical, and religious terminology. Three of these scholars we have already seen in the Hebrew repudiation: Baillie, Hatch, and Bultmann. We will add a fourth and more recent scholar, Dieter Lührmann.

Baillie looks at the lyric poets, at the tragedians, at the historians, at Socrates, and, finally, at Plato. He concludes:

> When Plato depreciated *faith* as contrasted with knowledge, he was doubtless using the word in a different sense from that which it had later in the vocabulary of religion. But the fact remains that classical Greek had no word, and required none, to express what we mean by faith . . . whereas in another environment, that of Hebraic-Christian piety, the word *pistis* naturally and inevitably came to be the name for the very central element in religion. The truth is that in the religious life and thought of ancient Greece (though it possessed a suitable word, and the Hebrew language did not), the idea of faith never emerged into clear consciousness at all.[39]

Hatch's survey is more comprehensive. He looks at the religions in Greece and Italy, at the mysteries, at the mystery cults, at Stoicism, at demonology and magic, and, finally, at Philo of Alexandria. His conclusion is this:

Religion in the Greco-Roman world took two fundamentally different forms—the state religions and the mystery cults. The former were public worships sanctioned

> by tradition and custom, and the latter were personal religions in which the sacramental principle and the assurance of bliss in the world to come were the prominent features. The mystic believed in the god or goddess of his cult, and was full of trust and confidence concerning the future; but his religious life was not based upon faith. Moreover, the ideal of the initiate was identification with the deity, whereas in Paul it is control by Christ or the Spirit and divinization without identification or fusion with Christ. Philo of Alexandria, who seems to have been influenced in this respect by the religious teaching of the Stoics, gave to the Old Testament idea of faith or trust as it appears in the LXX a mystical meaning; but it is highly improbable that Philo's conception of faith in any way affected Paul's view of it. Faith is occasionally mentioned in certain magical writings; but it is here of secondary importance, being regarded as inferior to knowledge, which was the all-important concern in such circles. Neither the philosophers nor the teachers of morals made any use of faith as a principle of faith or a source of goodness.[40]

Bultmann's survey is much more comprehensive than either of these two although it is more concise. Yet there are many more classical and Hellenistic references. He concludes as follows after the classical survey:

> The words in *pist-* did not become religious terms in classical Greek. It is true that faithfulness to a compact is a religious duty. . . . *Pisunos,* which means the same as *pistos* in the sense of "trusting," can have the deity as object. . . . *Apistos* = "unbelieving" can also carry a reference to deity . . . But in no sense is *pistos* used for the true religious relationship to God or for the basic religious attitude of man. Nor did *pistis* become a religious term. . . . Again, there are only the first beginnings of religious use in respect of *pisteuein, apistein* and *apistia.*[41]

The picture changed somewhat in the Hellenistic period, according to Bultmann. In philosophic discussions about atheism, both *pistis* and *pisteuein* could refer to belief and piety toward God. And in the mystery religions and in the area of magic, as well as in early Gnosticism, *pistis* took on religious overtones.[42] Stoicism also gave a somewhat religious meaninig to *pistis* and its derivates.[43]

We shall have more to say about Bultmann's coverage of *pistis* in the Hellenistic period in the second part of the present chapter. At present, suffice it to say that the weight of Bultmann's scholarship was added to the earlier work of Hatch and Baillie to confirm the repudiation of classical and even Hellenistic Greek as a source for the Christian notion. The general argument is that in Greek thought *pistis,* with a few exceptions in late Hellenistic writers, was not a religious term.

Dieter Lührmann is expressly concerned with the Hellenistic sources that Bultmann had used, some of which he had drawn from Richard Reitzenstein's *Hellenistic Mystery Religions: Their Basic Ideas and Significance* (first published in 1910).[44] He carefully examines the references that Reitzenstein had used to assert that *pistis* was a common religious Hellenistic concept; he then examines those that Bultmann had added. He rejects them as establishing anything like a common usage.[45] He also rejects a usage coming from the field of legal speech of the time.[46]

Rather than look for a pagan source for the Christian concept, Lührmann examines Hebrew authors writing in Greek in the Hellenistic period, particularly Philo, the translator of Jesus Sirach, the Wisdom of Solomon, and IV Macabees.[47] He finds that these authors show the increasing importance of *pistis* as a dominating virtue in religion. He next examines texts in the Old Testament that point in this direction. Then he concludes:

> The stronger emergence of faith in the Greek Sirach-Translation, in the Sapientia, in IV Macabees and in Philo corresponds therefore to a similar proceeding among non-Greek speaking Jews.[48]

Consequently, "[e]arly Christianity is clearly therefore linked to Judaism when it makes *pistis* its central concept."[49] It is in the internal speech of Judaic tradition, not in a coming to terms with the heathen world, that the horizon for understanding the early Christian speech about faith must be sought.[50]

Lührmann, therefore, weakens the not-too-strong link with Hellenistic thought that Bultmann and Reitzenstein had established. In so doing, he aligns himself with the position of Gerhard Ebeling, which he had announced at the beginning of his article, namely, that "faith" is not simply a general religious phenomenological category, but was exclusively coined to belong to the Christian language tradition.[51] Ebeling, therefore, could also be added to the list of those denying a Greek origin, almost on general principles. He has stated rather explicitly:

> Christian faith is not a special faith, but simply faith. Admittedly, as a preliminary thesis, this is much less illuminating. But the history of the word "faith" indicates that we are not dealing with a religious word of universal occurrence, but that the concept of faith comes from the Old Testament, and obtained in Christianity its central and decisive significance.[52]

A major exception to the second half of the traditional thesis, that of a denial of the Greek origin of the concept of faith, is the position of Martin Buber. Buber agrees with Hatch, Baillie, O'Connor, and Jacobs in categorically distinguishing between the kind of faith built on trust and that based on belief. Indeed, Buber begins his book *Two Types of Faith* (first published in German in 1950) with some strong statements that make the distinction between trust and faith more categoric and exhaustive. He says:

> The subject with which I am concerned in this book is the twofold meaning of faith.
>
> There are two, and in the end only two, types of faith.
>
> To be sure there are very many contents of faith, but we only know faith itself in two basic forms. Both can be understood from the simple data of our life; the one from the fact that I

> trust someone, without being able to offer sufficient reasons for my trust in him; the other from the fact that, likewise without being able to give a sufficient reason, I acknowledge a thing to be true. In both cases my not being able to give a sufficient reason is not a matter of defectiveness in my ability to think, but of a real peculiarity in my relationship to the one whom I trust or to that which I acknowledge to be true.[53]

The first type of faith has as its classic example the faith of the Old Testament and of Judaism. It consists in a "perseverance in trust in the guiding and covenanting Lord, trusting perseverance in the contact with Him."[54] It involves the whole person, and for this reason, it embodies the emotional aspect of trust. The second type is not based on an original contract; it is not a "matter of persisting-in but its opposite, the facing-about."[55] Although it is not wholly intellectual, its foundation is intellectual, and it had its origin in Greek thought.[56] Judaic faith, on the contrary, had its origin in the Old Testament.[57] Judaic faith was tribal, was based on a preexisting contract, and involved the entire person; Christian faith, especially in Paul, was individual, based on decision and conversion, and fundamentally, though not completely, intellectual.[58]

Eventually, Buber comes to use two different words for these two types of faith. He calls the first *emunah,* from the Hebrew word for trust; and he calls the second *pistis,* from the Greek word for persuasion or faith.[59] Buber's entire book consists in contrasts of these two types of faith. He aligns Jesus with the Judaic notion and continually contrasts Jesus' notion of faith to that of Paul. He notices the difficulty inherent in a faith that is fundamentally rational:

> Christian Pistis was born outside the historical experiences of nations, so to say in retirement from history, in the souls of individuals, to whom the challenge came to believe that a man crucified in Jerusalem was their saviour. Although this faith, in its very essence, was able to raise itself to a piety of utter devotedness and to a mysticism of union with him in whom they believed, and although it did so, yet it rests upon a foundation which, in spite of its "irrationality," must be described as logical or noetic: the accepting and recognizing as true of a proposition

> pronounced about the object of faith. All the fervor or ecstasy of feeling, all the devotion of life, grew out of the acceptance of the claim and of the confession made both in the soul and to the world: "I believe that it is so." This position, in it origins arising from a Greek attitude, a thorough acknowledgment of a fact which is beyond the current circle of conceptions . . . [is] yet an acknowledgment accomplished in a noetic form.[60]

Occasionally, Buber makes explicit the Greek origins of some aspects of the Pauline concept of faith. Thus, he sees in Greek philosophy the notion of proof used in the Epistle to the Hebrews.[61] He sees in the Greek notion of fate and in the Greek concepts of demons some of the wrath that Paul attributes to the Christian God.[62] Sometimes he finds Paul's Greek Bible the source of Paul's divergence from the Old Testament.[63] And sometimes Paul's notions derive from contemporary Rabbinic Judaism, derived partly from Alexandrian sources.[64] With the exception of the Biblical passages, however, the Greek sources are general.

More to the point of this book, however, is the fact that Buber does not refer to rhetorical origins for any of the components of the Christian notion of faith. I would like to extend Buber's thesis for a Greek origin of faith to include the area of Greek rhetoric. Furthermore, a good deal of what Buber considers of Greek origin can, I maintain, be found in Greek rhetoric in a fairly specific way.

Buber, however, is an exception to the theologians who write about the origins of the Christian concept of faith. Most of the major treatises on faith in this century that treat of its origin tend to follow the traditional thesis that the notion of faith in Christianity is basically neither Greek nor Hebraic. And the general reluctance of theologians to see in Greek thought a significant source for the Christian notion of faith lies in the marked contrast between the honorific status granted faith in Christian theology and the low esteem in which *pistis* was held in much Greek thought. Because this book is an attempt to reverse the theologians' position, it might be wise to present this negative view they found in Greek thought in a strong light. Later, in Chapter IV, the positive view taken of *pistis* in Greek history—generally ignored by the theologians—will be presented.

THE NEGATIVE VIEW OF PISTIS IN GREEK THOUGHT

Pistis, it may be recalled, means both belief and persuasion, that is, the mental conviction and the technique that evokes such a conviction. In this survey, only the former will be considered, reserving the latter for a later section. Theologians invariably consider only the former. From the point of view of the notion of belief or faith, the earliest statements, going back to Homer and Hesiod in the eighth and seventh centuries B.C., set a negative framework. From the beginning of recorded views on the matter there existed a notion that persisted from Homer to the Gnostics contemporary to Christianity that the gods possessed knowledge about truth that was certain whereas humans at best possessed beliefs about opinions. Bruno Snell, in *The Discovery of the Mind,* has traced the development of this contrast in a brilliant chapter called "Human Knowledge and Divine Knowledge Among the Early Greeks."[65] As he says at the outset of his chapter,

> "Human nature has no knowledge, but the divine nature has." Statements similar to this saying of Heraclitus (fr. 78 Diels) are made by a number of pre-Socratic philosophers, also by Socrates, Plato, and at the opposite end of the historical development the Christians may be cited to the same effect.[66]

And the contrasting words that were used by most of these writers were knowledge (*epistēmē*) of truth (*alētheia*) for the gods and belief (*pistis*) about opinion (*doxa*) for humans. Homer, typically, says in the prelude to the Catalog of Ships in the *iliad:*

> Tell me now, Muses that dwell in the palace of Olympus—for you are goddesses, you are at hand and know all things, But we hear only a rumor and know nothing—Who were the captains and lords of the Danaans?[67]

It is not necessary to catalog the other evidence for this point adduced by Snell. He instances especially Homer, Xenophanes, Heraclitus, and Alcmaeon (the physician who was a disciple of Pythagoras), Parmenides, and finally Empedocles.[68] There were some vital differences in the views of some of these. In particular, Xenophanes and Alcmaeon seemed to reconcile themselves to the limitations of belief and opinion and felt that the human enterprise, limited as it was, was still worthy of inquiry and search.[69] But all these writers placed belief in opinion and rumor and conjecture below the firm knowledge of the gods about truth.

The Sophists also, although they did not intend to, confirmed the negative associations attached to belief about opinions as opposed to certain knowledge about truth. Like Xenophanes and Alcmaeon, they recognized the inability of men to attain ultimate and certain truth recognized everywhere and at all times by all people. Consequently, they were often willing to settle for a local, provisional, temporal, and therefore somewhat subjective and relative view of reality. Protagoras, the first Sophist, subjected everything to the rule of opinion, denying absolute truth to any principle and insisting that there were two sides to every issue.[70] His dictum that "[M]an is the measure of all things" and his stated purpose "to change the lesser possibility of knowledge into a greater possibilily of knowledge" were used both by Plato and later by Aristotle to portray him as denying any absolute knowledge, asserting the subjectivity of opinion and the consequent importance of persuasion.[71] Gorgias also denied the possibility of science (*epistēmē*) and exalted persuasion, operating at the humbler area of human belief (*pistis*), capable only of arriving at probabilities.[72] It was, as we shall see, in treating of Gorgias that Plato made one of the three most violent attacks on the notion of belief (*pistis*) in the entire history of this issue.

The earlier violent attack on the level of belief and seeming as opposed to the way of truth occurs in Parmenides. In his poem "On Nature," Parmenides contrasts these two ways of inquiry, the way of truth, based on unaided reason, and the way of seeming, based on sense perception and the opinions of mortals.[73] This poem of Parmenides made him, Kirk and Raven point out, the most influential of the pre-Socratics.[74] In particular, he heavily influenced Plato on the whole nature of knowledge.

Plato himself, of course, was the major figure in the history of this matter who denigrated belief. He continued the association of *pistis* with opinion, sense perception, subjectivity, relativism, and probability. In the *Gorgias*, an early work, and in the *Phaedrus*, a late work, he attacked belief (*pistis*) as a level of knowledge based only on opinions and probability.[75] But it is in a middle work, the *Republic*, that Plato most vividly outlined the inferiority of belief to science. Bultmann carefully summarizes several of the important passages. Speaking of the element of uncertainty in *pistis,* he says:

> Cf. esp. Resp., VI, 511d-e, where *noēsis* ("insight"), *dianoia* ("understanding"), *pistis* ("belief") and *eikasia* ("probability") are listed in their graded relation to *alētheia* ("truth"). In Resp., VII, 533e–534a, the sequence is *epistēmē, dianoia, pistis, eikasia,* and the last two are summed up as *doxa* ("opinion"), the first two as *noēsis;* the relation of *noēsis* to *doxa* is that of *epistēmē* to *pistis.*[76]

The first passage adduced by Bultmann is illustrated in Plato by the parable of the cave, possibly the most famous single myth in Plato (514a ff.): "and those who live in the cave, chained, with their backs to the light of the fire and who see only shadows created by the light of the fire are those who live by belief and probability." Later, in 517e, Plato makes the association to the rhetoric of the law court very clear: "Such a man as before he has become accustomed to the surrounding darkness, is compelled to fight in courts of law, or in other places, about the images or the shadows of images of justice."[77]

In the light of this powerful dialectical myth, it is not surprising that *pistis* carried distinct derogatory connotations.

The almost fatal blow came when Aristotle basically adopted this schema of levels of knowledge. In particular, the early Aristotle distinctly repudiated belief, opinion, and probability as the bases for his theology, his ethics, and his politics.[78]

One final blow was yet to be delivered. In the period immediately preceding and accompanying the first Christian writings, Gnosticism flourished throughout the Mediterranean area. And, with but few exceptions, the Gnostics mirrored the Greek contrast of divine and human knowledge that was presented earlier: The knowledge (*gnōsis*) conveyed by their initiation ceremonies was highly superior to the knowledge of the Christians, whose insight was limited to faith (*pistis*).[79] In fact, the conflict over *gnōsis* and *pistis* became a major issue in the early Church.[80] *Gnōsis,* according to Jonas, one of the recognized experts in the field, was one of the major unifying concepts of Gnosticism, responsible, obviously for its name; and *gnōsis* meant the possession of a knowledge about God that was certain and that was given in revelation.[81] As has been the case consistently in this brief survey, *pistis* took on a derogatory connotation.

In the face of all this massive artillery ranging from Homer and the very early poets, through the Sophists, and including Parmenides, Plato, Aristotle, and the Gnostics, it is not surprising that theologians could arrive at the conclusion that the Christian notion of an honorific belief system and level of knowledge could hardly have come from the Greeks. And that has been their consensus conclusion in the face of this information. From a despised level of thought to the central concept of a religious system, from a nonreligious to a religious idea, from a low probability to a certainty (in the minds of some theologians)—these jumps were too much for the investigating theologians. And their stance is understandable.

Baillie had called faith "the very central element of religion,"[82] the "essence of religion."[83] Hatch had said that faith "is of divine origin"[84] and that by it one enters into mystical fellowship with Christ.[85] These honorific statements certainly form a striking contrast to the derogatory view whose history has just been outlined. This epistemological objection is part of the larger objection that *pistis* was not of much religious relevance in classical Greek thought.

A New Hypothesis

The new hypothesis of this book is that there is a major Greek origin for some of the fundamental characteristics of the Christian concept of faith as it is seen in the New Testament. This major source is the Greek concept of rhetoric at the time. It dominated the schooling of the time in Greek and Roman education, and it was conspicuous in Jewish schools also. It was an honorific concept, and it was a complex concept, much more complex than just a combination of intellectual and emotional appeals.

It may be objected that there is not a monolithic concept that can safely be labeled the Christian concept of faith. The concept is quite different in Paul as compared with the Synoptic Gospels or as compared with John or as compared with James, and so on. Nonetheless, Baillie, speaking of the concept of faith, can confidently say that the different parts of the New Testament doubtless reflect "different types of Christianity as well as different temperaments. But the deeper one gets into it, the more one is impressed by its deeper unity."[86]—

The next chapter will attempt to sketch a structural view of Christian faith that allows for a varying emphases but that still preserves what Baillie might call a "deeper unity." And the similarities and differences among the varying emphases in the different books of the New Testament will be carefully presented in Chapter IV.

The Greek concept of rhetoric was flexible and adaptable. It served as the framework on which different views of faith could be erected, with varying emphases in Paul, John, Peter, James, Mark, Matthew, and so on. It could accommodate Hebraic notions from the Old Testament, Greek notions from philosophical and school rhetoric, the peculiar amalgam of Greek and Hebraic notions that is found in some of the major Jewish authors of the time writing in Greek, and some of the concepts of the mystery religions.

THE STRATEGY OF THE BOOK

To arrive at this new hypothesis, we must take three major steps. First, it must be shown that the features of the notion of faith and the features of the Greek notion of persuasion were at least compatible enough to share fundamental characteristics. The semantic argument establishing this possibility is developed in Chapter II. Second, the historical argument contending that the rhetorical framework in all probability did influence the production of the Christian concept is developed in Chapter III. Finally, the analytical argument verifying the embodiment of the rhetorical framework in the various books of the New Testament is the subject of Chapter IV. The argument moves from possibility to probability to a measure of verification.

Common to all of the chapters is the idea of the mapping of one set of ideas onto another (faith onto rhetoric, understood as persuasion, or persuasion onto faith). For several reasons, the notion of persuasion has one complexity that is not frequently referred to in analyzing the concept of faith. And, to prevent three separate explanations of the same issue, we find it worthwhile to give a single explanation that will be relevant to all three forthcoming chapters.

In English the word "persuasion" refers to two related but different things: the process that brings about an eventual result and the result itself. "Persuasion" is a process (persuading) and the product (being persuaded). From the standpoint of the person doing the persuading, the *process* entails the techniques of persuading; from the standpoint of the person being persuaded, the *process* embodies the motivations for belief. Thus, it is not inaccurate to say that the *techniques* for persuading are, in this sense, equivalent to the *motivations* for belief (though from two different points of view). This curious equivalence is very important for understanding the evolution of the concept of Christian faith as I shall attempt to show.

The product (persuasion), which results from the processes of persuading, consists in the resulting conviction in the soul of the person being persuaded. It is the belief engendered because of the motivations presented in the process.

The same two components can be seen in the Greek word *pistis*, which is often translated as "persuasion" in English. Another translation used in the New Testament and in Christianity is "faith." In Greek, the processes of persuasion were called *pisteis* (the plural of *pistis*)—and we do not have an English equivalent of this plural (neither persuadings nor persuasions is used in English for these processes). Yet these "persuadings," these persuading techniques (motivations for the recipient), were carefully analyzed by Greek thinkers in the discipline of the study of persuasion that is called rhetoric.

Now it is quite interesting that these basic motivations for belief, as analyzed by Greek rhetoricians, turn up as the major components of the Christian concept of faith, this time viewed as a product, an epistemological state of conviction. In effect, what has happened is that the distinction of motivations for belief (processes) from resulting conviction (product) has been blurred. Such a conflation is understandable because both the Greek term (*pis-*

tis) and the English term (persuasion) carry this ambiguous connotation—and indeed the conflation extends to other languages.

Given such a conflation in both Greek and other European languages, it is not difficult to understand that some aspects of persuasion as process could be transferred to persuasion as product. That this is exactly what happened is what this study will attempt to show.

Graphically, this transfer can be shown in Figure 1. In this figure, the Greek concept of "persuasion" (*pistis*), is shown in the left-hand side of the diagram with both the product and the processes shown. The four processes will be established in the next chapter. In the right-hand side of the diagram is presented the Christian concept of faith (*pistis*), which does not usually distinguish process (motivations for belief) from product (belief as conviction). In fact, it incorporates the motivations into the resultant state of conviction; in effect, it incorporates the Greek components of the process into the product. This is completely understandable because the two were expressed in the same word in Greek (as they still are in English).

Another reason why the processes could be readily transferred into the product has to do with the nature of persuasive writing. Normally, the process appeals, the *pisteis* as such, are not called attention to in the persuasive speech or written document or advertisement, and so on. Demosthenes does not usually tell his audience analytically which persuasive technique he is using to persuade. Such terminology and reflective terminology are the province of the rhetorical analyst, not the practicing orator. For this reason, we do not find, either in Greek rhetorical practice or in the New Testament, reflective terms calling an emotional appeal a *pistis* or an authoritarian appeal an ethical *pistis*. To find these apppeals, we must analyze the context in which the persuasion is occurring. In other words, even in the Greek classical texts, the motivations are built into the resulting conviction, the product.

It is the search for these appeals accompanying the mental state of faith that we will attempt to undertake in the fourth chapter. There the processes, the motivations of faith, will be analyzed in each pericope or incident of the occurrence of the product *pistis*.

The justification for the categories under both Greek persuasion

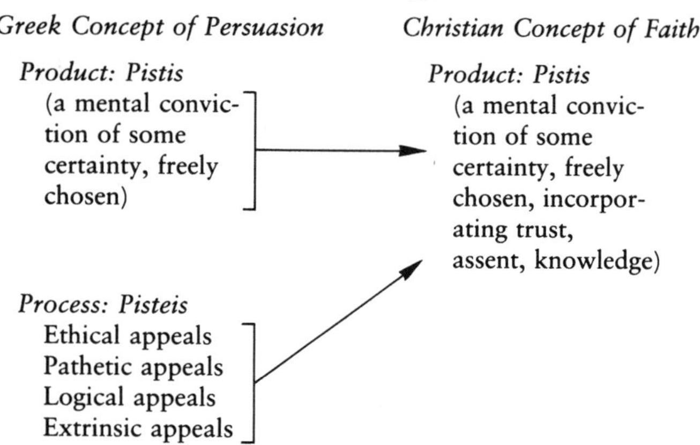

FIGURE 1. Greek persuasion and Christian faith: A transfer

and Christian faith will be given in the next chapter. The historical arguments for the probability of the transfer will be given in Chapter III. The textual evidence for the presence of the categories in the New Testament uses of the term *pistis* will be presented in Chapter IV, "The Analytical Argument: A Verification."

WHY THIS HYPOTHESIS IS NEW

I have often been asked the question, "Why has no one proposed this before if it is possible, probable, and susceptible of some verification?" The answer, I submit, has several plausible responses. In the first place, we now possess much more knowledge of the cultural and educational background of the Jews in Palestine than we did 60 or 70 years ago, when the first serious attempts were made to look for historical origins of the notion of faith. I trust that Chapter III will give sufficient proof of this response. We know much more about the Greek schools, the Hebrew schools, and the educational background of the authors of the New Testament books and of the readers of the New Testament books. This allows us to hazard suggestions that would have been unthinkable less than a century ago.

Secondly, we now have a much more favorable attitude toward rhetorical analysis than the scholars, either secular or religious, had even 30 years ago. At the beginning of the century, rhetoric was almost totally in academic eclipse on the Continent and in England. The decline of rhetoric in France has been examined in some detail by Paul Ricoeur in *The Rule of Metaphor* (1977) and by Gérard Genette in *Figures III* (1972).[87] The ambivalent attitude in nineteenth-century Germany toward rhetoric and its eventual disfavor have been chronicled by Joachim Goth in *Nietzsche und die Rhetorik* (1970).[88] At Oxford and Cambridge, despite the continuation of the weekly or fortnightly written essays presented to the tutor, rhetoric as a subject for reading and examinations was no longer required by the end of the nineteenth century. In Belgium, rhetoric as a required reading topic in universities was discontinued in the middle 1920s, as Chaim Perelman tells us in *The Realm of Rhetoric* (1982).[89] Sustained study by a group was carried on during this period only by scholars in the speech communication departments in the United States, and, except for studies in preaching, few of them ventured into theology. Theologians themselves usually participated in the intellectual climate of the period toward rhetoric.[90]

Consequently, neither the historical nor the rhetorical knowledge required by the task was available until rather recently. As we shall see, both have recently made their impress on Biblical studies in areas relevant to our concern.

CHAPTER II

The Semantic Argument
A Possibility

In this chapter the two concepts of faith and persuasion are compared in order to examine the possibility of a fusion between them. In the first part of the chapter, a summary view of the Christian elements of the notion of faith is sketched, drawn mainly from Lutheran, Presbyterian, Anglican, Episcopalian, Evangelical, and Jewish contemporary theological writers who have analyzed the notion of faith. All the modern scholars build their cases on Scriptural references, but this chapter will not attempt such a textual basis. The fourth chapter will provide the textual justification for the position arrived at in this chapter.

The second part of this chapter looks at the basic elements of the concept of *pistis* as it was used in Greek rhetoric and in the major Hellenistic philosophies of the period preceding and contemporaneous with the formation of the New Testament canon.

The third section of the chapter then attempts to show that the two concepts, faith and persuasion, are in many respects quite compatible with each other and share fundamental features. In a sense, they can be partially mapped onto each other. Thus, this chapter establishes the *possibility* of a rhetorical view of faith.

The Elements of the Christian Concept of Faith

It is probably impossible to reach a consensus definition of faith that would satisfy all sects of Christianity. However, it might be possible to reach a definition that would include the major elements but still allow for differences of emphases among these elements. That is what I shall attempt to do in this section.

TRUST (FIDUCIA)

The major heritage of the Old Testament notion of faith was undoubtedly the concept of a trust in God. In the New Testament the trust focused on the belief that God had promised salvation to the faithful. All the authorities whom we considered in the last chapter agree on this element of faith. Hatch, Baillie, Weiser, Bultmann, O'Connor, and nearly all Christian theologians would concur in this view. And Jacobs, studying Jewish faith, considers "belief *in*," the emotional and moral element of faith, as also anchored in the Old Testament, as we saw in the last chapter.

Karl Barth, in his systematic investigations of the nature of faith, uses the traditional Protestant term of the Reformation theologians for this aspect of faith: *fiducia*. This term was usually related to two others in the Reformation definitions of faith: *assensus* and *notitia*. *Fiducia* is usually translated "trust"; *assensus* is translated "assent" or "acceptance"; and *notitia* is translated "knowledge" or "doctrine." Together they make up what Barth calls the view of faith in "Old Protestantism."[1] He reverts to the trilogy at many instances in his discussions of faith,[2] traces its history in Protestantism and in medieval thought back through Peter Lombard to St. Augustine,[3] and states, "In the older dogmatics the classical definition of faith was that it takes place in the three acts of *notitia, assensus,* and *fiducia*."[4] In the context of a discussion of justification, Barth gives a quick summary definition of these three terms:

> Nor does it make any odds whether a man means by faith a mere knowledge and intellectual understanding of the divine work and judgment and revelation and pardon (*notitia*), or an assent of the mind and will to it, the acceptance as true of that which is proclaimed as the truth of this work of God (*assensus*), or finally a heart's trust in the significance of this work for him (*fiducia*).[5]

Much earlier, in the first volume of *Church Dogmatics*, Barth had taken the same stand as he takes in the preceding passage: Neither *fiducia* nor *assensus* nor *notitia* was particularly privileged although some Protestant theologians had given primacy to *fiducia*.[6]

The trust of faith was primarily a trust in salvation and justification, and most theologians emphasize the fact that faith itself, as well as justification and salvation are all three gifts from God to humanity. God's promise of the gifts of justification and salvation are central to the concept of faith even though there are quite differing views on whether faith alone justifies and on the certitude of the trust. Like the *pistis* notion in the Old Testament, the Christian faith is initiated by God.[7] Hatch,[8] Baillie,[9] Bultmann,[10] and especially Barth insist on the gratuitous nature of faith. Barth here goes further than Luther and Calvin, both of whom, in common with Catholic theologians had maintained that human beings had a predisposition to faith; Barth denies this natural predisposition and, thus, possibly more than anyone else at the present time, insists on the gift element of faith.[11] But all Christian theologians agree that faith is a gift of grace. We will have occasion later to return to the "gift" aspect of faith and to the certitude aspect of trust.

As O'Connor points out, traditionally Catholic theologians have given less attention to trust than to assent and knowledge in their studies of faith, but this tendency has changed recently.[12]

ASSENT (ASSENSUS)

The second feature of the concept of faith that modern and earlier theologians agree on is what Barth, following the traditional Protestant formulation, calls *assent*. His definition is given earlier; it incorporates three distinct facets: an intellectual assent, a voluntary assent, and an acceptance as true of the Biblical proclamation.

The intellectual assent is a part of the intellectual component that Hatch, Baillie, Jacobs, O'Connor, and Bultmann had established as a major point of differentiation from the Old Testament notion of faith, as was pointed out in the first chapter.

The voluntary assent is mentioned by Hatch,[13] by Baillie,[14] by Barth,[15] by O'Connor,[16] and especially by Bultmann. Bultmann's definition, in fact, makes it central to the definition of faith; specific to the Christian usage of the term is *pistis* as acceptance of the kerygma."[17]

Several important corollaries follow from the notion of a voluntary assent. Faith is a decision, a term frequently used by both Bultmann and Barth in describing the New Testament concept of *pistis*. Comparing the concepts in John and Paul, Bultmann says, "Faith, like unbelief, is, of course, a decision. It is thus an act in a true sense."[18] Barth uses very parallel expressions.[19] Consequent on this decision is the turning away of the Christian from his old beliefs to Christ. The *turn* constitutes another essential element of faith, *conversion* (the metaphor of the turn is present in both the Greek and Latin forms of the word). In the sense that the conversion is a total commitment to Christ, it is similar to the commitment of the Hebrew to the God of the Old Testament, involving obedience and allegiance,[20] but insofar as it is a change, a persuasion, it is a New Testament notion. It clearly involves a sense of mission, adopted from both pagan and Hellenistic-Jewish propaganda, says Bultmann;[21] to believe in "is to be construed on the analogy of *epistrephein epi* or *pros* [to convert to or towards]."[22] It is a mortification of the old self and a vivification in Christ, says Barth.[23] Some of the more interesting analyses of the concept of conversion, in relation to faith, are those of Hans Conzelmann in *The Theology of St. Luke,* of J. Behm and E Würthwein in *The Theological Dictionary of the New Testament,* and of Martin Buber in *Two Types of Faith.*[24]

The third element that Barth includes in his definition of assent is the acceptance as true of the Biblical proclamation. In a sense, some of the implications of this have been covered earlier; but the notion leads directly to the next component of the trilogy, *knowledge,* because the acceptance as true of the Biblical proclamation implies some knowledge of the extent of the proclamation.

KNOWLEDGE (NOTITIA)

In addition to the intellectual assent, the consequent knowledge that is gained is a further attribute of faith that is given attention by all of the theologians whom we have been considering. Hatch calls it knowledge,[25] and so does Baillie.[26] Weiser points at several instances to the cognitive aspect in Old Testament faith,[27] O'Connor prefers to call the resultant of faith understanding and analyzes it in several critical instances.[28] Barth uses the cognitive root *Kennen* in his adaptation to German of the Reformation trilogy: *Anerkennen, Erkennen,* and *Bekennen* (for assent, knowledge, and trust, respectively),[29] and Bultmann focuses on the proclamation itself as the content of faith in his analysis of this aspect of *pistis*.[30]

It might be worthwhile to point out a few of the pertinent points made by Barth and Bultmann. Barth insists strongly on the "cognitive event" that faith is.[31] In a lengthy survey, he points to many of the major figures in the theological tradition who have stressed the cognitive aspect of faith: Augustine, Aquinas, Bonaventure, Anselm of Canterbury, Luther, Calvin, Melanchthon.[32] Every Christian is, he says, in a rudimentary way a theologian—he or she knows something.[33]

Bultmann, after stating that "the primary sense of *pisteuein* [to believe] in specifically Christian usage is acceptance of the kerygma about Christ," then moves on to determine the nature of this kerygma or proclamation. The content of faith, as he calls it, is abbreviated at several critical texts in the New Testament, preeminent among which is Romans, 10:8–10,

> This means the word of faith which we proclaim [*kērussomen*]. If on your lips is the confession, "Jesus is Lord," and in your heart the faith that God raised him from the dead, then you will find salvation. For the faith that leads to righteousness is in the heart, and the confession that leads to salvation is upon the lips.[34]

An important final issue that relates both to knowledge and also to trust has to do with the certitude of the faith. The textual evidence on this point is examined most carefully by O'Connor and Bultmann, among the authorities being frequently cited in this chapter.

At several instances Bultmann calls attention to the "measure of faith," the weakness of faith, growth in faith, strength of faith, grades of faith, and so on.[35] As usual, he supplies ample documentation for his statements. He also insists on the provisional nature of the knowledge of faith, of its opposition to knowledge by sight (following Paul in 2 Cor. 5:7), of its being accompanied by fear, and of the danger of the believer's exposure to temptation.[36]

In a similar vein, O'Connor treats of the degrees of faith, as he phrases it. He notes the many passages that speak of a greater or lesser faith,[37] or of a greater or smaller introduction into the mysteries of faith.[38] Although he is treating only the Synoptic Gospels, he arrives at the same sort of generalizations as Bultmann does.

These careful analyses of the Biblical texts carry with them a caution about the certitude of faith. But not all theologians have been as cautious as Bultmann and O'Connor. Baillie, another of our authorities is somewhat ambivalent. After considering two opposing views, Baillie states the following:

> We need not analyse it here, or stop to ask whether any meaning can be attached to *absolute* certainty. The main thing is to avoid the fatal error of distinguishing religious faith from ordinary knowledge by making the former less certain. *We must be at least as certain of our faith as we are of anything.*[39]

Barth, on the contrary, is quite cautious. Speaking of this facet of Barth's concept of faith, Hamer says:

> The element of certitude, which is so characteristic of Luther's faith, has totally disapeared . . . Barth has chosen its direct opposite; he has not just appealed to a lower form of certitude. He is not content, for example, with simple probability. He has not reduced the degree of certitude. . . . Barth makes his own the statement of Paul Althous, who sums up the mystery of the Word of God and the corresponding human attitude thus: "I know not *whether* I believe, but I know in *whom* I believe."[40]

The contrast of Barth to Luther is paralleled by a contrast of Barth to Calvin. Whereas Calvin had written about a "sure knowledge" [*certa cognitio*] and a "sure confidence" [*certa fiducia*], Barth modifies the qualifier in each case.[41] As Hamer puts it, in Luther there is a certitude that the Christian has been justified in the past; in Barth there is the hope that he will be justified in the future.[42]

Barth's position in this matter is possibly closer to that of both Augustine and Aquinas, each of whom placed the level of certainty of faith below that of science. Aquinas placed it between knowledge (*scientia*) and opinion,[43] and Augustine says that it only has a plausibility because it is based on authority.[44]

EMPHASIS ON THE WORD

Bultmann's analysis of the different treatments accorded the Word of God in the Old versus the New Testament has already been referred to (Bultmann, p. 215). The new emphasis is epitomized in the Gospel of St. John, where the Word of God and Jesus are equated, says Bultmann.

This emphasis on the word, as opposed to the deed, is characteristic of the New Testament concept of faith according to most of the writers whom I have been following in this chapter. Hatch, in a succinct treatment sprinkled with abundant footnotes, calls attention to the many occurrences in Paul's epistles where this notion is stressed.[45]

Barth's first in a four-volume series on *Church Dogmatics* is significantly entitled *The Doctrine of the Word of God.* In it he makes the startling analogy of the three aspects of the Word of God to the Trinity:

> There is only one analogy to this doctrine of the Word of God. More exactly stated: the doctrine of the Word of God in its three-fold form is itself the sole analogy to the doctrine which will fundamentally occupy us in unfolding the concept of revelation: the doctrine of the three-in-oneness of God. In the facts that for revelation, Scripture, and proclamation we can substitute the divine "Person"—names of Father, Son, and Holy Spirit, and that in the one case as in the other we shall encounter the same fundamental relationships.[46]

Scholars writing about Barth reiterate his emphasis on the word, the verbal, signs, and language.[47] However, Barth is not alone in this—the long historical emphasis on Scripture, revelation, and proclamation attest to this feature of faith.

One final feature that almost goes without saying, but that may prove to be quite important in the historical section of this chapter has to do with the honorific nature of *pistis* in Christianity as opposed to the derogatory view taken of it by major figures in Greek thought. I have already called attention to some statements of Hatch and Baillie on this matter.[48] Anyone can match these with statements from the other experts whom I have been following in this chapter.

For the time being, this concludes the rapid survey definition of what some contemporary theologians of different persuasions think of the nature of faith. After a similar look at the nature of Greek rhetoric, the two will be brought together in the third section of this chapter.

The Elements of the Greek Concept of Persuasion in Rhetoric

The consideration of the elements of the concept of persuasion in Greek rhetoric must continually shift back and forth between two aspects of the concept: Persuasion sometimes is viewed as a technique that effects a change of mind, but sometimes persuasion is looked on as the resulting mental state of conviction. In the first case, persuasion is the cause; in the second case, persuasion is the effect. In their first definition of *pistis* in Greek, Liddell and Scott emphasize the effect: "trust in others, faith . . . generally persuasion of a thing, confidence, assurance."[49] But in the second definition they emphasize the cause: "that which gives confidence: hence, 1. assurance, pledge of good faith, guarantee . . . 2. means of persuasion, argument, proof . . . esp. of proofs of orators."[50] Persuasion, even in English, also has this same ambiguity.

Both meanings occur in the case of rhetoric: There is an epistemological knowledge level of *pistis,* the level that Plato opposed; and there is the technique of persuasion, often translated argument or proof. Some of the opposition that created a derogatory view of *pistis* in Greek thought was opposed to the epistemological result, and some of it was opposed to the rhetorical technique of persuasion itself. On the other hand, it is also possible to take an honorific view of either or both. Indeed, running through Greek history is a parallel current to the derogatory view of *pistis* that was outlined in the first chapter. Let us take a look at it throughout the classical period and then into the Hellenistic period. It is my contention that the honorific view of *pistis* in Greek thought has been neglected by theologians. It is also my contention that the Hellenistic view of rhetoric, both as epistemology and as rhetorical technique, has been slighted in favor of the earlier Hellenic view. Yet it is out of the Hellenistic period that the Christian view of *pistis* was derived.

AN HONORIFIC VIEW OF PISTIS IN GREEK THOUGHT IN THE CLASSICAL PERIOD

In addition to the derogatory view of *pistis* sketched in Chapter I, there is an accompanying honorific view in Greek thought. As will be shown, it is frequently identified with the study of persuasion, rhetoric. And because of the derogatory view of rhetorical studies taken in the nineteenth and twentieth centuries (see the end of the first chapter), theologians tended to neglect rhetoric as a possible source for the notion of *pistis*.

Persuasion nearly always has this double aspect. And Greek mythology, as usual, accurately reflects this schizophrenic nature of both persuasion and the kind of knowledge it engenders. The goddess Peitho (literally, '"I persuade"), like many Greek deities, was sometimes presented in quite a favorable light, but she often was presented disapprovingly. The discrepancy appears even in her genealogy. Hesiod says that she is one of the daughters of Oceanus and Thetis,[51] a respectable enough ancestry. But Aeschylus says, "Persuasion (Peitho) is a miserable creature not destined to reach maturity, daughter of Ate (the goddess of mischief) and the judgment at hand. All remedy is vain."[52] Another source makes her the daughter of Aphrhodite.

Generally, in earlier sources, Peitho is a member of the marriage circle of goddesses or a member of the circle of Aphrodite; often, in fact, her name is an alternate for Aphrodite.[53] Both associations are at least suspect. Persuasion is related to Aphrodite by the intermediation of the notion of seduction, and Aphrodite's legends bear this out. Persuasion as a part of the marriage ceremonies carries with it the suspicion of a kind of seduction again.[54]

With the fifth century B.C. and the realizations of the dangers of persuasion, Peitho takes on increasingly a more sinister picture. She is frequently equated with deception,[55] and although her associations with Aphrodite are not lost, she becomes the powerful goddess of Persuasion. "The ground for this fundamental turnabout in the interpretation of Peitho lies in the powerful role that the concept of *peithō* plays in technical rhetoric,"[56] as well as in the political life of the city: Sophocles, for instance, generally emphasizes more the fatal political power of persuasion.[57]

The other side of the picture, on the contrary, is often neglected. There are innumerable quotations from Democritus on that emphasize, as he did, that persuasion would be a better education than law or necessity.[58] This side of persuasion, the importance of free choice, became a significant part of the rhetorical tradition, but, seen less in the dramatists and poets than in the rhetoricians and historians, sometimes is neglected by Biblical scholars.[59]

Let us look at the notion of faith or persuasion in its historical development in Greece, for the goddess is only a reflection of some of these movements.

In the beginnings of Greek thought, a few of those who acknowledge the superiority of divine knowledge and the consequent inferiority of opinion (*doxa*) or belief (*pistis*) still recognize the possibilities and the importance of human belief and inquiry. Such thinkers such as Xenophanes, Alcmaeon, Empedocles, and the Sophists encouraged the systematic study of nature even if human beings could only attain to a limited kind of knowledge. Alcmaeon called this limited kind of knowledge *conjecture,* and he used it in his medical inquiries.[60]

But possibly the most influential of all the writers who spoke positively of *pistis* was Isocrates. Like the Sophists, Isocrates was convinced that absolute rules of science, promising certainty, were not a human possibility. In speech after speech he inveighed against the type of theory and science represented by Parmenides and Plato. But a combination of political events, a very successful rhetoric school, a famous speech at the right time, and especially a biting criticism of the practical inapplicability of the Platonic and early Aristotelian theoretical ideals of virtue and wisdom seemed to have turned the tide in a very critical way in favor of Isocrates' position as opposed to that of Plato and the early Aristotle. In his speech to the Assembly "On the Peace" between Athens and her former allies against Persia, Sparta and Thebes, in 355 B.C., Isocrates pointed repeatedly to attempts on the part of one or the other of the allies to impose absolute standards on the rest and referred to the persistent failures of these moves. Early in the speech he told the Athenians that

> they ought not to think that they have exact knowledge of what the result will be, but to be minded towards these contingencies as men who indeed exercise their best judgment, but are not sure what the future may hold in store.[61]

This was simply an application in the practical affairs of people of what Isocrates had consistently said of all human knowledge. Speaking of a legal case in which he himself was involved, he had defined his view of philosophy as follows:

> For since it is not in the nature of man to attain a science by the possession of which we can know positively what we should do or what we should say, in the next resort I hold that man to be wise who is able by his powers of conjecture to arrive generally at the best course, and I hold that man to be a philosopher who occupies himself with the studies from which he will most quickly gain that kind of insight.[62]

Immediately after this paragraph in the "Antidosis," Isocrates outlines his ideal of education. He does not propose an ethical theory, but rather, a notion that he says may seem so contrary to popular belief that he is concerned that his readers will not give it the consideration it deserves. He says:

> But I do not hold that people can become better and worthier if they conceive an ambition to speak well, if they become possessed of the derire to be able to persuade their hearers, and finally, if they set their hearts on seizing their advantage.[63]

He then proceeds to demonstrate how the art of persuasion can train to virtue and practical success in life—results that neither Plator nor Aristotle could offer.

It is this rhetorical idea that became the ideal of higher education in antiquity. At the heart of the ideal are two notions, the importance of persuasion as a methodology and the importance of the practical kind of knowledge that humans have, based on belief, not science. The educational ideal of Isocrates, then, was built on two meanings of *pistis* with which I have begun this paper: the notion of persuasion and the notion of belief.

Historians are quite specific on the subject that it was Isocrates who dominated higher education in antiquity. As Marrou says,

> For the vast majority of students, higher education meant taking lessons from the rhetor, learning the art of eloquence from him.
>
> This fact must be emphasized from the start. On the level of history Plato had been defeated; posterity had not accepted his educational ideals. The victor, generally speaking, was Isocrates, and Isocrates became the educator first of Greece and then of the whole ancient world. . . . Rhetoric is the specific subject of Greek education and the highest Greek culture.[64]

Rhetoric not only dominated Greek higher education. Speaking of Roman studies, Marrou says, "In practice higher education was reduced to rhetoric, in the strictest sense of the word."[65] And it was not limited to Greece and Rome:

> it ran through Hellenistic culture as a whole. For a thousand years—possibly two—from Demetrius Phalerus to Ennodius (later still in Byzantium), this was the standard type of teaching in all higher education.[66]

Symbolically, all of this ideal was the issue in "On the Peace," and, in several ways, it had some immediate effects.

Twenty-three years of war with Greek states fighting domination by Persia, 27 years with other Greek states fighting Athenian domination, 17 years of war with Athens and Thebes and other Greek states fighting Spartan domination, and 7 years of opposition to Theban domination, with each dominating agency attempting to impose absolutes on the others, had taught Athenians a hard-learned lesson: Some compromise was necessary. The issues were not pure falsehood versus pure truth. Opinion, conjecture, and belief were more practically reliable than absolutes, certainty, and science.

The word that Isocrates uses for conjecture and belief is usually *pistis*. An examination of the many occurrences of *pistis* and words of this root in Isocrates reveals an amazing fact: Every use is honorific. The contrast to the early poets, to Parmenides, to Plato, and to the early Aristotle is clear-cut. The noun is usually translated in the following ways: solemn pledges,[67] surety or guarantee or strongest assurances,[68] and evidence or arguments for or proofs of.[69] Whoever would read Isocrates—and many would, as can be shown—would receive an entirely positive concept of *pistis*.

Isocrates' speech (actually a circulated essay) made a tremendous impression on several very important people—as far as the issue we are investigating is concerned. Plato, after this time, recognized two separate types of wisdom, one theoretical and one practical,[70] and permitted Aristotle to teach rhetoric for the first time in the Academy. More importantly, the speech, the situation, and the practical success of Isocrates' school of rhetoric critically influenced the young Aristotle. It is at this time that Aristotle rejected the scientific ideal of Plato for rigid and theoretical sciences of politics, ethics, and rhetoric and opted instead for sciences or arts in these areas that would operate in the sphere of the *pistis,* in the sphere of the deliberative, that upon which there was difference of opinion, because the issues were not certain and predetermined.[71]

At this time, Aristotle's schema of the sciences developed, and the basic division was between (1) the scientific, involving the intellectual virtues of intuitive intellect, science and wisdom (encompassing metaphysics, mathematics, and physics; and (2) the deliberative or opinion-based, involving the virtue of good sense, *phronēsis* *(encompasing ethics, politics, and home management) and the virtues of art, *technē* (encompassing rhetoric and poetics).[72]

> Aristotle's development in his middle period, particularly in the fields of ethics, politics, and rhetoric, is clearly away from the dominance of a theoretical and nonempirical ideal, such as had dominated his treatment of these issues in the *Protrepticus.* It is much more in the direction of a deliberative and realistic science.[73]

He still retained the division of levels of knowledge into levels of certainty moving down to probability, but he no longer insisted on the primacy of the theoretical and the certain. In fact, he turned much of his attention precisely to the concerns of the areas of *pistis* (belief and probability and deliberation): ethics, rhetoric, and politics. There are several reasons why Aristotle turned his interest more to the individual viewed as a political animal. In the first place, as Isocrates had carefully argued, this was a more realistic view of humans, and Aristotle's general development is away from a utopian idealism toward a practical realism. This characterizes his development in ethics, in politics, and in rhetoric.[74] Secondly—and this may be more important—the sciences and arts that Aristotle included under his deliberative or opinion-based grouping, precisely because they are not predetermined, are areas in which the deliberations of people result in decisions that are free and that can change reality.[75] The emphasis on decison or choice is important here, for it introduces a new notion into the opinion-making (the term is Ando's) sciences and arts. These are the areas of reality where a free individual can make a decision. And rhetoric is important because, by rhetoric, a person can bring another to a decision and, therefore, change his or her mind or feelings about something. The emphasis on choice or decision making as the aim of rhetoric occurs continually throughout the *Rhetoric,*[76] and this is only natural because it is one of the deliberative arts. This facet of *pistis* reminds us of the goddess Peitho.

THE VIEW OF PISTIS IN GREEK THOUGHT IN THE HELLENISTIC PERIOD

The attitudes to *pistis,* whether viewed epistemologically as a level of certitude or rhetorically as a technique for persuasion, changed substantially in the period after the death of Alexander, 323 B.C. A few generalizations about the period should first be made in order to understand the sometimes paradoxical particulars of the era.

The general Hellenistic period can be characterized intellectually as a period in which practice rather than theory is emphasized. As von Arnim has pointed out, the move is away from the speculative and metaphysical and in the direction of the ethical, the political, and the pedagogical.[77] This is evident in the turning away from the Platonic and Aristotelian concern for the comtemplative life to the Stoic and Epicurean concern for the active and practical life. Such a concern is noticeable even in the Academy and the Lyceum as will be pointed out later. But it is even more evident in the epistemological bases of these ways of life. In all the major philosophical schools of the period (Stoicism, Epicureanism, Platonism, Aristotelianism, skepticism, and eclecticism), there is a move away from the rigidly scientific norm of certainty toward a more flexible norm of probability or belief. Thus, *pistis* becomes more respectable. It is this important change that I wish to document, particularly since it has not received the attention it deserves in theological discussions about the origins of *pistis*. Eduard Zeller, certainly one of the major historians of philosophy for antiquity, emphasizes the domination of the doctrine of probability during this period. Speaking of the move from the prevalent Stoic and Epicurean leadership in the middle Hellenistic period to the later eclecticism of the Hellenistic era, he notes the increasing dominance of the notion of probability.[78] He relates this dominance to the tendency of late Hellenistic philosophy to restrict itself to practical ethical questions.[79]

This *theōria-praxis* conflict is also seen in another arena, the temporary feud between philosophy and rhetoric, particularly from about 165 to 80 B.C. The success of the rhetoricians in the schools and with the politicians in the period immediately preceding this era worried the philosophers, who previously had assumed a superior educational posture. For a time, as will be shown, philosophical schools assumed a hostile attitude to the more practical rhetorical schools despite the fact that the philosophical schools themselves *all* continued to teach rhetoric (though some did so more than others).

The schools themselves, particularly toward the end of the period, cannot be too carefully distinguished, however. Antiochus of Ascalon, the teacher of Cicero, for instance, sought actively to unite the Lyceum and the Academy philosophically, though he was the head of the Academy. So did Eudorus, another head of the Academy, who also drew from the Stoics. Conversely, the Stoic Posidonius, who also influenced Cicero, drew heavily from Plato. This is typical of the eclecticism of the period.[80]

With regard to rhetoric, the immediate successors of Plato seemed to have continued his attitude toward persuasion's epistemology as being knowledge of the probable,[81] which they usually denigrated. But beginning with the Second Academy, under Arcesilaus, the epistemological foundations of the Platonists as a group shifted to skepticism. Under Arcesilaus and Carneades, founder of the Third Academy, probability became the epistemological and ethical norm. As Long points out, the word that Carneades used for probable, *pithanon*, "literally means 'persuasive' or 'trustworthy.' "[82] In fact, it belongs to the *pistis* family of words. Carneades worked out an elaborate hierarchy of probabilities for statements.[83] Both the Second and the Third Academy adopted the notion that certainty is unattainable and "thus probability is the highest standard for practical life."[84] Philo of Larissa and Antiochus of Ascalon somewhat muted this skepticism, but not totally; they were the founders of the Fourth and Fifth Academies, respectively. Thus, the Platonists of the period from 261 B.C. to 79 B.C. hardly continued the attitude to *pistis* of Plato in the *Republic*. Cicero, studying there in 79 B.C., adopted the position of Carneades, as Plutarch points out.[85]

Of these four figures, Arcesilaus, Philo, and Antiochus of Ascalon, all taught rhetoric, the last two being the major influences on Cicero's attempt to blend philosophy and rhetoric.[86] Carneades opposed the teaching of rhetoric for reasons that seem inconsistent with his own epistemology, as Kennedy remarks.[87]

The Stoics, though not a major influence on rhetoric, still did not generally oppose rhetoric. Their epistemological position was somewhat ambivalent. Theoretically, they favored a position of absolute certainty for the wise individual, but they recognized that, in particular cases, such certainty was not always possible. In our ordinary life, the probable or plausible proposition (*pithanon*) or the reasonable proposition (*eulogon*) were the actual guides.[88] The terms *pithanon* and *eulogon* were the terms that had been associated with persuasion, probability, and rhetoric in Greek thought and that had been traditionally opposed to *epistēmē*.[89]

Particularly in the later Stoics, the *eulogos* became the norm for their ethical and epistemological theories, though there was always the attempt to strive beyond it.[90] Cicero, encountering the notion of the *eulogos,* translates it "*probabilis.*"[91] Cicero particularly encountered the notion in the doctrine of the "fitting" or the "proper," which is the basis for his ethical and rhetorical systems. The "proper" can never be certain, but it can be quite probable; and it is the foundation for his treatise on duties.[92] More than any other single person, Panaetius of Rhodes, founder of the Middle Stoa, seems to have been Cicero's source in this doctrine, which we will also see in looking at Aristotelianism.

The Stoics were not generally hostile to rhetoric, and occasionally they were influential. Chrysippos and Cleanthes both wrote an *Art of Rhetoric;* and Posidonius, a strong influence on Cicero, was interesteed in the rhetorical stasis theory and in the concept of the philosopher-orator.[93] In any case, Stoics have been shown to have influenced Hermagoras, possibly the most prominent rhetorician of the period.[94] Unlike other philosophical schools, the Stoics included rhetoric in philosophy as a part of logic.

Epicureanism, like all the other contemporary philosophies, emphasized the practical and the ethical. In ethics, the Epicureans favored practical wisdom (*phronēsis*) over philosophy, and they emphasized the populist nature of their doctrines. One of Epicurus' disciples wrote about the unreasonable contempt for public opinion.[95] Epicureans, therefore, participate in the general sentiment of the period for the validity of opinion and probability rather than certitude although they attach certainty to some types of perceptions.

The Epicureans are generally hostile to rhetoric. Because Epicurus repudiated the public life, Epicureans rejected both legal and political rhetoric, considering these an abuse of language. However, Zeno of Sidon and his pupil Philodemus of Gadara (both bordering on Palestine) lectured and wrote on rhetoric as did Epicurus himself, emphasizing epideictic rhetoric.[96]

Aristotelianism, after a lethargic second century B.C., experienced a healthy Renaissance in the first century B.C. Paul Moraux's presentation of this Renaissance stresses the practical nature of the orientation of the school, its concern with ethics, with life forms (active, mixed, or contemplative life), and often with physical sciences.[97] The ethical orientation of three of the major figures is to the doctrine of the "fitting" or "proper," which we saw in the Stoics.[98] The practical tendencies of the period witnessed a movement toward the defense of the mixed life rather than the earlier preference for the contemplative life.[99] Both of these emphases are movements into the epistemological sphere of *pistis* and the intellectual virtue of *phronēsis* (practical insight, prudence) rather than *epistēmē* or *theōria,* with its claim to certitude.[100]

The Aristotelians were the most systematic and influential of the four Hellenistic philosophical schools in regard to rhetoric.[101] Sometimes the rhetorical training in the school was the "bread and butter" component of the Lyceum, supporting other efforts.[102] At the height of the philosopher-rhetorician conflict, Critolaus the Peripatetic joined with Carneades the Stoic and Diogenes of Babylon in a rejection of rhetoric.[103] But this was not characteristic of the school as a whole.

With the exception of a few references to Stoicism, most of the theologians completely ignore this entire period in Greek thought in their searches for sources or analogues for the Christian *pistis*. Even Bultmann, in his coverage of this period, refers to sources that postdate the appearance of the New Testament, with the single exception of Plutarch, who bridges the first and second centuries A.D.[104] Yet there is a fairly consistent picture of the relation of the schools to both the epistemological level of *pistis* and the *pistis* of rhetoric, which emerges from these authors, most of whom are minor figures in the history of philosophy. The picture is one of a strong perference for probability over scientific certainty and a practice and a tolerance for rhetoric within the four major philosophical schools in the Hellenistic period—not, in other words, a derogatory view of *pistis*.

This picture is strengthened by the emergence in some of the religions of the period of a trio or foursome or occasionally a quintet of virtues, each containing faith as a member. Bultmann points to a foursome in Porphyry and a trio in the Chaldean Oracle;[105] but Reitzenstein also calls attention to the trio of Philo, the quintet in the Iranian Soghdian, and a Manichaean quintet.[106] All these are similar to Paul's faith, hope, and charity of I Cor. 13. The concept of *pistis* as having a religious basis in these contexts is similar in respect to the honorific attitude taken to it and in respect to the virtues with which it is aligned.

Finally, the view from the top may be indicative of the honorific position of rhetoric in the last 150 years that we are studying. During this period the orator becomes a standard "form in imperial sculpture and the iconography borrows from the rules of gesture and delivery," reports Kennedy in a discussion of the attitude to rhetoric during the Empire from Augustus till the end of the first century A.D.[107] He calls attention to the fact that nearly all the emperors had studied and were patrons of rhetoric. Caesar had studied it and knew Cicero's works at firsthand. Augustus had also studied rhetoric. Tiberias, Caligula, Claudius, Nero, Galba, Otho, Vespasian, Titus, and Domitian all were interested in rhetoric and oratory and were patrons of orators and of teachers of rhetoric. Galba brought Quintilian to Rome, and Vespasian, Titus, and Domitian were his patrons. Only Vitellius is missing from this survey by Kennedy.

THE RHETORICAL CONCEPT OF PISTIS

There are numerous rhetorical treatises from the Hellenic and Hellenistic period, but not all of them deal with *pistis* as a rhetorical technique of persuasion. At least a third of the extant rhetorical treatises in Greek deal almost exclusively with style, particularly with schemes and tropes. These figurist rhetorics obviously deal with stylistic techniques of persuasion, but, for reasons that are not clear, style was not considered a *pistis* in rhetorical texts. Another third of the treatises deals with the type of stand that the lawyer or politician should take in a given case. These "case" or "issue" treatises, called *stasis* in Greek, also did not deal with *pistis* as such though they assumed it. Only what might be called the comprehensive rhetorics handle *pistis* in any detail. In Leonardi Spengel's three-volume edition of Greek rhetoricians, these comprehensive rhetorics occupy the first volume whereas the *stasis* rhetorics take up the second volume, and the style rhetorics are in the third volume (with a few minor exceptions).[108]

If one excepts Longinus' treatise "On the Sublime," which is not really a rhetorical text, one is left with ten treatises in Spengel's first volume, some fairly lengthy, some quite short. Of these, *pistis* is treated in seven. In most of these, it occupies the central part of the book, the section having to do with proof or argumentation or techniques of persuasion (they are not limited to logical proofs as the terms used in English might imply). Furthermore, there seems to have been considerable agreement, even before Aristotle, on the major distinctions of kinds of *pistis* and even on some of the subdivisions of the major types. Thus, the *Rhetoric to Alexander,* probably written by Anaximenes of Lampsacus before Aristotle's completed *Rhetoric,* uses many of the same categories of *pistis* that Aristotle uses.[109] So do both Rufus in his short rhetorical treatise and the anonymous author of the *Art of Rhetoric.*[110]

Aristotle, however, gives the most complete presentation. Consequently, let us look at the full schema of *types* of *pistis* given by Aristotle in Book II of the *Rhetoric.*

Aristotle begins the systematic presentation of the *pisteis* (plural of *pistis*) by distinguishing between methods of persuasion that are actually extrinsic and those that are intrinsic to the use of the art of speech as a means of persuasion. Among those extraneous means of persuasion are torture, oaths, laws, witnesses, and contracts. Because they are external to the art or technique of rhetoric, they are usually called the extrinsic or inartistic or nontechnical means of persuasion (*atechnoi pisteis*). I will use the term "extrinsic" for these in the sequel. Aristotle considers these *pisteis* in the last chapter of the first book of his *Rhetoric* (Chapter 15).[111] The point of these extrinsic means of persuasion is that the verbal message does not produce the persuasion. For instance, slave evidence taken under torture in Greek courts was clearly a method of getting someone to admit something, but it didn't operate mainly through the verbal art. And, although witnesses in a court deliver their information in a verbal transmission, it is the fact that they were witnesses to the act that bears the burden of proof, not the verbal transmission itself.

Among the methods of persuasion intrinsic to the art of rhetoric (*rhetoric* derives from a word meaning speech), Aristotle distinguished four: those techniques deriving from the influence of the speaker as a personality, those deriving from the subject matter under consideration, those deriving from the appeals to the emotions and interests of the audience, and those based on the stylistic techniques of the speaker. To each of these, Aristotle devotes one or several chapters in his rhetoric. It is clear that they are based on the components of the process of communication: the author, the audience, the subject matter under consideration, and the stylistic potentials of the language. The first three of these techniques of persuasion are what concern us here.

A simple model of this communication process that is often used is called the communication triangle. It can be used to make a graphic presentation of the three persuasions (see Figure 2). The speaker is at the left vertex, the listener is at the right vertex, and the subject matter being discussed is at the bottom vertex.

Persuasion can be effected by the high credibility of the actual speaker—Aristotle calls this the ethical *pistis*. Or persuasion can be effected by appealing to the emotions or interests or type of character of the listener—Aristotle calls this the pathetic *pistis*. And persuasion can be effected by logic related to the subject

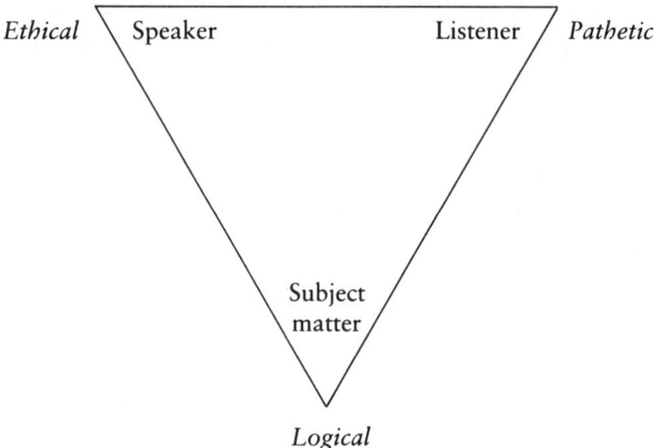

FIGURE 2. The basis of the three rhetorical appeals in Aristotle's *Rhetoric*

matter at issue—Aristotle calls this the logical *pistis*. To these various techniques of persuasions or "*pisteis*" Aristotle devotes 26 chapters, and they make up the largest, the most significant, and the most innovative chapters of the *Rhetoric*. Each of the terms is a jargon term and must not be interpreted according to its usual meaning in ordinary English. "Ethical" does not mean moral or virtuous, as it usually does in English, although it includes these meanings. It refers to the type of credibility generated by the *character* of the speaker. Nor especially does "pathetic" mean what it ordinarily does in English. It means "emotional" or "audience-interested." Finally, even "logical" does mean rational or scientific, as it would normally in English; it means plausible or seemingly rational according to the opinion of the audience—in actuality, the argument might be very fallacious, but it *appears* logical. On the other hand, it might actually be very logical in itself and also appear so to the audience: The appearance of the argument is all-important—if it *seems* logical, whether it is or not, it is called a logical argument.[112]

Each of the arguments or persuasions is broken down into subdivisions. The ethical argument, says Aristotle,[113] is achieved by the speaker's conveying a favorable impression of himself to his audience. The speaker does this by emphasizing his personal knowledgeability about the matter under discussion, showing that he or she is a person of *good sense,* in a practical way. Secondly, obviously or subtly, the speaker lets the reader know that he is interested in the concerns of the audience as a person of *goodwill.* Thirdly, the speaker gives evidence in the speech itself of being a trustworthy person and having, in this situation at least, *moral character*. This is the most nearly "ethical" part of the ethical. All of these characteristics add up to establishing the speaker as a person of trust and as a person of authority—in fact, Quintilian uses the term *auctoritas* for the ethical argument.[114]

The treatment of the pathetic or emotional argument in Aristotle is quite lengthy. Aristotle here transfers his treatment of the emotions, which he had handled in his treatise on ethics, to the matter of persuasion. He considers anger, calmness, friendship, fear and confidence, shame and shamelessness, kindness and unkindness, pity, indignation, envy, and emulation in ten chapters of Book II. Then he turns to a consideration of the types of social groups or characters a speaker might usually encounter in typical audiences. He devotes a chapter to each of the following: the young, the elderly, men in their prime, aristocrats, the wealthy, and the powerful.[115] In effect, the pathetic argument might be called the audience-interested argument: It involves promises or threats.

For his treatment of the "logical" argument in persuasion, Aristotle transfers much of his expertise in scientific logic to the popularized logic of persuasion. He speaks of the use of different kinds of examples, whether historical or fictional. Under this head he also lists fables and parallels. Examples are to persuasion, he says, what induction is to scientific logic because, in the use of examples, we are generalizing from the particular to the general.[116] The logical argument is the subject matter argument; it provides information and evidence about the issue at stake.

If examples are a kind of rhetorical induction, then Aristotle's next method, the enthymeme, is rhetorical deduction. It consists in the use of premises that the audience will concede to be true as the basis for conclusions. Usually, such premises are at best probable, and often they are unstated in the discourse. One particularly useful type of enthymeme is the maxim.[117]

Finally, Aristotle discusses some of these premises that Greek society takes for granted and some of the kinds of conclusions that can be drawn from them. These commonly used techniques of arguments he calls topics.[118]

Summarily, these techniques of appeal (*pisteis*) can be presented in graphic form in Figure 3.

The Compatibility of Christian Faith and Greek Rhetoric

This section attempts a partial semantic mapping of the notion of Christian faith onto that of Greek persuasion, given the structural similarity that they are shown to share. Then a brief survey of the uses of the term "to persuade" in the New Testament will be made, as well as an assessment of these uses with regard to the notion of faith.

PRELIMINARY CONSIDERATIONS

One prima facie bit of evidence that suggests a semantic similarity between the notion of faith and the notion of persuasion is the common etymological origin of the two terms in Greek. The verb for "to believe" in Greek is *pisteuein* (and it has adjectival and nominal forms also). The usual verb for "to persuade" in Greek is *peithein*. Etymologically, *pisteuein* derives from an early form of the root of the verb *peithein*.[119] It is not, therefore, surprising that the noun form survived in both root systems as the same word (*pistis*). In other words, in historical Greek "to believe" was semantically related to "to persuade."

It is not difficult to find examples in the New Testament of instances of the approximation of the two concepts. The following is a typical illustration:

> And Paul went in [to the synagogue], as was his custom, and for three weeks he argued with them from the scriptures, explaining and proving that it was necessary for the Christ to suffer and to rise from the dead, and saying, "This Jesus, whom I proclaim to you, is the Christ." And some of them were persuaded [epeisthēsan], and joined Paul and Silas; as did

I. Intrinsic: Ethical, Pathetic, Logical

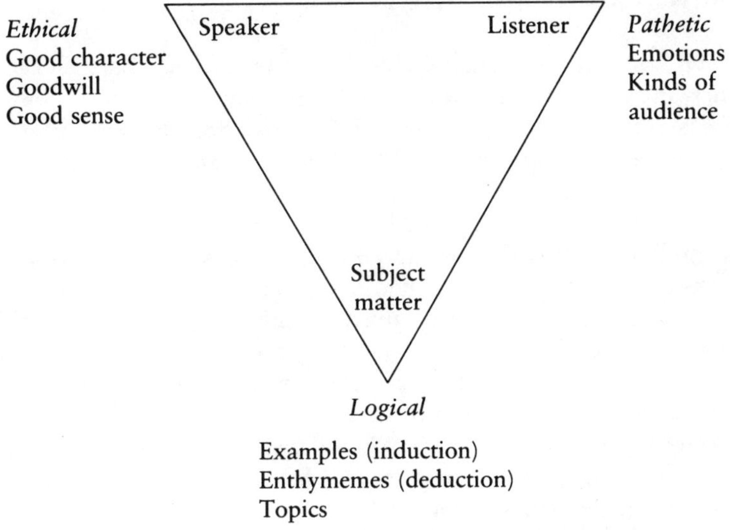

II. Extrinsic
- Torture
- Oaths
- Laws
- Contracts
- Witnesses

FIGURE 3. The Rhetorical appeals in Aristotle's *Rhetoric*

> a great many of the devout Greeks and not a few of the leading women [Acts 17, 2–4].[120]

In this case, it is clear that being "persuaded" is equivalent to accepting the faith. As will be shown in the third section of this part of the chapter, this is a common use of the word "persuade" in the New Testament. But it is not a use of the term in the Old Testament at all. Interesting in this case also is the phrase "as was his custom." Such a hermeneutic of the Old Testament to persuade the Jews was a frequent technique of the apostles and Paul.

Let us turn to the common components of the two notions.

THE STRUCTURAL SIMILARITY OF THE TWO NOTIONS: PISTIS AS FAITH AND PISTIS AS RHETORICAL TECHNIQUE

In an interesting sidelight to his discussion of faith, Barth suggests that, in the matter of faith, God can be viewed as faithful (*pistos,* the adjective); that in "to believe" (*pisteuein,* the verb), humans make the decision; and that "the faith" (*pistis,* the noun) is the divine teaching revealed. This distinction seems to parallel the trilogy that Barth uses in his discussion, the "Old Protestant" formulation, as he calls it, of the trust, the assent, and the knowledge. For it is God who is trusted, the individual who assents, and knowledge that is given in "the faith," using the term as it has just been used.

In fact, it was possible, given the earlier discussion establishing the elements of the notion of faith, to group most of the constitutive components around these basic elements if to them we add the notion of a verbal message (the Scripture and revelation) and the notion that such a view of faith was honorific.

If the establishing of faith is viewed as a process in which God, through a verbal message, reveals knowledge to assenting humans, then faith is seen as a communication process involving the same components as other communication processes: a sender, a receiver, a message, and a subject matter. In this case, God is the sender (usually through an intermediating Scriptural writer); the assenting human (using the term generically for all humans given the gift of faith) is the receiver; the Scriptures, revelation, and proclaiming constitute the verbal message; and the resulting knowledge of the proclamation constitutes the subject matter.

It is not surprising that one can analyze faith in this way; any communication process can be so handled. And simply having in common these elements would not suffice to establish a common semantic base for the notions of persuasion and faith. What faith and persuasion have in common, besides this genus structure of communication, is the species nature of persuasion as a particular kind of communication.

If one looks at the books of the Bible in the light of the historical distinctions between science, rhetoric, and poetic, one would have to say that the Bible largely is rhetorical. These distinctions, of course, have heavy overlaps. And certain books of the Bible are obviously poetic in some measure. On the other hand, the Bible does purport to contain information that could be viewed as scientific information in the culture that produced it. To use the term that is sometimes used in these distinctions, the Bible is partly *ethnically* scientific, and partly *ethnically* poetic, judged by the standards of the producing culture. Nonetheless, both the poetry and the information in the Bible are not usually ends in themselves; they are nearly always oriented toward persuading the reading audience of the religious message of which the "science" and the "poetry" are simply the vehicles. In other words, the science and poetry of the Bible are *very* persuasively ordered. For this reason, among others, it is called the *Holy* Bible. This is a contention that seems fairly safe to make. In this sense, the Bible is not primariy scientific, nor is it primarily poetic.[121]

If one adopts these distinctions, which are not the distinctions of the culture that produced the Old Testament, then the statement can be made that, in the context of such a set of distinctions, the criteria of persuasion would seem to fit the Bible more than the criteria of science or of poetic belles lettres as such. It is in the context of these distinctions that it can be said that the Bible is a persuasive document and shares with other types of persuasion the characterics of this kind of discourse rather than those of poetry and science.

In this context, it can be said that the message of the Bible is a persuasive message. Like other persuasive messages, it elicits a strong trust in the credibility of the speaker (the ethical argument); it elicits a free assent from the recipient of the message who must believe that it is to his or her good to assent (this is the essence of the pathetic argument); and it passes on information and some knowledge about the subject matter involved (the logical argument). For this reason, it is possible to erect the structure of the concept of faith in the same model as that of the structure of the concept of persuasion. Viewed in this light, the concept of faith, with the ancillary notions attached to each component can be presented as seen in Figure 4.

The validity of the structure, it might be pointed out, does not depend on the distinctions among rhetoric, poetic, and science in either Greek or later European cultures. What is necessary for the

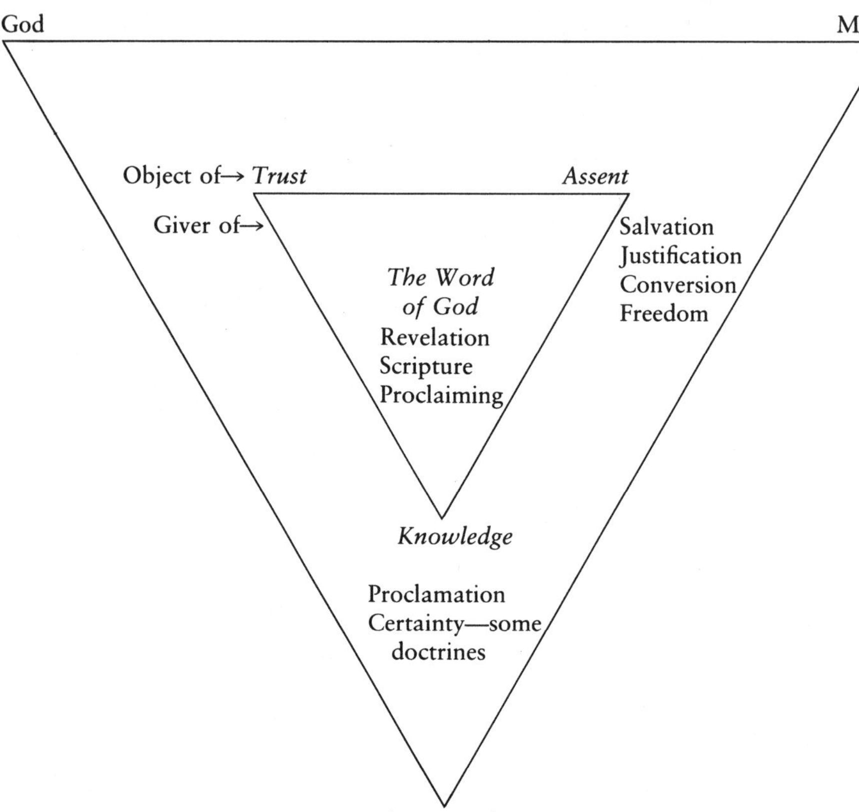

FIGURE 4. The rhetorical structure of an honorific concept of faith

validity of the structure is the presence in both *faith* and *rhetoric* of a common element of persuasion. The presence in both notions of *pistis*—of a notion of trust in the speaker, of a promise of good to be achieved by the listener who freely assents to the message, and of the acquisition of some knowledge—constitutes this basis. These are the ethical, the pathetic, and the logical arguments in rhetoric, and they also exist in the concept of faith.

In addition to the three basic appeals of the rhetorical situation, the diagram also attempts to call attention to some other facets of the congruence of the two notions. The concept of freedom *present* in each is in evidence. So also is the centrality of the verbal emphasis. So also is the notion of a change or a turn. All these facets had been emphasized in the treatment of the individual elements in the two prior sections of the chapter.

It also might be pointed out that the mapping of the two structures need not be perfect at any one area of the structure. It seems clear that "logical" argument and "ethical" argument and "pathetic" argument are not quite parallel in all respects to the facets of the doctrine of faith as shown in Figure 4. The closer approximation of the two structures will be presented in Chapter IV, when a rhetorical analysis of the occurrences of the verb and the noun is attempted (See Figure 6 later, p. 107). However, even then, the mapping makes no pretense to be complete in all respects.

THE CONCEPT OF PERSUASION IN THE OLD TESTAMENT AND THE NEW TESTAMENT

That something like the partial congruence of the two concepts of persuasion and faith occurs in the New Testament is rather remarkable in view of the fact that no such structural congruence can be found for these concepts in the Old Testament. Indeed, as a reflective and analytical concept, persuasion is nonexistent in the Old Testament. As G. Bertram says in the article "Peithō" in *The Theological Dictionary of the New Testament,*

> The typical G[ree]k concepts of persuading and convincing are notably absent from the Heb[rew] tongue. In transl[lating] books, therefore, *peithein* and *peithesthai* [to persuade and be persuaded] are rare, and there is no true Heb[rew] equivalent. On the other hand *pepoitha,* which expresses confidence, is relatively common in the G[reek] OT.[122]

Bertram is obviously speaking of the concept as a reflective and analytical concept, for which there would be a word. No one can read the Old Testament, particularly the books of the prophets, without realizing that there was a marvelous sense of persuasion. The prophets were certainly trying to persuade their audiences to return to God. And there was a wonderful stylistic and rhetorical use of persuasive techniques in the books of the Old Testament. These include everything from the overall use of complete persuasive genres, such as the lawsuit speech, the call to repentance speech, and so on, to stylistic techniques of parallelism at the entire book level down to such techniques at the line level. These techniques have of late been the object of careful and rewarding study.[123] And, of course, the authors who used such techniques were acutely aware, reflectively and analytically, of their own techniques.

But such an awareness does not constitute an awareness of a reflective and analytical concept of persuasion as such. Such awareness may not come to a civilization at all. The author has been told by a teacher in Tokyo University that what surprised the Japanese students most of all in studying his *A Theory of Discourse* was the reflective and conscious analytical awareness of the notion of persuasion. Yet the Japanese have for millenia been experts at persuasion.

It is not, therefore, surprising that there is no word for persuasion as such, as Bertram has said, in the works of the Old Testament written in Hebrew before the period of Greek influence. In Edwin Hatch and Henry A. Redpath's *A Concordance to the Septuagint and the Other Greek Versions of the Old Testament (Including the Apcoryphal Books),* there are many entries for the verb *peithein* (to persuade).[124] But if one subtracts those that were not translations of a Hebrew original (in other words, belonged to the apocryphal books of the Hebrew canon) and those that are not forms of the past aorist form *pepoitha,* expressing confidence, as Bertram pointed out, there is left only *one* instance of the verb that is a translation of the Hebrew original. That particular text reads in translation, "When his words are gracious, do not *trust* him," (Prov. 26:25). Some versions of the Septuagint do not give this verse. In any case, it means the same as the *pepoitha* (trust) forms of the verb.

This survey confirms the judgment of Bertram: There is no reflective *concept* of persuading or convincing in the Hebrew tongue.

The situation is quite different in the New Testament. Taking all the forms of the root "persuade" in the New Testament (this will include the negative forms of *apeitheia* [nonpersuasion] and *apeitheō* [not to believe] and *apeithēs* [disobedient, inflexible, not persuasive]), we find that there are 82 such occurrences.[125] Of these, 12 are practically synonymous with "belief," "believe," or "faith" in a religious sense (much like the quotation from Acts 17:4 with which this section was begun).[126] Of all of the occurrences, 48 out of 82 are related to the notion of persuasion to a religious faith or confidence and obedience to a Christian God.

Of the 82 occurrences, about half are translated as "trust," "obey," and so on. The other half are used in the sense of verbal persuasion. This is quite a contrast to the Old Testament, where such a concept was lacking, as we have seen.

What brought about this change? Almost 300 years of Hellenization intervened between the completion of the last Hebrew book of the Old Testament and the first Greek epistle of the New Testament. It is this process that will be examined in the next chapter.

Chapter III

The Historical Argument

A Probability

The purpose of this chapter is to establish the historical background of the writers of the New Testament in order to suggest the strong probability that they were quite acquainted with the rhetorical meaning of *pistis* as persuasion. To do this, we must outline the extent of the Hellenization that Palestine had reached at the time.

Because the Hellenization of the Mediterranean world at this period was brought about by the instrumentality of the so-called Greek cities, it will be useful to look at the many Greek cities in Palestine during the period from approximately 200 B.C. till A.D. 100 In particular, the spread of Greek as a language used by Jews in Palestine at the time will be looked into. Then the political organization of the Greek city and the extent of participation of the Jews in the political life of these cities will be examined. Because this political life presumed an education to citizenship in the *ephēbia,* the academic center of the Greek city, a look at the kind of education pursued in that institution will be taken. Finally, the influence exerted on Hebraic education by this enveloping Hellenism will be examined. Generally speaking, the conclusions of these surveys might be summarized as follows: Greek was a language that was widely used at all levels of society, particularly in Galilee; the Hellenization of Palestine, particularly on the coast and in the north, due to the presence of the Greek cities, was massive; the Jews participated actively in the political life of the majority of the Greek cities in the northern part of Palestine; the education of the Jews, whether they went through the *ephēbia* or through a rabbinical school or a study group like the rabbinical school, would ordinarily have included an introduction to some Greek rhetoric.

With this as a background, we will then take a look at the kind of environment in which the writers of the New Testament wrote in a more specific way. The results of modern scholarship reenforce the Greek influence that the first section of the chapter establishes.

Given this sort of background, it would seem logical, if the thesis of this book is true, that other writers at the same period, combining the Hebraic notion of *pistis* as trust and the Greek notion of *pistis* as persuasion, would arrive at a notion of faith quite similar to those of the New Testament. The notion of faith in Philo and in Josephus is examined and found to contain many of the same characteristics as that of the New Testament.

The conclusion of this lengthy historical survey is that there is a strong probability that the writers of the New Testament were quite aware of the current notion of *pistis* as persuasion, coming from Greek rhetoric, and could well see similarities with the notion of *pistis* as trust, coming from the Septuagint.

Hellenistic Culture in Palestine

THE GREEK CULTURE AND LANGUAGE IN PALESTINE

After the death of Alexander the Great in 322 B.C., his generals established rival empires centered in Antioch and in Alexandria, the former governed by the Seleucid dynasty and the latter by the Ptolemaic dynasty. Generally, Palestine was under the control of the Ptolemies from 322 B.C. until 198 B.C. and under that of the Seleucids until the revolt of the Maccabees in 167 B.C. From this time until the conquest of Syria by Pompey, Palestine was an autonomous state under the rule of the Hasmonean or Maccabean dynasty. In 63 B.C., Pompey annexed Syria and Palestine to the Roman Empire; and, from that time until the destruction of the

Temple, Palestine was governed by rulers appointed by Rome, most of them being descendants of Herod the Great.

The Seleucids and the Ptolemies were both Greeks and worked systematically at spreading the Greek language, political ideals of the city, and culture throughout their respective empires. Pompey also viewed himself as the emissary of Greek culture. All of them used the institution of the Greek city to achieve the Hellenization of the lands under their control. The result was the Hellenized Palestine of the first century of the Christian era.

Let us take a more careful look at this hybrid civilization. In general, regardless of some differences, the experts agree that the outward aspects of the hybrid culture were quite Hellenic. Speaking of the Hellenism of this period (his book uses the years 175 B.C. to A.D. 135 in its subtitle), Schürer says:

> It was a civilizing power which extended into every branch of life. It shaped the organization of the constitution, the administration of justice and government, public institutions, art and learning, commerce and industry, the customs of early life down to fashion and dress, and thereby set the stamp of the Greek spirit on the whole of existence.[1]

He is here speaking specifically of the effects of Hellenism on the Jews, not just of Hellenistic influence on the Mediterranean area in general. The Hellenization in some areas affected all levels of society, not just the rich and aristocratic members, as we shall see in speaking of the use of the Greek language. Because of the use of Greek in trade and industry, the language of the monetary system was Greek as was the language of many of the materials that were bought and sold, such as clothing materials, household utensils, and the like.[2]

Because much of the life centered in the Greek city, the architecture of the period reflects that influence. As Schürer says, in this regard:

> Architecture, in generally, especially that of public buildings, was an important aspect of Hellenization. . . . In the Hellenistic cities in the environs of Palestine this is, of course obvious. All had their temples, theaters, gymnasiums, covered walks, pillared cloisters, public forums, aqueducts, baths, fountains, and colonnades in the Greek style.[3]

Some of these public buildings involved the political life of the city, and some of them, the educational life. We will look into both aspects later. Both of these assume a common language, a facet of Hellenistic civilization we will look at soon.

The presence of theaters in the Greek cities in Palestine (there have been remains of 20 discovered in archaeological findings) indicates another interesting aspect of life in these cities. Many of these were large: The theater at Scythopolis, some 20 miles southeast of Nazareth, could accommodate 8000 spectators;[4] that at Sepphoris, 3 miles north of Nazareth, could accomodate 5000;[5] larger cities sometimes had several theaters, with Gerasa having 3 and Gadara 2.[6] Caesarea had a very elaborate theater, an ampitheater, a stadium, a circus, and a hippodrome. All the theaters came after the accession of Herod the Great to the position of ruler of Palestine (39 B.C.). Usually, Greek plays and speeches by orators were given in these theaters.

In addition to the educational establishments, some of the Greek cities in Palestine were also famous for the writers and scholars whom they produced. This was particularly true of the cities of the Decapolis (see the map on p. 67). Philodemus, one of the few Epicurean rhetoricians, was from Gadara; so was the epigrammatic poet Meleager and the Cynic and satirical poet Menippus of Gadara. The rhetorician Theodorus of Gadara, tutor to Tiberius, was from the same city.[7] All of these were from the first century B.C. except Menippus, who was from the third century B.C. Gerasa likewise produced some philosophers of note at the time. Ascalon, on the coast, produced four Stoic philosophers of note, one of whom we have mentioned already, Antiochus, the teacher of Cicero.[8] Ascalon also produced two somewhat prominent grammarians, Ptolemaeus and Dorotheus, as well as two noted historians of the period, Apollonius and Artemidorus. Most of these writers we now know little or nothing of except from references by contemporaries. From these references we can infer that most of these writers flourished in the first century B.C. or the first century A.D.[9]

A most extensive coverage of the Jewish writers of the period is that of Schürer, *The Literature of the Jewish People in the Time of Jesus*.[10] In this work, Schürer moves beyond the borders of Palestine and includes writers from anywhere in the Mediterranean area. After covering in the first part of the book Jewish writers who wrote in Hebrew, he considers Jewish writers of the period who wrote in Greek. He includes historians, epic and dramatic poets, philosophers, apologists, propagandists, and translators of the Scriptures. Some of these writers considered in this book are from Palestine, as Schürer notes at several places,[11] and they are not considered in his brief survey in *The History of the Jewish People in the Age of Jesus Christ.*[12] Finally, of course, Josephus, the historian, was also from Palestine. Many of these writers used the Greek language quite effectively. And, as Goodenough points out, nearly all of them use a Greek rather than a Hebrew name.[13]

Not too long ago, it was customary to concede the Hellenization of many of the intellectuals and aristocrats but to deny it of the rural and common people. After a lengthy survey of the Greek cities in Palestine, Tcherikover, the author of one of the most extensive analyses of the Hellenization of the Jews at this period, concludes as follows.

> In this hybrid culture, which was very far from classical Hellenic civilization, the external garb—speech, nomenclature, and architecture—was generally Greek; the content—religious customs, art, opinion, Weltanschauung—remained oriental in origin. . . . we must be careful not to set too high an estimate on the cultural value of the Greek towns of Palestine and on their influence over the country's population. It must be emphasized that when modern historians describe the Greek Palestine cities as points radiating the light of Greek culture in the Orient, their view does not fit historical reality; and Greek names do not always constitute evidence of the Greek content of a civilization.[14]

He continually makes the point that the Hellenization party of the Jews was aristocratic and urban.[15] A. H. M. Jones, in an older work, *The Greek City from Alexander to Justinian,* takes essentially the same view when he comments on the Hellenization of the Egyptian cities, namely, that the peasants were "untouched by Greek culture of the cities. There is evidence that the urban proletariat was but little affected by it."[16] Even Tcherikover, however, admits that the Palestinian Greek cities were more Greek than the Egyptian Greek cities.[17]

Indeed, with the accumulating evidence, most of it archaeological in the form of funerary inscriptions, the position of Tcherikover and Jones is being seriously contested. Because these inscriptions lead directly to the language spoken in Palestine, especially northern Palestine, during this period, let us consider this issue.

What is accepted by nearly everyone today is the fact that Greek was a very common language in Palestine during these centuries. The only serious difference of opinion between the authorities is between those who maintain that Galilee—and other sections of Palestine like it—was almost completely bilingual and those who maintain that, as Schürer puts it, a "rough familiarity with it [Greek] was fairly widespread"[18] though it was not current among the common people.

The evidence presented by the bilingualists is largely archaeological, as Sevenster maintains.[19] As Dalman remarks, most of the funerary inscriptions from Jewish people in this period are written in Greek.[20] As a specific case, Saul Lieberman instances Jaffa:

> Of the Jewish inscriptions found in the coastal town of Jaffa (mostly in the cemetery) sixty are in Greek and only six are in Hebrew and Aramaic. . . . The Greek accompanied the dead to their eternal resting place. In the midland towns of Palestine as well a great many Greek inscriptions have been discovered in the synagogues and the cemeteries. . . .
>
> The very poverty and vulgarity of the language of these inscriptions show that it was spoken by the people and not written by learned men only. We shall presently see that the learned and cultured Jews of Palestine spoke a good Greek as the educated Jew in England speaks a literary English.[21]

Another of the main contentions of Lieberman's book is this:

> In proof of the assertion that Greek was familiar to the Jewish masses in the synagogue we shall try to show that Biblical events were elucidated by the Rabbis in the light of Greek sources . . . and that preachers used Greek translations of the Bible in their sermons.[22]

These types of evidence have led many to the conclusion that, particularly in northern and coastal Palestine, Greek was familiar to all levels of the populace, urban as well as rural, and aristocratic as well as peasant.

Sevenster, Hochner, Wikenhauser, Grosheide, Dalman, and others, therefore, make statements like the following by Sevenster:

> it is quite natural to assume that an inhabitant of Galilee in particular was by nature bilingual, since anyone who lived in Galilee came into the closest contact with Greek culture and must certainly have known Greek.[23]

Such a position would explain the rather adequate *koinē* (popular) Greek of such writers of the New Testament as Peter, James, and Jude. Hoehner and Sevenster have some interesting remarks on this issue.[24] Sevenster considers the Greek of James to be the one of the best examples of Greek in the New Testament.[25] James uses rhetorical figures characteristic of the period, says Sevenster, quoting a recent authority.[26] St. James, he reminds us, was, like Jesus, a humble carpenter's son from Nazareth.[27] St. Peter, a fisherman from Galilee, also wrote a good workaday *koinē* Greek although he might have had some assistance from a scribe.[28]

This would also explain the several instances in the New Testament in which Jesus appears to talk Greek, especially at Mark 7:26, where he talks to the woman who was a Greek, a Syrophoenician by birth. Dalman clarifies this passage by saying that she was a Greek-speaking, but Syrophoenician (Canaanite) by birth.[29] Sevenster also discusses other instances.[30]

Yet such a stance would be consistent with the usual supposition that the native language of Jesus and his disciples was Aramaic[31] and that when some Greeks desired to speak to Jesus (John 12:20), they approached Him through the mediation of two disciples with Greek names, Andrew and Philip.

The instances of Jesus occasionally speaking to people in Greek, despite the fact that it was not His native language, are consistent even with the more moderate approach of an authority like Schürer, who considers the basic language of Palestine at the time of Christ to be Aramaic and who considers the evidence of funerary inscriptions throughout Palestine to be in favor of this position.[32] However, Schürer does assume a familiarity with Greek as a certainty in Jerusalem and in the Hellenistic cities of Palestine.[33]

Finally, the hybrid character of speech in northern Palestine would also explain the frequent Greek names among Jewish families. Even in the immediate entourage of Jesus, there were four or five instances of such names. Andrew, Philip, Thaddeus, and Simon (Peter) all have Greek names.[34] Simon is a native Greek name close enough to the Hebrew *Simeon* to serve as its substitute. However, it is not improbable that Peter had been originally given a Greek name because his brother, Andrew, had one.[35] And Paul used the Greek form instead of Shaul in his converse with Gentiles.

Possibly the most curious instance of a Greek form is the name *Iēsous* itself. It was a common name at the time and was not accidentally given to the son of Mary;[36] Joseph was advised by the angel, "you shall give him the name Jesus (Saviour), for he will save his people from their sins" (Matt. 1:21). Yet, as Dalman points out, the Aramaic-speaking members of the Church of Palestine, when writing of Jesus Christ (the first a Hellenized rendition of a Jewish name and the second a Greek translation for *anointed*), referred to him as Iēsous Meshiha (Jesus Messiah), a form that retains the Hellenized rendition for the first word but that reverts to the Aramaic for the second word. The full Aramaic form would have been Jeshua Meshiha. This strongly suggests that Jesus, even to those who spoke Aramaic, was known by his Greek name.[37]

In any case, it is clear that, at least in the case of language, the civilization of the Greek cities had reached the ordinary people of Palestine, especially Galilee, largely through, it might be pointed out, the influence of the Greek cities in Palestine.

THE GREEK CITIES IN PALESTINE

Christian and Jewish writers seem to agree on the central importance of the Greek city in any discussion of Hellenization of the Jews. Bevan, for instance, practically equates the spread of Hellenism with the "creation of cities."[38] Tcherikover says that the foundation of Greek cities was the "root of Hellenism."[39] These are typical statement that are echoed in all the authorities.[40] Possibly the most incisive statement has been made by Jones in *The Greek City from Alexander to Justinian:*

> The essence of Greek civilization was civilization in its literal sense, life in a city community. The new cities were to provide models for the barbarians to imitate, and to be centres from which Greek culture was to penetrate the surrounding country.[41]

The establishment of the Greek cities was systematically begun by Alexander in Alexandria. After his death, both the Ptolemies in Alexandria and the Seleucids in Antioch continued the foundation of Greek cities. Most of the cities were not new placements, but rather preexisting cities of Oriental backgrounds. For our purposes, one of the most important of the Seleucids who built Greek cities was Antiochus Epiphanes IV, who ruled from 175 B.C. until 163 B.C. and whose attempt to enforce the worship of Zeus and Dionysus in the Temple itself led to the revolt of the Maccabees in 167 B.C. Although the Hasmoneans defeated Antiochus and his successor, they still preserved the structure of the Greek cities that he had established.[42] One of the most important innovations of Antiochus had been the extension of the citizenship of the Greek cities to non-Greeks.[43] In other words, he created some Greek cities without introducing Greek immigrants.[44] This was to have far-reaching consequences, as we will see in the sequel.

Although, at the beginning of the Maccabean period, Jews had been driven from Galilee and some of the Greek cities, Galilee and the Greek cities in it, as well as other Greek cities on the coast, were eventually Judaized, with most of the cities having a healthy proportion of Jews in the population.[45]

When Pompey conquered Syria with Palestine in 63 B.C., he continued the policy of favoring Greek cities, as Jones points out:

> On the one hand, Pompey fancied himself as a missionary of Greek civilization; he was carrying forward the traditional policy of the Roman republic, which had always been the friend of free people against kings, and he was himself a second Alexander, a founder of cities and a promoter of Hellenism. On the practical side, the freeing of cities was a convenient way of weakening the native kingdoms which had grown over-powerful, and in general cities were better subjects of the Roman empire than dynasts.[46]

Even within the old Jewish cities, Pompey built "amphitheaters, and gymnasia in the Greek style."[47] Gabinius (57–55 B.C.) continued the policy of Pompey and was responsible for some of the important Greek cities. Finally, Herod the Great (39 B.C.–4 B.C.) further continued this expansion; he was responsible for some of the most important Greek cities of the time of Christ.[48] It was Herod, who, in Caesarea and elsewhere, introduced the theaters of which we spoke earlier. The Hellenistic period, almost without interruption, witnessed a growth and encouragement of the Greek cities.[49] After Herod and well into the third and fourth centuries, the Greek cities continued to flourish.

But this carries us beyond the period of the formation of the New Testament canon. The canon was born at the height of the phenomenon of the rise of the Mediterranean Greek cities. The early Gospels were directed to the Greek-speaking Christians of Galilee in cities like Sepphoris, Tiberias, Caesarea, Antioch, and Damascus (all Greek cities); and the epistles were sent to Greek-speaking Christians in places like Thessalonica, Ephesus, and Corinth (also all Greek cities). Consequently, it might be worthwhile to learn more about these cities.

What Was a Greek City? It is possible to take a legal or a cultural definition of "Greek city." Jones takes the second view: "By the 'Greek city' I mean not only cities Greek by origin and blood, but any community organized on the Greek model and using Greek for its official language."[50] Tcherikover and Schürer limit their discussions to the more legal definition: A Greek city was a city that was empowered by the emperor or ruling power (e.g., Pompey) to govern itself, to consider its citizens Greek citizens, to issue coins, and so forth. Legally, the city states were allies of the ruling power and were, in effect, petty states, acting quite autonomously. They had to recognize the military supremacy of the ruling power and pay tribute or certain taxes. Otherwise, they could act quite on their own. Tcherikover describes their autonomy as follows:

> Questions of war and peace, the making of allegiances with other cities, monetary arrangements, the drafting of laws and statutes, the internal authority—all these were conducted by the members of the city with complete freedom and without coercion from outside.[51]

Citizens could express their opinions in the general assembly (*ekklēsia*); they elected a city council (*boulē*) of several hundred members to make decisions of an executive nature; they usually were granted the right to live according to their ancestral laws; and they built their own temples, stadiums, theaters, and educational establishments (though some of these constructions were privately financed).

A city often governed not only its own territory but also all the villages and towns within the surrounding area, which could be quite extensive. It is evident that a good deal of Galilee was at one time subject to the domination of either Sepphoris (three miles north of Nazareth) or Tiberias.[52]

These villages and towns were themselves relatively autonomous. The inhabitants were free subjects of the emperor or ruling power. The structure of the government reflected, in part, that of the Greek cities. As Rostovtzeff says, "The administration of most of the villages was not theocratic at all but a sort of combination of tribal organization with that of a Greek city-state."[53]

Size, Number, and Locations of the Greek Cities How large were these Greek cities? We sometimes tend to think of most cities in Palestine in antiquity as sleepy little villages with a few houses nestled in hills or alongside roads or the sea. In actuality, many of the cities were quite sizable, even by modern standards. We have already given one norm of judgment, the size of the theaters: a city that could use a theater of 8000 people, such as Scythopolis, had to be a sizable city. Another norm we have is the number of Jews who were killed at the time of the insurrections in the war of 66–70 B.C. At Caesarea 20,000 Jews were killed, at Damascus 18,000 were killed, at Ascalon 2500 were killed, and at Scythopolis 13,000 were killed, according the Josephus.[54] Even after discounting for Josephus' exaggerations, we still can conclude that cities with such minority populations of Jews had to be fairly large. At any rate, they certainly weren't sleepy little villages.

The number of Greek cities in the Hellenistic and Roman periods was quite large. Tcherikover says that we know of over 350 Greek cities, and "many others are still covered by deep drifts of desert sand and their very names are unknown."[55]

The number of these cities present in Palestine during the Hellenistic period and up through the first century of the Christian era varies, though not greatly, according to the authority consulted. In the map of Greek cities (Figure 5), I have generally followed Schürer's list although I have given strong considerations to cities mentioned by both Jones and Tcherikover even if they are omitted

FIGURE 5. Palestine in New Testament times, A.D. 6–70.

by Schürer.[56] I have tried to follow the general area of Palestine, and for this reason I have omitted such cities as Antioch, Damascus, Tyre, and Sidon, which are included by Jones (and Damascus by Schürer). I have also omitted cities that came later than the general end of the first century A.D. (such as Capitolias, also listed by Jones; it became a city only in A.D. 97–98). Consequently, my list is larger that Tcherikover's by 7, larger than Schürer's by 3, and smaller than Jones's by 10. I have also included Jerusalem because it was probably a Greek city, and it certainly for a short time had a *gymnasium*.

Jerusalem was an exception to the general location of the Greek cities in Palestine. It is fairly clear that they cluster along the coast, in Galilee, and on an eastern sort of frontier from Kanawat in the north to Esbus in the south. In fact, if one were to draw a circle from Nazareth as center, with a radius of 25 miles, one could include 12 of the Greek cities, including some of the largest.

The map makes it fairly obvious that the position of those who regard Galilee as very Hellenized has a geographic justification, particularly when one considers the sphere of influence of each city. At a later period, the territory of Sepphoris extended westward all the way to the sea and that of Tiberias to Samaria.

THE CASE FOR CITIZENSHIP IN TWO GALILEAN CITIES

The reason for this treatment of Greek cities is to establish a connection between the citizenship of the Jews in the cities and the corollary education to citizenship. In Greek cities, the education to citizenship involved a training in rhetorical persuasion. Consequently, if it can be shown that Jews participated in the political activities of these cities *as citizens,* then it can also be inferred that some education in political rhetoric took place.

To establish the first half of this argument, let us now take a look at the case for citizenship in Galilean cities, particularly in the two most important cities of Galilee, Sepphoris and Tiberias. Galilean cities are chosen for several reasons. They played such an important background in the rise of Christianity initially because the greater part of the private life of Christ and a good deal of the public life of Christ took place in this district. Secondly, all but one of the apostles came from Galilee. Thirdly, it is now known that the audience of Galilee and the neighboring areas was the audience for several of the Gospels; this will be discussed later.

The two cities just mentioned, Sepphoris and Tiberias, were the two largest cities in the area and between them alternated as the central legal city for the district between 64 B.C. and the middle of the second century A.D.[57] Sepphoris was probably the capital for a longer time.

Sepphoris and Citizenship. Sepphoris was an ancient site, extending back to the Iron Age. Its Aramaic name was Zipporin, but Josephus, from whom we get much of our information about it, uses the Hellenized form Semphoris.[58] Today it is called Saffuriyeh.

Sepphoris was first established as a capital city by Pompey in 64 B.C.; it was one of the five district capitals he established for Palestine.[59] Gabinius in 55 B.C. reaffirmed its status in this regard. It submitted to Herod the Great in 38 B.C. but rebelled after his death and was sacked by Varus, who sold the inhabitants into slavery.[60] Herod Antipas, however, rebuilt it in 8–10 A.D. and made it, as Josephus says, "the ornament of all Galilee,"[61] Hoehner thinks it highly probable that all available carpenters from the area would have worked on this reconstruction and says that it is quite likely that Joseph and Jesus from Nazareth, only three miles away, would have assisted in the work.[62] Antipas also reestablished it as the capital of Galilee; he probably conferred Greek city status on it as well.[63] Later, when he built Tiberias, Antipas transferred the capital to the new city that he had constructed, giving freedom and housing to many peasants and compelling them to live in Tiberias.[64]

Although predominantly a Jewish city, with a city council that at one time was completely Jewish, Sepphoris supported Rome in the revolt of A.D. 66. After Nero's death in A.D. 68, Sepphoris was again made the capital of Galilee, and Vespasian reaffirmed its *polis* status.[65] Later, in the second century A.D., Hadrian made it more autonomous and renamed it Diocaesarea.[66] It was an important city for centuries after that.

Sepphoris is important for this investigation for several reasons, not the least of which is the clear evidence of the role of the citizens of Sepphoris, primarily a Jewish city,[67] in its political fortunes. The fact that it had different levels of independence throughout its history from 64 B.C. on through the first centuries of Christianity is clear from the preceding historical sketch. What is important in this matter is that the Jews themselves in the assemblies and in the councils made the major decisions. Several critical quotations bear this out. A statement in the Mishnah, cited by Schürer, makes it certain that at one time during this period, *all* the government council-members of Sepphoris were "pure-blooded Israelites."[68] Avi-Yonah says that this probably refers to the period of the revolt of Bar Kokhba (135 A.D.) against the Romans, as a result of which the "Jewish members of the municipality were replaced by Gentiles. . . . However, within one generation, the Jewish preponderance among the population resulted in the restoration of a Jewish city council."[69] Indeed, it was shortly after this revolt that Hadrian reaffirmed its autonomy and renamed it.

Tiberias. In this matter of Jewish participation in the government of the city, Sepphoris was similar to Tiberias, the alternate capital of Galilee from A.D. 23 to A.D. 68 Tiberias was the largest city of Galilee, and it had been inhabited by a good number of peasants, as we saw earlier. It had a preponderantly Jewish population although its "constitution was entirely Hellenistic."[70] Its city council was made up of 600 members, and it was headed by an archon.[71]

We get a vivid glimpse of the activity of the citizens of Tiberias at the time of the Jewish rebellion in A.D. 66–70. At that time, Josephus tells us, the archon was Jesus, the leader of "a seditious tumult of mariners and poor people,"[72] "a wicked man . . . a seditious person . . . indeed."[73] Despite the presence of an influential faction of Romans on the council and in the city, Jesus and another "innovator," Justus, prevailed on both the council and the assembly to take up arms against Rome. Josephus acknowledges that both men could move the citizens by their speeches and in particular that Justus in his "craftiness and fallacies . . . was not unskilful in the learning of the Greeks."[74]

Just as at Sepphoris, it seems evident that here was a council dominated by Jews, headed by a Jew, and yet politically associated with Romans.[75] Two of the Jews address the council and the assembly (almost certainly in Greek), and the council and the assembly are swayed by their arguments and take the suggested measures.

Caesarea. The old city of Straton's Towers, rebuilt by Herod and renamed Caesarea in about 22 B.C., is an interesting comparison and contrast to Sepphoris and Tiberias in the matter of Jewish citizenship. Jews and Gentiles enjoyed equal citizenship rights until A.D. 61, at which time a conflict between the two groups arose, with each group claiming sole rights to citizenship in the city, the Jews on the basis of the city's reconstruction by Herod, a Jew, and the Gentiles on the basis of the earlier population of Straton's Towers, which had not been Jewish.[76] When an appeal was made to Nero, he was persuaded "to disannul that equality of the Jewish privileges of citizens which they had previously enjoyed," as Josephus puts it.[77] This was probably in A.D. 61, as Schürer says.[78] As in Sepphoris and Tiberias, citizenship was granted to Jews in Caesarea (until the revocation by Nero in A.D. 61). What is curious here is the claim of the Jews to sole rights to the citizenship.

It is worthy of note here that all three of these cities, because of their heavily Jewish populations, were important religious centers for Judaism both before and after the war of A.D. 66–70. Sepphoris, for instance, had 18 synagogues and a number of greatly revered religious teachers.[79] Tiberias later became an important rabbinic city for scholarship.[80]

Other Cities in Asia Minor. We know from various sources of several cities in the environs of Palestine where Jews were given the privilege of citizenship: Antioch,[81] Jamnia, [82] Joppa,[83] Iasus,[84] Sardis,[85] Hypaipa,[86] Ephesus,[87] some unidentified cities in Asia,[88] and, of course, Tarsus ("I am a Jew, a Tarsian from Cilicia, a citizen of no mean city," says Paul in Acts 21:39).

It seems obvious, from the extant information that we have, that Jews, particularly in Galilee, had citizenship rights and that they also had such rights in other cities in the environs of Palestine. We also know that it is highly probable that Jews possessed citizenship in Alexandria, in Cyrene, and in Corone (see later, p. 78). Schürer also points out that there were some cities in which Jews had exclusive rights to citizenship, such as Jerusalem at certain times.[89]

I am not hazarding any generalization from these facts. It is enough for my purposes to point to the obvious fact of citizenship in Galilee and in some of the major cities in Asia Minor, both inland and coastal. It is manifest that we can point in these cities to a Greek-speaking populace of some rhetorical sophistication.

However, I have gone to some trouble to collect these data in one place because at least one major authority has questioned Jewish citizenship *on principle* in these places. It must be granted that there were some cases in which Jews were excluded from citizenship: Caesarea after A.D. 61 (as was pointed out earlier); Rhodes (because the "Greeks" there forbade any foreigner to belong to the *gymnasium*),[90] and probably, says Schürer, some of the ancient Philistine and Phoenician cities, such as Ascalon, Ptolemaïs, and Tyre;[91] and probably also Alexandria after the Jews were excluded from the *gymnasium*.[92] Some of these cases were only temporary, and others are only educated guesses (e.g., Schürer on the older Philistine and Phoenician cities).

Consequently, it is surprising that W. W. Tarn could maintain that it is inconceivable that the Jews were citizens of Alexandria or any other Greek city because full citizenship entailed worship of the city gods, and this meant apostasy to the Jews.[93] Tarn's position, which is somewhat paralleled by that of Wolfson, who also *on principle* contends that the Jews did not join the *gymnasium* because of the many statues of the gods,[94] has been questioned because of the kinds of facts given earlier. It is indubitably clear that many Jews were citizens of Greek cities despite the assumption that the worship of the city gods should have excluded them, and it is also clear that some Jews also joined the *gymnasium* despite the oath of the young men on entering and the presence of the statues of gods and goddesses on the premises of most *gymnasia*. Such a priori reasoning has to be questioned on two grounds. First, the facts are against such theorizing: as has been shown, Jews in many cities were among the citizen voters and councillors. It is practically inconceivable that the hundreds of councillors in Sepphoris and Tiberias all were apostates. Tarn has to acknowledge this. Second, it is known that the laws of worship of the city gods and the obligation to take the oath of the ephebes were usually disregarded in view of the tolerance of the Seleucid, Ptolemaic, and Roman authorities in these matters. Schürer and others recognize this tolerance in the Greek city.[95] We know that the Romans exempted the Jews from worshiping the emperor and that the Seleucids had permitted the establishment of Jewish "tribes" (with their own religious ceremonies) in the Greek cities and absolved Jews from participating in the city cultus and from observing laws and regulations contrary to their religion.[96]

Hellenistic Education in Palestine

Given the general ambience of the Greek city, it is time to turn to the more specific issues of Greek education in these cities. First the Greek educational schools in these cities preparing the citizens for legal and political duties will be examined. Then the indirect contributions of Greek rhetoric and law to rabbinical and synagogue education during this period will be looked into.

THE TRAINING FOR CITIZENSHIP: THE EPHĒBIA AND THE GYMNASIUM

In a famous passage in the "Panegyricus," Isocrates had given a definition of a Greek that moved from an ethnic basis to an educational basis: "The man who shares our paideia [education] is a Greek in a higher sense than he who only shares our blood."[97] As Hengel remarks, Eratosthenes, one of the heads of the library at Alexandria, takes the same position as Isocrates.[98] Hengel himself and Marrou seem to agree that Hellenism is a "civilization of paideia."[99] Earlier we have seen that Bevan, Tcherikover, and Jones had defined the city as the foundation of Hellenism.[100] The two positions are completely compatible, for, as we shall see, the educational establishment, the *gymnasium,* and the educational experience, the *ephēbia,* are the central elements of the Greek city.

The Gymnasium, *the Center of the City's Activity.* Nearly everyone who writes on Hellenistic culture agrees with this basic fact: The training for citizenship happened in the *ephēbia,* the (usually) two-year educational experience of the (usually 17- and 18-year-old young man, and it normally took place in the facility called the *gymnasium*. As Merkelback says, in a recent lengthy article,

> The *gymnasium* was the central place of the Greek *polis*. There the young men were educated to be sportsmen and warriors and to be able to defend their homeland and to preserve its freedom. The *gymnasium* was the school of the hoplites, who had marched alongside one another and had sworn not to desert their comrades. In the *gymnasium* was also found the spiritual education of the young men; many of the philosophical dialogues of Plato take place in the *gymnasium*. Only he who has gone through this school has the right to citizenship in a Greek city. In Hellenistic and Roman times, when the whole eastern Mediterranean area was settled by Greeks, Greeks could be distinguished from the natives by the fact that they had benefited from the *gymnasium;* they were called *hoi apo gymnasiou,* "those from the *gymnasium.*"[101]

The life of the young man was spent in the *gymnasium,* he goes on to say.[102] Feldman,[103] Delorme,[104] Jones,[105] and Hengel[106] agree: the *gymnasium* was the center of activity for the Greek city.

As Delorme says,

> From the sporting clubs that they were at the beginning, they became at the end true universities, active centers of political, religious, and social life.[107]

This statement must be taken to be true of the first century A.D., of which Delorme is writing; actually we will shortly see the religious and military origins of the *ephēbia,* long before it was a sporting club. However, at the period that he is considering as a terminus, the era of Augustus, the statement is quite accurate. By this time, not only had the young men arriving at citizenship come to spend their time at the *gymnasium,* but the other age groups of the society had also established *gymnasium* roots. The younger boys (and occasionally girls), the *paides;* the young men who had gone through the *ephēbia* and graduated to citizenship, the *neoi;* and the mature men and older men, the *gerontes,* often had their associations and sometimes their own *gymnasia* in which to meet and socialize and engage in sports and intellectual gatherings and musical festivities.[108] Innumerable associations of all sorts had their roots in the *gymnasium:* banquets for city functions, speeches by visiting orators or rhetoricians or scholars, scientific conferences, music recitals, men and women reciting poetry, rhetorical conferences, and such—all were frequently held at the *gymnasium.*[109] In addition, religious festivals were often centered around the *gymnasium,* as we will see shortly. But the main activities of the *gymnasium* for the city at large were the sports spectacles whether they were just local competitions or were regional Olympiads. Not unlike many colleges and universities in America today, the Greek *gymnasium* was an intellectual, a social, and a sporting center for the town.

Ephebic Training a Condition for Citizenship. Originally in Athens and other Greek cities, the two years at the *gymnasium* culminated in the initiation into political manhood: the ephebe was granted citizenship. Aristotle and Pausanias both assure us of this.[110] However, later on, in Athens at least, the attendance at the *ephēbia* became voluntary and was not required (presumably) as a condition for citizenship. Probably that is why Pausanias tells us that attendance at the *ephēbia* was *formerly* a condition for the full exercise of the rights of citizens.[111] Most of the authorities on the Hellenistic city agree that in some of these cities the *ephēbia* was a required condition for full enfranchisement. In any case, Tcherikover,[112] Jones,[113] Smallwood,[114] and Zeitlin[115] look on the *ephēbia* in the Hellenistic city as a procedure for citizenship.

Consequently, for both social and educational reasons, wherever there was a Greek city, it was almost inevitable that there were both a *gymnasium* and the *ephēbia.* In fact, for over half of the 300 Greek cities that we know of in the Hellenistic period, there is some evidence of the *gymnasium* either in historical records or archaeological remains. This is Delorme's estimate, which he admits is quite cautious;[116] Marrou mentions that we know of over 200 cities for which we have the names of gymnasiarchs, the heads of the *gymnasia,* a very honored position in the city. Consequently, he says, we can assume that the office was universal.[117] The figure, however, confirms the large number of *gymnasia* at the time.

Particularly in the cities of non-Greek inhabitants, the *gymnasium* was the place in which the Greek way of life was learned. When a Greek city was first established, the ruling power simply bestowed citizenship on anyone; but after this initial move, the regular procedure was attendance at the *gymnasium.*

OUR LATE KNOWLEDGE ABOUT THE ORIGIN AND DEVELOPMENT OF THE EPHĒBIA

Despite the figures given earlier the widespread existence of the *ephēbia* and the *gymnasium,* much of the information we have about these institutions is fairly recent. Aristotle's systematic treatment of the subject in *The Athenian Constitution* was discovered only in 1880, and it is the only sustained (a half-page or so) reference to the topic in antiquity; most of our current information comes from archaeological findings in this century. Indeed, many histories of education well into this half of the century do not mention the *ephēbia* at all. And theologians have almost totally ignored the topic as well although the phenomenon endured for more than seven centuries.

Yet the *ephēbia* probably had a religious origin, and it was, initially at least, a fairly religious experience. The initiation oath was quite religious, there were religious feasts and processions in which the ephebes took place quite frequently, and there were many statues of gods and goddesses throughout the usual *gymnasium.* Pélékidis' chapter on the religious aspect of the *ephēbia* is, in fact, the largest in his book.[118] It might be worth recording the oath taken by the ephebe:

> I shall not dishonour these sacred arms, nor shall I abandon my comrades in battle; I shall fight for the gods and for hearth and home, and I shall not leave my country smaller, but rather [I shall leave it] greater and stronger than I found it, either by my own efforts or in company with my comrades. I shall submit to whosoever has authority [over me and exercises it] with wisdom, and I shall obey the existing laws and those that the wisdom of the rulers may enact and if anyone should attempt to subvert them I will not tolerate it, but I will fight for them, either by myself or in company with my comrades; and I shall venerate those whom my fathers venerated. [Be] my witness—Agraulos, Hestia, Enyo, Enyalios, Ares and Athena Areia, Zeus, Thallo, Auxo, Hegemonde, Heracles, my country's frontiers, its cornfields, its barley, its vines, olives and fig-trees![119]

Subjects Taught in the Ephēbia. Religion, however, did not remain for long the major concern of the *ephēbia.* Military training and police duty, then education, and finally sports became controlling aims of the *ephēbia* as it spread throughout the Mediterranean area. In the first century B.C. and the first century A.D., sports and education, probably in that order, were the main concerns of the *ephēbia.*

The educational orientation of the *ephēbia* came early. In Athens, Lycurgus managed passage of a law that required some philosophy and rhetoric in the training of the ephebes;[120] this was within the first 50 years of its foundation as a military training and "civic novitiate," as Marrou calls it.[121] And these subjects seem to have persisted if we judge by the types of teachers appointed and library books that we have some knowledge of, although the *ephēbia* did adapt differently to different host countries.[122] These are the two subjects that the Romans most emphasized[123] and teachers in these areas are the kinds of scholars from the schools of the time, who left their names as we saw them earlier.

Thus, the schools maintained the consistent theme of higher education in antiquity; higher education meant taking lessons from a rhetor. Speaking specifically of the *ephēbia,* Marrou describes the program:

> However, let it be understood, the program consisted essentially in the two disciplines characteristic of higher education, those taught by the philosophers on [the] one hand and by the rhetors on the other. We have seen the one and the other mentioned side by side regularly at Athens; one rediscovers them elsewhere: a philosopher speaks to the ephebes at Haliartus, some rhetors teach at Delphi, at Eretria; and almost at the extremity of the Greek world, at Histria . . . on the Black Sea, a physician comes from Cyzicus [in Asia Minor] to give conferences on his discipline to the ephebes of the city (first half of the second century B.C.).[124]

Other subjects were undoubtedly taught, but rhetoric remained a constant. Plutarch, in the second century A.D., mentions rhetoric, alongside letters, geometry, and music, as being taught in the *ephēbia.*[125] The "letters" here must certainly refer to Homer, the dramatists, and the historians, always listed in the papyri remains of the period from schools or from other sources.[126] Homer remained the educator of antiquity; even at Rome, Martial lists the order of popularity for gifts as being Homer, Vergil, Cicero, Livy, and Ovid.[127]

Nonetheless, the major thrust of higher education in antiquity was rhetoric. As Marrou says,

> Hellenistic culture was above all a rhetorical culture, and its typical literary form was the public lecture. . . and it ran through Hellenistic culture as a whole. For a thousand years—possibly two—from Demetrius Phaleron to Ennodius (later still at Byzantium), this was the standard type of teaching in all higher education.[128]

Jews and the Ephēbia. If we can assume the presence of the ephebic training in the Greek cities of Palestine and its environs during the Hellenistic period, we can also assume the presence of the *gymnasium* throughout the area. We know of the existence of *gymnasia* in some cities: Jerusalem, Kanawat, Gerasa, Ptolemaïs, Jericho, Philadelphia, Scythopolis, Damascus, Petra, Tyre, and Sidon.[129]

Generally, we can assume that where there was a Greek city, there were both a *gymnasium* and the ephebic training for at least some of the inhabitants. Hengel and Marrou believe that we can accept the fact that there were *gymnasia* even in the larger villages, in addition to the cities, whether they were official *poleis* or not.[130]

How did these affect the Jews in Palestine and Asia Minor? There are very few records of Jews participating in the *ephēbia;* of course, as we pointed out earlier, there are so few records, comparatively speaking about the *ephēbia* generally that it was an ignored topic in history until this century. There are a few documented cases of Jews in the *ephēbia* or *gymnasium* or both. Philo and Aristeas speak of the Jews belonging to the *gymansium* in Alexandria.[131] We also know that there were Jews in the *gymnasium* in Iasus in Asia Minor,[132] in Cyrene (modern Libya),[133] in Corone (Greece),[134] and in Jerusalem at the time of the Maccabees.[135]

Whether the Jews actually attended the *ephēbia* or participated in the *gymnasium* is impossible to say with any degree of generality at all. For my purposes, it is sufficient to establish the general ambience of these institutions in the cities of Palestine during the period of the formation of the New Testament canon. What does such an ambience mean to writers like Mark, Matthew, Luke, John, and Paul and to their *audiences?* The answer to this question is the critical issue. Specifically, what did the word *pistis* mean to the people of these cities whether they were Greeks or Jews or Romans or Syrians, and so on?

At the schools of these cities the students learned that *pistis* was the central notion of their education; it meant the persuasive technique of being able to operate successfully in the council, in the assembly, or in the courts. Later, in the practical life of the *polis,* it meant the exercise of these persuasive techniques as speakers or as listeners. Thus, to generations of Greek-speaking Jews in Sepphoris who sometimes completely dominated the city council, to those in Tiberias who often held a majority in the council of 600 members and in the assembly of thousands, to the Jews in Jamnia and Joppa who also often were in the majority, the primary meaning of *pistis* was the meaning it had in the life of the *polis*. This was also true for the many Jews in the surrounding Greek cities though possibly less critically because of less personal involvement. *Thus, for the many Greek-speaking Jews—and indeed Gentiles as well—in Palestine and Asia Minor and in the Mediterranean world at large, faith (pistis) meant the faith one could have in the personal credibility of a political speaker addressing the council; it meant the faith that one could give to the promises or threats of a speaker before the city assembly; it meant the faith one could put in the seemingly logical arguments of a person in the law courts; it meant the faith that one could put in a witness in a legal case. These are the primary meanings of pistis in a Greek polis.* They were taught theoretically in the schools, and they were practiced every day in the council, the court, and the assembly.

This is the historical context and the usual situational context for the primary meaning of *pistis* for the *authors* and for the *audiences* of the works of the New Testament. These are not esoteric meanings; they are the familiar currency of the citizens and noncitizens of Greek and non-Greek in the Hellenistic *polis*. *Pistis* means the techniques of persuasion for political, legal, and display rhetoric and the resulting level of belief (faith) accorded these persuasive messages. It is out of this semantic background that we must interpret the additional meanings of *pistis* that we see in the New Testament.

Does the picture change radically when we turn to the rabbinical, synagogue, and other educational agencies of the Jewish culture in its own right? That is the object of the next section of the chapter.

Jewish Education in Palestine

The educational system of the Greek cities, featuring the *ephēbia,* was paralleled in Palestine with a systematic and extensive Jewish educational system, featuring a type of elementary training in reading, a secondary introduction to interpretation of the Torah, and a higher education for scholars and leaders.

Training in the ability to read the Torah and then to explicate and apply it had been a major preoccupation of the Jews since the earliest times. Josephus traces the tradition back to Moses although there is no other documentation to confirm his statement.[136] Rabbinical tradition also alleges that the Great Sanhedrin, at the time of Ezra (ca. 458 B.C.), had legislated higher education for some of the leaders of the nation; Schürer, however, discounts this claim.[137] There are historians who make strong affirmations about the early spread of literacy in Palestine. Simon, for instance, says, "By the Maccabean Era, elementary education was accessible to all, so that we can appreciate the conclusion of Wellhausen, 'Whoever could not read was no true Jew.' "[138] Simon makes this statement in the context of a discussion about the influence of the synagogue.

Drazin is more cautious, but he does point to a recommendation by Simon ben Shetah (ca. 90 B.C.) that there be education beyond the rudiments of reading and memorizing the Torah; Gerhardsson calls attention to the same prescription.[139] One may question the trustworthiness of this tradition, as does Schürer,[140] without doubting the underlying implication: Secondary education, largely because it was associated with the spread of the synagogue, was probably further advanced as a communal enterprise than elementary education, which frequently took place in the family.

Schürer does grant that there were elementary schools in some towns of Palestine at the time of Jesus.[141] We do know that Joshua ben Gamla (fl. A.D. 63–65) ordered teachers "to be appointed in every province and in every town, and children to be brought to them from the age of six or seven."[142] Because of this and of confirmatory evidence, Gerhardsson can conclude as follows:

> We may be quite sure that at the time of the fall of the Temple there were private elementary schools in all the Jewish towns of Palestine, and that the larger villages of Judaea all had such schools.[143]

There is considerable agreement on the type of education pursued at each level. Elementary education was concentrated on the ability to read and memorize parts of the Torah. Secondary education consisted in becoming acquainted with the collection of the Oral Laws of the traditions. And higher education consisted in the ability to become acquainted with and engage in explication and application of the Law to everyday situations.[144]

The structural similarity of this model to that of the parallel Greek educational system of the day has been emphasized by several writers, especially Gerhardsson.[145] The two systems both initially stressed memory and reading, then writing and some interpretation skills, and finally careful interpretation skills in a rhetorical situation. Substitute Homer for Torah, literary for Biblical exegesis, and orator in the *boulē* for rabbi in the synagogue, and the partial parallel becomes even more apparent. Even the Greek terms for schoolmaster at each level transferred quite neatly.[146] For it was quite true that the main object of elementary Greek education was an introduction to the reading of Homer and the memorization of large parts. The principal concern of the secondary stage was exegesis of the text in four stages: textual criticism (establishing the text), oral interpretation, explanation, and criticism.[147] The third stage of the process in Greek education we have already outlined earlier in describing the rhetorical training in the *ephēbia,* which was a preparation for the council and the assembly. The third phase of the educational system of the Hebrews was the application of the exegesis to the practical life of Jew, and the application was made in the synagogue.

Three central concerns of the two systems have to do with law

(Torah and democratic legislation in the *polis*), with interpretation of an accepted educational ideal (from Yahweh and from Homer respectively in the "books" of the culture), and with rhetorical techniques of making better subjects of the populace (either of Yahweh or of the *polis*). Let us turn our attention to each of these in turn in order to examine the Greek influence on the Hebrew educational milieu of the period. This analysis cannot be at all exhaustive, among other reasons because not enough has been done in a comparative way with the two coexistent systems.[148] In any case, some illustrative material from each facet can be taken to suggest strong influences.

THREE CENTRAL CONCERNS: LAW, INTERPRETATION, AND RHETORIC

The Primal Issue of Law At the heart of both educational systems, though in a vastly different way, was the concern with law. The Law as given by Yahweh to Moses, with its continual reinterpretation and application, was the major preoccupation of the Jewish world. And the free legislation of law in the council and the assembly was the final function of the Greek *polis*. In a curious manner, however different these two approaches were, they converged into a common problem and a partial common solution.

The common problem had to do with the relation of written to unwritten law. Among the Greeks the first to face up to the problem were the Sophists, the wandering wise men who moved from city to city in the fifth century before Christ. They could not help but notice in their peregrinations, even in the restricted Greek world, that the laws of one city sometimes contradicted the laws of another; what was virtuous in one place was demeaned in another; what was viewed as just in one province was not rewarded in another. Some of the Sophists jumped to the conclusion that all law (*nomos*) was culturally relative. Others, however, hypothesized a more basic unwritten law underlying these various cultural customs and codifications. This unwritten basis was nature (*physis*), and both custom and the codification of custom into law were attempts to adapt to nature. And sometimes these adaptations of custom and code became outmoded or never worked in the first place, and a return to nature was called for. The various views of the nature-custom-law trilogy was a pivotal issue (possibly *the* pivotal issue) for several centuries of Greek philosophy and rhetoric, and it has been brilliantly handled by Guthrie in the third volume of his *A History of Greek Philosophy.*[149]

It is not difficult to see the similarity of the Greek problem to that of the Hebrews. The Hebrews were inheritors of a code of laws (the Torah) and an unwritten tradition of interpreting these laws (the Mishnah). Both systmes continually required interpretation and application of the laws—in the case of the Greeks, even abrogation of the laws. But though the two legal systems in one sense were almost reversed, in another sense they were similar. The notions of nature-custom-codification were applicable to both.

It is not surprising, therefore, that two of the major influences of the Hellenistic educational system were in the fields of law and rhetoric. Henry A. Fischel, compiling an anthology of essays on "Greco-Roman and Related Talmudic Literature," emphasizes both of these areas, along with philosophy, but does not include the legal field in the accompanying bibliography because of its "incredibly vastness."[150] Let us take one of these more fascinating studies and relate it to our enterprise.

One of the aspects of the written-unwritten law disputes in Greek had to do with the actual written statement of the law as opposed to the basic intent of the lawmaker. In *Jewish and Roman Law,*[151] Cohen traces the history of the distinction in Greek thought to Protagoras and Lysias, but especially to Aristotle and Hermagoras. The last two, in their rhetorical treatises, had dealt with this critical distinction and pointed out how a rhetorician could exploit it in a given case. Roman rhetoricians, particularly Cicero and Quintilian, had also taken over the distinction and had also introduced it into Roman law.[152] The terms used in Greek for the distinction were "word and thought" (*rhētos kai dianoia*), the stated and the unstated. Cohen shows how Paul adopts this distinction, which is not Hebraic, but uses the notion of the letter of the law, which is very common in Jewish thought, and a phrase "undoubtedly suggested to Paul by Isa. 28:5–6 where it is said that the Lord of Hosts will be a crown of glory and a diadem of beauty unto the remnant of his people and *the spirit of the law* (inspiring) him who sits in judgment."[153]

Cohen's summary of his own argument is difficult to improve on:

> Paul was eminently imbued with the culture of his day, and was undoubtedly familiar with the current doctrines of Greek rhetoric and Roman law, which was natural for a man raised in Tarsus, the seat of a university where Stoic philosophy and Roman law were taught.
>
> As a protagonist of a new religion, Paul was as much interested in reaching the Jews as well as the Gentiles. Consequently he used his Jewish and Greek learning to discredit Jewish law, by methods employed by advocates in the law courts to win a case. Hence he coined the antithesis between letter and spirit, which is an amalgam of the familiar Greek antithesis of *rhētos kai dianoia* [word and thought] and dressed it in a Hebrew garb woven from *ruah mishpat* and *ot min ha-torah* [spirit and letter of the law].[154]

Cohen's article supplies an example of Christian expression that is a marvelous convergence of Hebraic and Greek thought, and in Greek thought a brilliant illustration of the convergence of legal theory and rhetorical practice. It exemplifies many of the principles that we have been exploring.

The issue of the Hebrew Law and the Christian challenge to it is a fundamental theme in the entire New Testament, handled quite dissimilarly by the different writers of the book. But the Hebraic and Greek distinctions of written and unwritten law haunt all of them.

Interpretation. If knowledge of the Torah was the central focus of the elementary stage of Jewish education, knowledge of the unwritten interpretations and applications of it embodied in the Mishnah and an introduction to interpretation skills were the focus of the secondary stage. And the interpretations and teaching of them to others were the heart of the higher education. Later, in the third century A.D., the Mishnah was to be written down; and the interpretations were recorded, with their presumed Scriptural bases, in the Jerusalem and Babylonian Talmuds. However, during the time we are investigating, neither the oral tradition nor the interpretations with their Scriptural foundations had been committed to writing.

Interpretation of texts, particularly Homer, was the focus of the secondary stage of Greek education. And it had become a fairly advanced discipline that incorporated elements of philosophy, of logic, and of rhetoric. Hebraic hermeneutics, which had always been practiced, had, however, not been given the analytic treatment that the Greeks had bestowed on their problems of interpretation. In a sense, the distinction is similar to the practice and intuited rhetoric of the Hebrews as contrasted to the analytic and conscious techniques of the Greeks in rhetoric itself that we have talked about earlier and will return to later.[155]

In the interchange of the two cultures, it was, therefore, natural to expect a borrowing of terminology and some concepts from the Greeks in this area. The person who has most thoroughly investigated this facet of the Hellenization of Palestine has been David Daube, who in a series of brilliant and painstaking studies, startled the scholarly world with his thesis that the hermeneutic system of Hebraic exegesis was heavily indebted to Greek thought. He states his thesis concisely at the beginning of one of his major articles.

> The thesis here to be submitted is that the Rabbinic methods of interpretation derive from Hellenistic rhetoric. Hellenistic rhetoric is at the bottom of both of the fundamental ideas, presuppositions, from which the Rabbis proceeded and of the major details of application. This is not to detract from the value of the work of the Rabbis. On the contrary, it is important to note that, when the Hellenistic methods were first adopted, about 100 to 25 B.C., the "classical," Tannaitic era of Rabbinical law was just opening. That is to say, the borrowing took place in the best period of Talmudic jurisprudence, when the Rabbis were masters, not slaves, of the new influences. . . . It is the kind of thing which, mutatis mutandis, happened at Rome in the same epoch. . . . However, in its beginnings, the Rabbinic system of hermeneutics is a product of the Hellenistic civilisation then dominating the entire Mediterranean world.[156]

Daube pursued this study centrally in a number of major articles and peripherally in many others. His thesis, which had been suggested in the Middle Ages,[157] was supported by others, such as Armand Kaminka.[158] Even those who disagreed with him, such as Saul Lieberman, conceded that the definition of the method, the terminology, and the application of the method to particular questions may have been borrowed from the Greeks.[159]

The curious irony about the phenomenon of borrowing from the Greeks in this and other educational areas is that the borrowing often was for defensive purposes. Rengstorf and Boyd both comment on this educational irony.[160] Rengstorf's analysis is very useful for our purposes:

> Scribal learning was a reaction by conservative Judaism to the disintegrating force of Hellenism. Its aim was to maintain the faith of the fathers through every peril. It was thus constrained from the very outset to use the methods of its opponents. A closed philosophy and a detailed order of life were needed if, as the Rabbis saw it, Judaism was to be effectively protected against the danger of absorption. This meant that the main emphasis of Rabbinic scholarship came to be put on exegesis, not in the practical or ethical sense, but rather in the theoretical. Thus it is understandable that the Rabbis were increasingly characterised by learning as the continually necessary presupposition of teaching, and not so much by exemplary action. . . . The upshot of this imposed development, which is reflected in the attacks of Jesus on the Rabbis in the NT (Lk. 11:46 ff. and par.; 20:46 and par.) is to found in a resolution proposed by Aqiba, and adopted by the authoritative Rabbis in Lydda during Hadrian's persecution, to the effect that a higher rank is to be conceded to studying the Law than doing it. . . . Basically, however, this is a Greek or Hellenistic attitude rather than a Jewish, since in it the intellectual becomes the predominant principle and there is a falling short of the whole man.[161]

The emphasis on exegesis, which Rengstorf indicates comes from Greek sources, is critical to an understanding of the New Testament. Indeed, some of the most telling work in the study of the New Testament in this century has been the analysis of the interpretation techniques of the various writers of the New Testament, particularly their interpretations of versions of the Old Testament that differ from the Septuagint. In the hands of redaction critics, such analyses have brought to light large structural frameworks hitherto unperceived for many of the books of the New Testament.

Nearly all the writers of the New Testament have been examined from these perspectives, and there can be little doubt that they had some kind of schooling in Scriptural exegesis. It isn't known where or when such study took place, but its evidence cannot be denied. For some writers, there have been claims of study groups or "schools" where such skills were learned in company with other scholars or scribes. Thus Stendahl's *The School of St. Matthew and Its Use of the Old Testament* posits such a group for Matthew and uses as one of its main arguments the type of formula quotation that Matthew employs in significant places and that is not the usual rabbinical kind of commentary (*midrash*), but rather a type of commentary favored by the Qumran sect, a type more heavily Greek in origin than the ordinary rabbinic genres.[162] Similar claims have been made for a Johannine school, and in this case there is also a strong Hellenistic bent.[163] Hellenistic claims in this area have been made for all of the evangelists, for Paul, for Luke, for Peter, and, of course, for the writer of the Epistle to the Hebrews.

As the knowledge of the Hellenistic background is to an understanding and interpretation of the Greek concepts of written and unwritten law, the acquaintance with the Hebraic and Greek exegetical techniques must be seen as permeating the New Testament. Because this type of study was rhetorically based, it must be granted to those who used these methods, that is, most, if not all, of the writers of the New Testament. Such a conclusion supports the general contention of this chapter that there is a strong probability that the writers of the New Testament had some knowledge of the Greek rhetoric of the period and, consequently, of some of its fundamental concepts.

Rhetorical Genres and Techniques. A third area of investigation that testifies to the presence of Greek rhetorical study in Jewish schools and study groups, synagogue or otherwise, in this period is the field of rhetorical genres and techniques. Particularly in the study of the New Testament and in the Talmudic scholarship, these areas of investigation have taught us a good deal about the rhetorical tools available to the speaker and writer of the period.

This third area includes the types of oral persuasion genres available in the culture, such as the stories about the wise man, miracle stories, parables, apocalyptic and eschatological sayings, proverbs, diatribes, chria, virtue stories, exempla, and so on. In addition, this area is meant to include here such rhetorical techniques as the use of *topoi,* sorites, examples as logical argument, authority arguments, *typoi* (types or models as forerunners), and the like. The second techniques do not constitute genres as such, but rather rhetorical appeals found in classical rhetoric.

Studies by form critics Martin Dibelius[164] and Rudolf Bultmann[165] and others have attempted to reconstruct the oral tradition forms or genres that the evangelists used to construct the gospels. In so doing, they have carefully analyzed the existence of rhetorical genres present in the Jewish tradition and rhetorical genres paralleling them in the Hellenistic culture of the time. Many of the fundamental building blocks of the Gospels can be traced to these oral genres or forms. Consequently, one has to assume an acquaintance with these materials in the evangelists' stitching together the Gospels into different types of frameworks. Sometimes the Gospels use the Hebraic genres, but frequently they use Hellenistic variations on the Hebraic genres or even the Hellenistic forms themselves. Dibelius and Bultmann differed somewhat on terminology, but their basic categories of the oral tradition were the following: examples (Bultmann called them apothegms and subdivided them into controversy-dialogues, scholastic dialogues, and biographical examples), miracle stories, historical stories and legends, myths, wisdom sayings, prophetic and apocalyptic sayings, laws and community regulations.[166] Dibelius located these genres in a generic function of preaching, and he includes in this "all possible forms of Christian propoganda . . . mission preaching, preaching during worship, and catechumen instruction."[167] Others later emphasized the instructional function more heavily.

The early research of Dibelius and Bultmann has generated numerous additional studies on variations and additions to these lists. Some of the work has been done with an eye to immediate New Testament influences, but some of the work simply relates to the Greco-Roman influences on Judaism in the two centuries before Christ and the first centuries of the Christian era. Thus, more work has been done on the figure of the sage, on virtue stories (aretologies), on martyrologies, on the diatribe, and on the Hellenistic romance.[168] In the field of larger genres, of course, there has been further work on the Hellenistic epistle and the genre represented by the Acts of the Apostles.

There has been an increase of studies looking at particular techniques of classical rhetoric that were current at the time and may have been used in the New Testament and in other Greek works by Jewish writers of the period. Possibly the most ambitious of these is that of Hans Dieter Betz, *Galatians: A Commentary on Paul's Letter to the Churches in Galatia.*[169] In this extensive work, Betz argues that the organization and the logic of the argument are not difficult to perceive "because the letter was composed in accordance with the conventions of Greco-Roman rhetoric and epistolography."[170] Not only are the conventions of the apologetic letter as a genre considered,[171] but the traditional rhetorical arrangement of a speech is also shown as the basic organizational structure of the letter,[172] and the logic of rhetoric is discussed in an introductory section and at the relevant sections of the commentary.[173] Other epistles are now being analyzed by these criteria.[174]

Less comprehensive studies have analyzed the use of sorites,[175] of *topoi,*[176] of types (as models or forerunners),[177] and other techniques of Hellenistic rhetoric. All these were traditionally aspects of invention, as it was called, in classical rhetoric although *typoi* could also be considered under style. I have consistently avoided the issue of style because style was not considered a *pistis* in classical rhetoric although it might well have been. Since, however, I am trying to arrive at an understanding of *pistis* in the period, I have avoided stylistic considerations.

Where did the student of Scripture during this period encounter these rhetorical genres and these rhetorical techniques? Either in one of the "schools" of which we have already made mention or in the synagogue schools. The synagogue itself was primarily a center of instruction even more than of worship before A.D. 70.[178] And when both functions had reached full development, provisions for both functions were made. Thus, Dalman reports that at the period of full development, all of the 480 synagogues of Jerusalem had a Bible school and a Mishna school (elementary and secondary) attached to them.[179] In fact, both Philo and the New Testament refer to the synagogues as *didaskaleia* (schools).[180]

The scribes who taught in the synagogue schools might themselves have studied at Jerusalem or have studied with scholars who had. What was the extent of the Hellenization of the schools at Jerusalem, that is, of the school of Hillel and that of Shammai? The early period of these schools, that is, until well after the destruction of the Temple in A.D. 70, was heavily influenced by Greek wisdom, that is, as we have seen, Greek rhetoric and law. Hillel himself drew on the Greek exegetical system in constructing his first set of systematic rules for interpreting Scripture.[181] His successors continued this borrowing. Indeed, the notion of successors in a school may well have come from the Greek concept of a school; it fitted in very well with the Hebraic notion of oral transmission. In this sense, Bikerman calls both Beth Hillel and Beth Shammai Hellenistic schools.[182]

But the Hellenism was considerably more pervasive. We get a glimpse of this for the school of Hillel at the time of Paul's studying under Gamaliel the Elder. Gamaliel's son, R. Simeon ben Gamaliel, speaks of a "thousand young men in my father's house, five hundred of them studied Torah while the other five hundred studied Greek Wisdom and out of all of them only I have remained here and the son of my father's brother in Asia."[183] The startling effect of the figures is surpassed only by the poignancy of the concluding statement. In any case, it shows how likely it was that Paul, studying either in a Greek school at Tarsus or in Gamaliel's house in Jerusalem, would encounter Greek rhetoric and law.

Because of recent studies like those of Saul Lieberman, from whom the last quotation was taken, scholars today believe that, as Schürer says,

> recent research has shown that the rabbis possessed an undeniable but limited knowledge of Greek culture. "They probably did not read Plato," writes S. Lieberman, "and certainly not the pre-Socratic philosophers. Their main interest was centered on Gentile legal studies and their methods of rhetoric."[184]

Sevenster, also using some of the material of Lieberman and others, points to the use by the rabbis of Greek in some written discourses, in sermons, and in important prayers in the synagogues, and so on. His conclusion is: "Hence it is highly probable that many rabbis were completely familiar with Greek."[185]

Our survey of the schools in Palestine in the Hellenistic period shows that they were massively under the influence of Greek education. Particularly in law and rhetoric, Greek education found its way into the Greek schools of the free city-states and into the Hebrew schools, both at the secondary and at the higher level, in the schools and in the synagogues.

With this widespread omnipresence of Greek rhetoric in the Mediterranean area and with Jews in many localities encountering the same dual cultural confluence of the Greek meaning of *pistis* in the pervasive rhetorical atmosphere and the meaning of *pistis* as it came through in the Septuagint (in the verb form of the root), it would be logical to expect other writers and thinkers to come up with some Greco-Jewish concepts of *pistis* somewhat similar to that of the evangelists and Paul.

Two Contemporary Jewish Concepts of Faith Similar to Those of the New Testament

Given some of the same seeds and the same soil, one should expect similar results, but not the same results. Indeed, even in the New Testament, although there may be elements common to all the notions of faith in all the writers of the New Testament, there are certainly differences among them. Baillie, whose treatment of faith we drew heavily from in Chapter I, speaks of the "deeper unity" of the idea of faith in all the books of the New Testament, even though that "body of early Christian literature doubtless reflects different types of Christianity as well as different temperaments."[186] No one would attempt to defend the position that Paul's stand on the juxtaposition of faith with works is the same as that of James's, at least in emphasis—or even that Matthew's and Mark's positions on the same issue are the same.

Nonetheless, it is not surprising that there are some similarities among other views of *pistis* among writers contemporary to the authors of the New Testament. There are distinct contrasts also. Thus, though Philo considers *pistis* a virtue, in fact, the queen of virtues, the Gnostics (somewhat later for the most part) often demean it in contrast to their superior *gnōsis*. Again Philo and the author of 4 Maccabees undoubtedly intellectualize faith more than do Josephus or the authors of the New Testament, as we will shortly see. However, all these contemporary notions of faith are quite distinct from the notion of faith in the Old Testament. And they point to a generic similarity with the components of faith of the New Testament. They share the notion of faith as honorific (except some of the Gnostics), the notion of a trust in God, the notion of an intellectual assent, and the notion of some corollary doctrine (these are the elements we saw in the framework sketched in Chapter II). They also share the subsidiary concepts of faith as a gift, of faith as being a free assent, and of only a limited measure of certainty in faith. In these senses, we may speak of a generic concept shared with the writers of the New Testament.

I have chosen two of these authors to illustrate my thesis, Philo and Josephus, each representative of a different genre of writing in Greco-Jewish literature. Josephus certainly towers among the historians and Philo among the philosophers. Each is obviously, though in very divergent ways, a product of the two cultures. For Philo and Josephus, at least, there is a large corpus, probably the two largest of this era in antiquity for Jewish writers in the Greek language. The two represent quite contrastive attitudes to the convergence of Hellenistic and Hebraic cultures.

Philo sees a remarkable union possible in the two cultures. Josephus, a Jew, sides politically with the Romans eventually in the war, opposing what seems to have been the majority feeling among the contemporary Jews. Consequently, the two give diversified, sometimes discordant, perspectives of the events or ideas under consideration, and yet they exhibit a view of faith much closer to that of the New Testament than to that of the Old Testament. This similarity, I contend, is due to the common infusion of Greek thought.

PHILO, THE ALEXANDRIAN THEOLOGIAN

Philo is usually classified a philosopher, and the classification may reflect the presupposition of the persons making the categorization. Schürer classifies him as a philosopher,[187] and Wolfson's two-volume work on Philo uses the term "religious philosophy."[188] Certainly, Philo was dominated by a religious viewpoint. Sandmel says:

> Yet more to the point is that his writings, except for the historical ones, are all deeply rooted in Scripture, and again it is the Book religion which animates and shapes, and even dictates, the tremendous expansion that Philo represents.[189]

I classify him as a theologian because I believe that, like, for instance, Aquinas or Augustine, his religion uses his philosophy as a handmaiden, as the medieval terminology put it.

The similarity of Philo's view of faith to that of the Epistle to the Hebrews has been carefully investigated by three scholars, J. B. Carpzov,[190] C. Spicq,[191] and Ronald Williamson.[192] Consequently, I shall use the data they supply and attempt to draw some inferences. Carpzov's overenthusiastic treatment in 1750

> finds so many parallels between Hebrews and Philo that the reader begins to feel at times that if he is right then the only adequate answer to the problem of Hebrews is to say that Philo himself wrote it or that its Writer deliberately set out to embrace within his Epistle as many of Philo's terms and ideas as he could possibly include.[193]

Nonetheless, both Spicq and Williamson concede that Carpzov's work is still a useful storehouse of information. Spicq's two-volume commentary on the Epistle to the Hebrews also contends that there is a heavy Philonic influence on the entire epistle and particularly on the concept of faith in Chapter XI. Williamson's *Philo and the Epistle to the Hebrews* is a direct response to Spicq's claims, attacking his arguments seriatim. Indeed, in the section on faith in the epistle, the structure of Spicq's arguments is the framework for Williamson's lengthy reply. Consequently, it will be useful to consider them together.

Spicq takes four specific characteristics of faith in the Epistle to the Hebrew to be somewhat different from those of Paul and to be similar to those of Philo. (1) Chapter XI eulogizes faith as the fundamental attitude of the soul towards God (whereas Paul in Roman 8 and 1 Corinthians 13 had seemed to accord that position to either hope or charity, respectively). In addition, Spicq points to the similarity of treatment of Philo's treatment of faith in

Abraham to that of the epistle.[194] (2) The faith of the epistle is solid and secure, just as Philo's was.[195] (3) Faith in both the epistle and in Philo has a double object: God's existence and his providence. Spicq uses Heb. 11:6, "for anyone who comes to God must believe that he exists and that he rewards those who search for him" as the basis for this argument. This double emphasis is peculiarly Philonic, he says.[196] (4) The concept of faith in Philo and the epistle is an ensemble of many qualities: reception of divine teaching, confidence in divine power, especially in trials, fidelity, assurance of providence, and so on. These are also Pauline. But in Philo and Hebrews, as distinct from Paul, faith is the last step, not the first in religious life; it also is closely related to vision; and it carries a negative attitude to the sensible word.[197]

In response to these points respectively, Williamson concedes that faith is honorific in Philo and Hebrews,[198] that faith in Philo is solid and secure (though in a different sense from that in Hebrews),[199] that faith in Philo "undoubtedly meant belief that He existed and belief in His providential government of the universe,"[200] and he does not deny that Philo's concept of faith had the same *general* qualities that Spicq had enumerated in his last point.[201] Williamson's quarrels with Spicq center on the more specific differences between the doctrines of faith in Hebrews and Philo on the one hand and between Hebrews and Paul on the other. With these particular polemical points I am not presently concerned. For the purposes of this chapter, it is enough to recognize that even Williamson sees in Philo's doctrine of faith many of the same characteristics that the doctrine of faith in the New Testament manifests. One of Williamson's disagreements with Spicq, namely, that there is no use of *pistis* in the sense of proof in Hebrews, will be returned to later. In any case, it is clear that the three major studies of the comparison of Philo's concept of faith to that of the Epistle to the Hebrews conclude that there are some similarities.

JOSEPHUS

As far as I can determine, there is no extended study of faith in Josephus. Schlatter, in his study of faith in the New Testament, does draw up a list of quotations from the New Testament that parallel citations from Josephus,[202] a procedure he had also followed for Polybius and Philo.[203] His references, 31 in all, constitute only a small number of the 425 occurrences in Rengstorf's concordance, and most of the parallels he indicates are covered in the following survey.

To supplement Schlatter's analysis and to arrive at the possibility of making some generalizations, something Schlatter had not done, I surveyed all the verb (*pisteuō*) and noun (*pistis*) references in Rengstorf's concordance. This I felt was necessary because there had been no scholarship on Josephus' concept of faith at all paralleling the careful work of Spicq and Williamson on Philo. At least I could not find any listed in Schreckenberg's comprehensive bibliography from 1470 till 1968.[204]

Such a survey obviously has its limitations. It is restricted to considering the context of the incidents that contain the *belief* and *believe* terms and does not consider synonyms or phrasal equivalents or larger discourse contexts. And in this survey I did not look at the adjective and the privative forms of the root *pist-* such as *apistos* (unbelieving), and so on. Nonetheless, such a survey does tell something comprehensive about the concept of *pistis* in Josephus, given these limitations.

The first and immediately noticeable remark to be made has to do with the semantic density of the two words in Josephus as compared to the Septuagint. Even if we make allowances for the size of the corpus in each case, it can be shown that Josephus uses the verb and the noun about 10 times more often than does the Septuagint (considering only the canonical books in the Septuagint). What this means is that the concept of *belief generally* is much more pervasive in Josephus than in the Old Testament although it is not as pervasive in Josephus as it is in the New Testament. Using the same proportions as given earlier, for every 1 occurrence of the root in the Septuagint, there are 10 in Josephus and 16 in the New Testament (taking account of the size of the three corpora).

What differentiates Josephus from the New Testament, however, is that the references in Josephus are overwhelmingly secular whereas in the New Testament they are overwhelmingly religious. Thus, of the 425 combination noun and verb occurrences in Josephus, only 39 are used in a religious context. By "in a religious context," I mean in the context indicating the relation of God to humans or vica versa. Thus, to take a negative example, after re-creating Jeremiah's promise to the Jews of a return to Jerusalem, Josephus adds:

> In saying these things Jeremiah was *believed* by most of the people, but their leaders and the impious men ridiculed him as though he were out of his mind.[205]

This passage may have some indirect religious reference to belief in God, for the prophet can be looked on as His representative, but I have not counted such an instance as religious in the sense used here though, in a more general sense, it has a religious context. The positive norm of inclusion in a religious sense of indicating the relation between God and humans will be illustrated by several examples to be examined shortly.

The somewhat low ratio of religious meanings of *pistis* to general meanings of *pistis* can be explained by the nature of much of the material Josephus is covering. His historical accounts of much of the Old Testament in *The Jewish Antiquities* and of the *War of the Jews* does not call for the heavy intrusion of the notion of religious faith as other types of material might, such as some of the treatises of Philo.

Characteristics of Josephus's Concept of Faith. Although the major focus of this section of the chapter will be on Josephus' concept of religious faith, it will sometimes be useful to look at his concept of faith in general. In Josephus' case, the generic concept of faith sheds some light on the religious concept of faith.

Of the 425 occurences of *pistis* (generically used to indicate the verb *pisteuein*) in Josephus, almost half (202) emphasize the trusting relationship. The ratio is almost the same for those with religious connotations (33 percent). Josephus, in this respect, continues the Old Testament concept of faith as should be expected. However, comparing only the verbs (Weiser, in his analysis reported earlier, did not look at the nouns[206]), we find that, whereas all the Old Testament verbs related to trust, only 33 percent of Josephus' did. This is an interesting change. Something obviously has taken the place of the other 67 percent. That something is the logical appeal, as opposed to the ethical appeal (viewed rhetorically). In the religious references to faith in Josephus, 17 out of 39 have a distinctly logical appeal. Because this issue is a controversial one in Williamson's disagreement with Spicq (see earlier), let us first examine a case of logical appeal used in a secular context; then we will examine the logical appeal in a number of religious contexts. An illustrative example in the secular realm is the following passage, which speaks of the discovery by Herod that a certain Joseph had engaged in intimacies with his wife.

> When these words came out, the king became violently indignant and at once released her from his arms, crying out and tearing his hair and saying that he now had clear and damning proof [*pistis*] of Joseph's sexual intimacy with her, for he would not have disclosed what had been privately told if there had not been full confidence between them.[207]

Schlatter uses this passage to relate to Matt. 15: 28, "Woman, what faith you have! Be it as you wish."[208] He also relates it to Matt. 8:10: "I tell you this: nowhere, even in Israel, have I found such faith." I believe Schlatter is interested in showing the degree of faith or belief in these passages. But the passage about Herod is a clear illustration of *pistis* used in the rhetorical sense of a logical appeal.

Some illustrative citations in which *pisteuein* is used in a religious context in this sense are the following:

> God exhorted him [Moses] to be of good courage, to be assured that His might aid would be ever with him, and to use miracles *to convince* all men.[209]
>
> and, tasting it [the manna], he bade them thus too *to convince* themselves.[210]
>
> For the books which he wrote and left behind are still read by us even now, and we are *convinced* by them that Daniel spoke with God, for he was not only wont to prophesy future things, as did the other prophets, but he also fixed the time at which these would come to pass. And whereas the other prophets foretold disasters . . . Daniel was a prophet of good tidings to them [the people].[211]

There are many other passages, both religious and secular, that take this view of *pistis*.[212] It is worth noting that the verb *pisteuein* in each of the three cases just given is translated by "convince." The rapprochement of *pistis* to persuasive rhetoric is not difficult to establish in such cases. Sometimes *pisteuein* is translated "persuaded."[213]

Another rather conspicuous connection with rhetoric can be

seen in the frequent conjuctions of *pistis* in the sense of loyalty with either goodwill or virtue.[214] The tradition coming from both Isocrates and Aristotle, which viewed the elements of the "ethical" *pistis*, that is, the credibility argument, as constituted by good character, goodwill, and good sense, can be here seen repeated time and time again.[215]

Another rather patent overlap with both traditional rhetoric and the Christian concept of faith is the consistent emphasis in Josephus' concept of *pistis* on the verbal aspect. The noun *pistis* in Josephus in translated "pledge," or "oath" or "sworn assurance" some 38 times; other terms used are giving one's "word" or "keeping faith."[216] These are frequent meanings of *pistis* in Isocrates. There is also the emphasis on the written documentation, often in conjunction with the logical appeal. At the outset of his polemical essay *Against Apion*, he speaks of the unimpeachable *evidence* of the witnesses from Egypt and Phoenicia that he will use, then of the annals of the Jews, then of the Greek historians.[217] He makes a similar appeal for his sources in *The Jewish Antiquities:*

> Now, there are many other such decrees, passed by the Senate and the Imperators of the Romans, relating to Hyrcanus and our nation, as well as resolutions of cities and rescripts of provincial governors . . . all of which those who will read our work without malice will find it possible to take on *faith* from the *documents* we have cited.[218]

This verbal concern carries right over to the religious context usages of *pistis*. The following example combines the emphasis on the verbal message of the prophet and the request for a miracle to support belief:

> When the prophet [Isaiah] at God's command told him [Hezekiah] these things, he would not believe him because of the severity of his illness and because the news brought to him surpassed belief, and so he asked Isaiah to perform some sign or miracle in order that he might believe in him.[219]

Here the miracle supports the verbal message and thus brings on belief. Another passage combines the same three elements, this time in a section in which God reassures the faith of Moses by promises and then by miracles:

> But God exhorted him to have perfect confidence, promising Himself to assist him and, when words were needed, to lend persuasion, when action was called for, to furnish strength; and He bade him cast his staff to the ground and to have *faith* in his *promises*. Moses did so, and lo, there was a serpent crawling and coiling itself.[220]

As a final example of the insistence on the verbal message, I would refer the reader to the citation earlier referring to the books of Daniel and used to illustrate the logical appeal meaning given to *pistis*.

One final aspect of Josephus' view of faith has to do with the *free assent* given by the believer to the Word of God. The freedom of the person being persuaded was, as was pointed out earlier, a traditional concomitant of persuasion, particularly the persuasion of the council and the assembly.[221] Josephus, continually concerned about the rights of Jews as citizens in the Greek cities, is very aware of this aspect of citizenship and, indeed, is the authority whom we used earlier on several occasions to establish the fact of citizenship.[222] In fact, in our detailing of the actions of the councils and the assemblies, there is the implicit assumption that the voters are free in their persuasions despite the circumstances of the times and the blandishments of orators. Josephus even speaks of his own success with the populace and of the freedom he gave the people of Sepphoris.[223]

There is also indirect evidence of freedom in religious faith. Thus, the blame that attaches to failure to believe implies the guilt of choosing not to have faith. Schlatter calls attention to several texts in Josephus that parallel the threat of the angel to Zacharias in Luke 1:20: "You will lose your power of speech . . . because you have not believed me." In the next passge, Josephus is speaking of the end of the famine during the reign of Jehoram:

> The only one who did not enjoy any of these good things was the commander of the third division, for . . . [he was] trampled to death . . . as Elisha had prophesied when this man alone of them had refused to believe what he said concerning the abundance of provisions that was to be.[224]

Schlatter calls attention to two similar passages and more could be adduced.[225] It must be conceded, however, that more explicit conjunctions of freedom and faith, whether natural or supernatural, or more general arguments about freedom in political and in religious life would more securely establish the position I am supporting here. However, I believe that there is enough indirect evidence to establish, both in the realms of natural and supernatural faiths, a link to freedom of assent.

The final aspect of faith on which I should like to focus relates to the notion of a measure of certainty. In Greek thought, as has been pointed out at some length earlier, *pistis* did not indicate a total certainty; such a certainty was reserved for *epistēmē* or, in some contexts, *gnōsis*.[226] The limited certainty of *pistis* was partially responsible for its denigration at the hands of theologians as was pointed out.

Attention has already been called to several passages in Josephus, cited by Schlatter, that focus on this issue.[227] Another citation, instanced by Schlatter, could add support to this notion of a restricted certitude. Speaking for Joshua and Caleb, addressing the people, Josephus writes:

> Go we then, forward . . . against the foe, with *no lurking misgivings; trust* in our leader, God, and follow us who will show you the way.[228]

Indeed, the many passages which speak of distrust or disloyalty or suspicion in connection with *pistis* give evidence to this aspect of the notion of *pistis,* and they are legion.[229] In fact, the dubiety of allegiances, of treaties, of pledges, all of which have been considered earlier, lend credence to the concept of a limited measure of certainty attached to the faith (*pistis*) that these verbal messages carry.

This rather protracted analysis has shown, it is hoped, that the concept of *pistis* in Josephus is, on the one hand, quite different from that of the Old Testament and, on the other hand, similar in many basic respects to the generic concept of faith in the New Testament. Josephus, therefore, joins Philo as a Jew contemporary to the writers of the New Testament who joined Hebraic and Greek notions of *pistis* to produce a new concept of faith.

CHAPTER IV

The Analytic Argument
A Verification

The function of this chapter is to test analytically the hypothesis that has been suggested by the two preceding chapters. Chapter II attempted to show the possible congruence of the notions of faith and persuasion; Chapter III gave evidence that made a probable case for the awareness of the Greek notion of persuasion by the writers of the New Testament canon.

If this is so, then the text ought to support such a reading. If the noun and verb occurrences of the root *pist-* manifest such a reading, then some verification of the hypothesis of the two preceding chapters will have been established. I am not using the word "verification" here in the sense of definitive corroboration, but rather in the sense of a different kind of confirmation of the hypothesis. That is, the analytical argument will lend support to the semantic and the historical arguments. The hypothesis will have been strengthened, but it will remain a hypothesis. Much more evidence in these three areas and in other fields must by accumulated before the hypothesis can be creditably called a working theory.

In this chapter a rhetorical analysis of the 491 occurrences of *pistis* and *pisteuein,* in the incidents or expositions or exhortations in which they are found, will test the hypothesis. Concretely, this is tantamount to taking a particular passage and asking if the word *pistis* in that passage exhibits a sense of persuasion. For instance, Mark has Jesus begin His public ministry with these words: "the time has come; the kingdom of God is upon you; repent, and believe in the Gospel" (1:15). If "believe in" here can be construed to mean "be persuaded by" by using the normal contemporary Greek criteria of persuasion, then this passage will be offered as evidence of the coalescence of the meaning of Christian faith and persuasion. To put it another way, the New Testament meaning of *pisteuein* in this case will be construed as embodying an element of persuasion.

The generic application of the contemporary Greek criteria of persuasion, established in Chapter II, to the rhetorical situations of the New Testament will be presented in tabular form in Figure 6 after a brief introduction to the notion of persuasion itself in the New Testament.

Such a construction of a given passage is really making a very modest claim. It simply asks that the dominant contemporary meaning of a term be considered in interpreting a given text. As I shall attempt to show, it does not abrogate previous meaning given the term; it is usually quite compatible with the traditional meaning of the term. In fact, it may enrich the meaning of the term by giving to it a dynamism and a personal meaning that may sometimes have been overlooked.

For interpreting these passages with a notion of persuasion as a semantic backdrop, it will be useful to survey the meaning of persuasion in the New Testament.

The Concept of Persuasion in the New Testament

The first thing to be said about the concept of persuasion is that there is one and that there is a name for it. Unlike the Old Testament, the New Testament has a clearly articulated, conscious notion and semantic cluster of terms for persuasion. Concerning the Old Testament, G. Bertram has stated, "The typical G[ree]k concepts of persuading and convincing are notably absent from the Heb[rew] tongue."[1] For that reason, the verb "to persuade" (*peithein*) is not used in the Septuagint except in the perfect tense meaning of "trust" or "be confident" (*pepoitha*).[2] The situation is quite otherwise in the New Testament. There are 89 occurrences of the root *peithō* in the New Testament—not counting all the forms of *pistis* and *pisteuein,* which are also listed under it in Stegenga's concordance, because of the root origin of *pistis*[3] (see earlier Chapter II).[4] Of the 89, only 18 are of the perfect tense form meaning "trust" or "be confident." The others have the usual meanings of persuade, both in the active and the passive moods. The "trust" occurrences are an expected continuation of the Old Testament notion and, of course, contribute to the semantic cluster of words surrounding the New Testament concept of faith. The other meanings, however, are a semantic innovation since the Old Testament.

They are normally translated "persuade," with "believe" and "obey" occurring occasionally, particularly in the compound forms. Many of the meanings occur in a secular context: The elders and the chief priests *persuade* the people to ask for the release of Barabbas and the death of Jesus (Matt. 27:20); the Jews *persuade* the people to stone Paul and Barnabas (Acts 14:19); the chief priests tell the guards at the tomb that they will *persuade* the governor that the disciples stole the body of Jesus (Matt. 28:14); and so on. But more than half of the occurrences are used in the sense of a religious persuasion (54 out of the 89 instances). In Acts 17:2–4, when Paul argued with the Jews from the Scriptures for three weeks in the synagogue, as was his custom, some of the Jews "were *persuaded,* and joined Paul and Silas." Here "persuaded" clearly means "believed." A similar occurrence can be seen in Acts 28:23–24, in which Luke relates Paul's discussion with the Jewish leaders at Rome:

> So they fixed a day, and came in large numbers as his guests. He dealt at length with the whole matter; he spoke urgently of the kingdom of God and sought to convince [*peithōn*] them about Jesus by appealing to the Law of Moses and the prophets. This went on from dawn to dusk. Some were won over [*epeithonto*]; others remained skeptical [*ēpistoun*].

The Revised Standard Version translates the last sentence: "And some were convinced by what he said, while others disbelieved." The juxtaposition in the Greek of *persuade* for "believe" and *disbelieve* for its opposite is interesting. The passage also illustrates the frequent use of persuasion in a context of a sustained argument about the Old Testament and its Christian interpretation. There are quite a few citations similar to this one.[5]

Particularly noteworthy are the privative forms of the root *peithō*. All the uses of *apatheia* (usually translated "disbelief" or "disobedience") are religious; so are all the uses of *apeithō* (translated "disbelieving" or "disobedient" or "believe not"), and most of the *apeithēs* references (though there are only six).

This brief survey does provide some evidence for two important contentions: (1) The New Testament has a concept and a semantic cluster for the notion of persuasion; (2) this notion is frequently applied to the specific meaning of religious persuasion. Because the term *pistis* (and related terms) are etymologically related to the concept of persuasion and because the term was in widespread use at the time in the sense of rhetorical persuasion, it is not surprising that the religious concept of persuasion should borrow the secular term *pistis* just as it borrowed the secular term *peithō*.

One final preliminary question remains to be considered. A few scholars in America have recently approached the issue of a specifically rhetorical analysis of the Bible as distinct from more general philological or literary analyses. In particular, James Muilenberg and his disciples, on the one hand, and Yehoshua Gitay, on the other, claim a certain novelty in their rhetorical approaches to the Bible. Jack R. Lundbom, a disciple of Muilenberg, claims that the priorities in rhetorical criticism are (1) the necessity of defining the literary unit and (2) the determination of the structure of this unit.[6] The particular literary unit that Lundbom and Muilenberg focus on is the *inclusio*, a segment of the Old Testament balanced at the beginning and end by a phrasal repetition.[7] Lundbom analyzes such units in *Jeremiah: A Study in Ancient Hebrew Rhetoric*, paying particular attention to parallel and chiasmic structures in these units. He acknowledges Muilenberg as his major source for this work, which he considers rhetorical and novel.

Gitay recognizes the work of Muilenberg and his disciples, as well as previous genre studies in the Old Testament, deriving from form criticism and other approaches.[8] However, he distinguishes his work from such research by stressing in his work the act of persuasion, which he considers to be the heart of rhetorical study as such. Previous rhetorical study of the Bible, he states,

> does not understand rhetoric in the act of persuasion. That is to say, both Muilenberg and his followers are concerned with style as a functional device for determining the literary unit and its structure, but their analysis is not oriented towards rhetoric as the pragmatic art of persuasion.[9]

Because Gitay directly orients his analysis of Isaiah to the art and act of persuasion, he considers his work a new direction in Bible study. To ensure that his investigation is distinctively rhetorical, Gitay adopts the rhetorical structure of classical rhetoric and then proceeds to analyze Isaiah. Consequently, for each chapter of Isaiah, he considers invention (the traditional rational, ethical, and emotional appeals), arrangement, and style. The three appeals, it might be recalled, are the three areas of *pistis* in classical rhetoric. In addition, Gitay emphasizes the importance of the context of the situation and especially of the audience in that situation. The "context" is Gitay's attempt to stress the relevance of the *Sitz im Leben* of form criticism and the "matrix" of other Biblical studies. The audience makes a choice, a free decision. All these elements are outlined in Gitay's second chapter, "Rhetoric as the Art of Persuasion."[10]

Gitay's approach is quintessentially rhetorical from the standpoint of classical rhetoric. And, in emphasizing the three appeals, arrangement, style, the situational context, and the audience, Gitay approaches Biblical studies with a rhetorical purity that no one can deny is distinctively original. The approach of my book is quite compatible with Gitay's position. Nevertheless, it is quite possible to recognize the rhetorical relevance of much other work done in Bible studies as indeed the three preceding chapters have made clear. Dibelius' position that the material of the New Testament is oriented primarily to preaching is intrinsically rhetorical;[11] so is the position of later form critics who differentiated preaching from religious instruction. And the many genre studies in messenger speeches, judicial speeches, disputations, and priestly oracles of salvation in Isaiah, cited by Gitay,[12] are inherently rhetorical studies. So are the many studies that we instanced in the last chapter having to do with the rhetorical genres of the period. And the hermeneutical and Midrashic studies of both the Old and the New Testaments are more than peripherally rhetorical. Indeed, given a distinct twist, many of the studies that Gitay calls literary could be oriented to rhetoric.

One more issue raised by Gitay calls for attention. He is quite aware that he is imposing a Greek analytical technique of rhetorical study on cultural documents that were written by authors having no connection with Hellenic or Hellenistic notions of persuasion. They did not follow any school; in particular, the prophet Deutero-Isaiah "obviously did not follow any classical conventional school of rhetoric."[13] Yet Gitay feels that the Greek analytical model is a useful instrument for looking at the persuasive techniques of a prophet of the Old Testament. Such a position assumes some cross-cultural validity to the Greek rhetorical model.[14] Actually, I believe that Gitay has found out a good deal about the persuasive techniques of the author Isaiah.

But Gitay's assumption does raise the question broached in the preceding chapter about the validity of a rhetorical approach used to analyze the persuasive productions of a culture that did not possess an analytical and conscious awareness of the concept of persuasion although it certainly possessed a conscious awareness of the use of some of these techniques.

Our analysis, however, does not encounter this difficulty. The entire intent of the preceding chapter has been to establish the probability that the writers of the New Testament were in contact with the Greek rhetorical tradition in some form or other. Consequently, the imposition of the Greek model for rhetorical analysis on the works of the New Testament does not have to assume any cross-cultural validity or quasi universality in the Greek rhetorical system.

The Analytical Model for Rhetorical Analysis

The problem of this chapter is to apply the symmetrical models of faith and persuasion, established in Chaper II, to the occurrences of *pistis* and *pisteuein* in the New Testament. Figure 6 is thus a combination of the rhetorical structure of the concept of faith, given in Figure 4 with the rhetorical structure of classical persuasion, given in Figure 3. Using Aristotle's categories for classical rhetoric, Figure 6 relates them to the corresponding appeals in the New Testament. Thus, the classical appeal to the authority of the

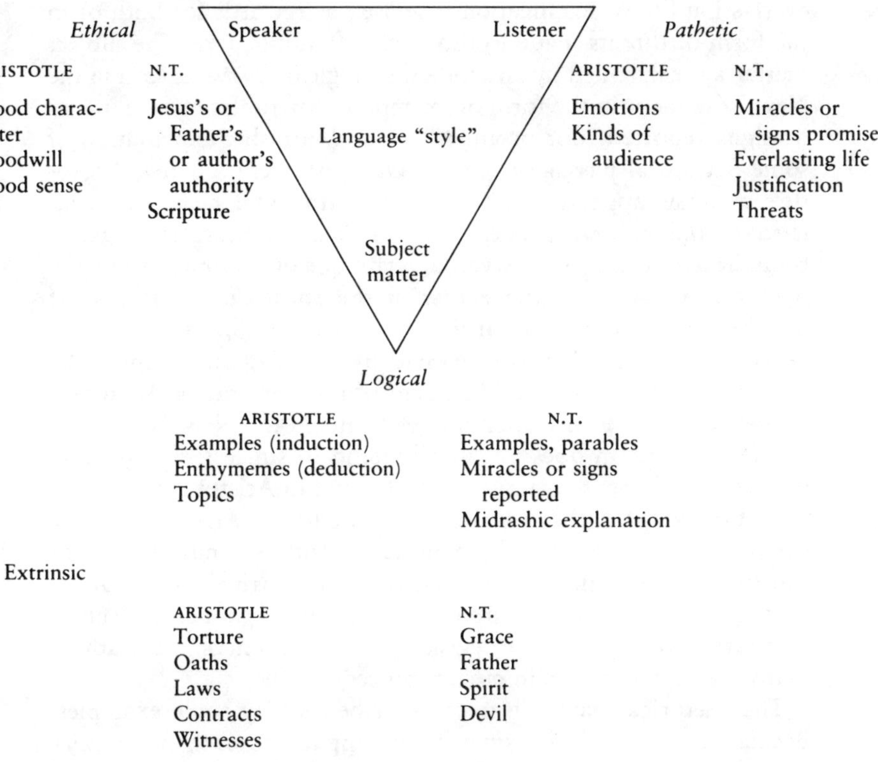

FIGURE 6. Rhetorical appeals: Classical rhetoric and the New Testament compared

speaker, which Aristotle called the "ethical," is related to the use of the authority argument in the New Testament. The author of the Gospel or Epistle, for example, may appeal to the authority of Jesus or of the Father or of the Spirit, or Jesus Himself may appeal to the authority of the Father, or the writer of the work or the person he is quoting may appeal to the authority of the Scriptures. All these are classified as "ethical" in the analysis that follows. Second, the appeal that is based on the interests and emotions of the audience, which Aristotle called the "pathetic" appeal, is most frequently seen in the New Testament in the form of miracles or signs promised to the audience or the reader or in the form of everlasting life or justification proposed as rewards for faith or in the form of threats made to those who do not believe. The subject matter appeal, called by Aristotle the "logical" *pistis,* is seen in the New Testament in the form of examples or parables or as miracles or signs reported (not promised) or as Midrashic explanation of some Scriptural passage from the Old Testament. Finally, Aristotle's extrinsic appeals such as torture, oaths, and such, are paralleled in the New Testament by examples of persuasion (faith) brought about, not by any verbal technique of rhetoric, but by the operation of grace or the Father or the Spirit or, in the case of unbelief, by the operation of the Devil or of the Spirit.

The parallelism that is suggested by the diagram, it might be pointed out, is not a rigid alignment of the elements of Aristotle's elements with the corresponding elements in the New Testament. Thus, the diagram does not at all intend to suggest that grace in the New Testament corresponds to torture in Aristotle or that the operation of the Father parallels that of oaths in Aristotle. But the persuasion of grace and of the Father to faith is similar to that of torture and oaths in court in that both are extrinsic to the art of speech. (Oaths, of course, are verbal, but their *legal* persuasiveness in court derives from the legislative recognition of the truth of oaths taken under certain circumstances).

The rhetorical parallelism can best be seen by some examples. Because the rhetorical framework is applied to each of the 491 occurrences of the verb and noun in the New Testament, it will probably help to explain the category system aligned alongside the list of occurrences given by *The New Englishman's Greek Concordance,* which has been followed in the analysis.[15] The italicized word in the English quotation indicates the word translating either a form of *pistis* or of *pisteuein* in the King James version (see Figure 7).

In addition to the ethical, pathetic, and logical arguments labeled in the middle columns of Figure 7, the analysis also records three other facets of the rhetorical situation. The three are labeled "conversion," "measure of certainty," and "extrinsic" appeal—as opposed to the "intrinsic" appeals of the rhetorical verbal art, that is, the ethical, pathetic, and logical arguments.

FIGURE 7. Rhetorical Analysis of the Occurrences of the Verb *Pisteuō* and the Noun *Pistis* in the New Testament (Citations are from George V. Wigram, *The Englishman's Greek Concordance of the New Testament,* Ninth ed. (Zondervan Publishing House: Grand Rapids, Mich.: Zondervan Publishing House, reprinting the 1903 ed., 1971).

KEY: **Ex,** Extrinsic; **L,** Logical; **P,** Pathetic; **Eth,** Ethical; **M,** Measure of Certainty; **C,** Conversion.

C	M	Eth	P	L	Ex		*πιστεύω, pistūo.*
	√	√	√	√		Mat.	8:13. and as thou *hast believed,*
√	√	√	√	√			9:28. *Believe* ye that I am able to do
							18: 6. little ones *which believe* in me,
√			√	√			21:22. ye shall ask in prayer *believing,*
√							25. Why *did* ye not then *believe* him?
√	√		√	√			32. and ye *believed* him not: but the publicans
√	√			√			and the harlots *believed* him:
√				√			— that ye might *believe* him.
√		√	√	√			24:23. *believe* (it) not.
√		√	√	√			26. *believe* (it) not.
√				√			27:42. and we *will believe* him.
√		√	√			Mar.	1:15. and *believe* the gospel.
√	√		√				5:36. Be not afraid, only *believe.*
√	√		√				9:23. If thou canst *believe,* all things (are) possible
√	√		√				to him *that believeth.*
√	√		√				24. Lord, I *believe;* help thou mine unbelief.
							42. little ones *that believe* in me,
√	√	√	√	√			11:22 but *shall believe* that those things
√	√	√	√	√			24. *believe* that ye receive (them),
√							31. Why then *did* ye not *believe* him?
√	√	√	√	√			13:21. *believe* (him) not:
√				√			15:32. that we may see and *believe.*
√		√		√			16:13. neither *believed* they them.
√	√	√		√			14. because they *believed* not them
√		√	√				16. He *that believeth* and is baptized
√		√	√	√			17. these signs shall follow them *that believe;*
√	√	√	√	√		Lu.	1:20. because thou *believest* not my words,
√		√	√	√			45. blessed (is) she *that believed:*
√	√	√			√		8:12. lest they should *believe and* be saved.
√	√	√		√	√		13. which for a while *believe,*
√	√	√	√	√			50. *believe* only, and she shall be made whole.
							16:11 who *will commit* to your *trust*
√							20: 5. Why then *believed* ye him not?
√		√					22:67. ye will not *believe:*
√	√	√		√			24:25. O fools, and slow of heart *to believe*
√	√	√		√		Joh.	1: 7. all (men) through him *might believe.*
√		√	√		√		12. to them *that believe* on his name:
√		√	√	√			50(51). Because I said unto thee, . . . *believest* thou?

FIGURE 7. (cont'd)

C	M	Eth	P	L	Ex	
√				√		2:11. his disciples *believed* on him.
√		√		√		22. and they *believed* the scripture.
√	√			√		23. many *believed* in his name,
	√					24. Jesus *did* not *commit* himself unto them,
√	√	√				3:12. and ye *believe* not, how
√		√		√		*shall* ye *believe,* if I tell you (of) heavenly things?
		√	√			15. *whosoever believeth* in him should not
		√	√			16. *whosoever believeth* in him should not
√		√	√			18. He *that believeth* on him is not condemned:
√		√	√			but he *that believeth* not is condemned
√		√	√			already, because he *hath* not *believed*
		√	√			36. He *that believeth* on the Son hath
√		√		√		4:21. Woman, *believe* me, the hour cometh,
√		√		√		39. of the Samaritans of that city *believed*
√		√		√		41. many more *believed* because of his
√		√				42. Now we *believe,* not because
√			√	√		48. ye will not *believe*
		√	√			50. the man *believed* the word
√		√	√	√		53. himself *believed,* and his whole house.
		√	√			5:24. and *believeth* on him that sent me,
√		√				38. him ye *believe* not.
√						44. How can ye *believe,*
√		√				46. For *had* ye *believed* Moses, ye would
√		√		√		*have believed* me:
√		√		√		47. But if ye *believe* not his writings, how
√		√		√		*shall* ye *believe* my words?
√		√	√			6:29. that ye *believe* on him whom he hath
√				√		30. that we may see, and *believe* thee?
		√	√		√	35. he *that believeth* on me shall never thirst.
√			√			36. ye also have seen me, and *believe* not.
		√	√			40. and *believeth* on him, may have
		√		√		47. He *that believeth* on me hath
√		√				64. some of you that *believe* not.
√		√			√	— who they were *that believed* not,
√		√	√			69. And we *believe* and are sure that thou art
√				√		7: 5. neither *did* his brethren *believe* in him.
√				√		31. many of the people *believed* on him,
√		√	√	√		38. He *that believeth* on me, as the
		√	√			39. which they *that believe* on him should
√		√				48. or of the Pharisees *believed* on him?
√		√	√		√	8:24. if ye *believe* not that I am (he),
√		√			√	30. many *believed* on him.
√		√	√			31. to those Jews *which believed* on him,
√		√		√	√	45. ye *believe* me not.
√		√		√	√	46. why *do* ye not *believe* me?
√		√		√		9:18. the Jews *did* not *believe*

C	M	Eth	P	L	Ex	
✓		✓				9:35. *Dost* thou *believe* on the Son of God?
✓		✓		✓		36. that I *might believe* on him?
✓		✓		✓		38. Lord, I *believe.*
✓		✓		✓		10:25. and ye *believed* not:
✓		✓		✓		26. But ye *believe* not,
✓		✓		✓		37. *believe* me not.
✓		✓		✓		38. though ye *believe* not me,
✓				✓		*believe* the works: that ye may know,
✓				✓		and *believe,* that the Father
✓		✓		✓		42. many *believed* on him there.
✓		✓	✓	✓		11:15. to the intent ye *may believe;*
✓		✓	✓	✓		25. he *that believeth* in me.
✓		✓	✓			26. and *believeth* in me shall never die.
✓		✓	✓			*Believest* thou this?
✓		✓	✓			27. I *believe* that thou art the Christ,
✓		✓	✓		✓	40. if thou *wouldest believe,*
✓		✓		✓	✓	42. that they *may believe* that
✓				✓		45. *believed* on him.
✓				✓		48. all (men) *will believe* on him:
✓				✓		12:11. and *believed* on Jesus.
✓			✓	✓		36. *believe* in the light,
✓				✓	✓	37. yet they *believed* not on him:
✓		✓	✓	✓	✓	38. who *hath believed* our report?
✓				✓		39. Therefore they could not *believe,*
						42. many *believed* on him;
✓						44. He *that believeth* on me,
✓						*believeth* not on
✓		✓	✓			46. that *whosoever believeth* on me
✓		✓	✓			47. and *believe* not,
		✓		✓		13:19. ye *may believe* that I am (he).
✓		✓	✓			14: 1. ye *believe* in God,
✓		✓	✓			*believe* also in me.
✓		✓			✓	10. *Believest* thou not that I am in
✓		✓		✓	✓	11. *Believe* me that I (am) in the Father,
✓				✓		— or else *believe* me for the very works'
✓		✓	✓			12. He *that believeth* on me, the works
✓		✓		✓		29. when it is come to pass, ye *might believe.*
✓		✓	✓			16: 9. because they *believe* not on me;
		✓	✓			27. and *have believed* that I came out
		✓		✓		30. by this we *believe* that thou camest
	✓	✓				31. *Do* ye now *believe?*
✓		✓			✓	17: 8. and they *have believed* that thou didst
✓		✓	✓			20. for them also *which shall believe*
		✓	✓		✓	21. that the world *may believe* that thou
✓		✓		✓		19:35. he saith true, that ye *might believe.*
✓				✓		20: 8. and he saw, and *believed.*
✓				✓		25. I *will* not *believe.*

FIGURE 7. (cont'd)

C	M	Eth	P	L	Ex			
✓				✓			29.	thou *hast believed:*
✓		✓					—	and (yet) *have believed.*
✓		✓		✓			31.	that ye *might believe* that Jesus
✓		✓	✓	✓			—	and that *believing* ye might have life
✓				✓		Acts	2:44.	And all *that believed* were together,
✓		✓	✓	✓			4: 4.	which heard the word *believed;*
✓							32.	of them *that believed* were of one heart
✓			✓	✓			5:14.	and *believers* were the more added
✓		✓	✓	✓			8:12.	But when they *believed* Philip
✓		✓	✓				13.	Then Simon himself *believed* also:
✓	✓	✓					37.	If thou *believest* with all thine heart,
✓	✓	✓		✓			—	I *believe* that Jesus Christ is the Son of
✓							9:26.	*and believed* not that he was a disciple.
✓				✓			42.	and many *believed* in the Lord.
✓		✓	✓	✓	✓		10:43.	*whosoever believeth* in him shall
✓		✓	✓	✓	✓		11:17.	*who believed* on the Lord Jesus Christ;
✓					✓		21.	a great number *believed, and* turned
✓			✓	✓			13:12.	when he saw what was done, *believed,*
✓		✓	✓	✓	✓		39.	by him all *that believe* are justified
✓		✓	✓	✓			41.	which ye shall in no wise *believe,*
✓		✓	✓		✓		48.	were ordained to eternal life *believed.*
✓		✓					14: 1.	and also of the Greeks *believed.*
✓							23.	on whom they *believed.*
✓							15: 5.	certain . . . of the Pharisees *which believed,*
✓		✓			✓		7.	hear the word of the gospel, and *believe.*
✓		✓	✓		✓		11.	But we *believe* that through the grace
✓		✓	✓	✓			16:31.	*Believe* on the Lord Jesus Christ,
✓		✓	✓	✓			34.	*believing* in God with all his house.
✓		✓		✓			17:12.	Therefore many of them *believed;*
✓		✓		✓			34.	clave unto him, and *believed:*
✓		✓					18: 8.	*believed* on the Lord with all his house;
✓		✓					—	many of the Corinthians hearing *believed,*
✓		✓		✓	✓		27.	helped them much *which had believed*
✓							19: 2.	received the Holy Ghost *since ye believed?*
✓		✓					4.	that they *should believe* on him
✓				✓			18.	And many *that believed* came,
✓							21:20.	of Jews there are *which believe;*
✓							25.	touching the Gentiles *which believe;*
✓							22:19.	them *that believed* on thee:
		✓	✓				24:14.	*believing* all things which are
		✓					26:27.	King Agrippa, *believest* thou the prophets?
		✓						I know that thou *believest.*
		✓	✓	✓	✓		27:25.	for I *believe* God, that it shall
		✓				Ro.	1:16.	to every one *that believeth;*
							3: 2.	unto them *were committed* (lit. they *were intrusted with*) the oracles of God.
		✓	✓	✓			22.	unto all and upon all them *that believe:*

C	M	Eth	P	L	Ex			
		√	√	√	√		4: 3.	Abraham *believed* God, and it was
		√	√	√	√		5.	but *believeth* on him that
		√	√	√	√		11.	the father of all them *that believe,*
		√	√	√	√		17.	before him whom he *believed,*
√	√	√	√	√	√		18.	against hope *believed* in hope,
	√	√	√	√	√		24.	*if* we *believe* on him that raised
			√	√			6: 8.	we *believe* that we shall also (live)
		√	√	√			9:33.	*whosoever believeth* on him
			√	√			10: 4.	to every one *that believeth.*
		√	√	√			9.	and shalt *believe* in thine heart
		√	√	√			10.	with the heart man believeth (lit. *is* it *believed*)
		√	√	√			11.	*Whosoever believeth* on him
√		√	√				14.	in whom they *have* not *believed?*
√		√	√					and how *shall* they *believe*
√		√	√				16.	who *hath believed* our report?
			√				13:11.	nearer than when we *believed.*
	√						14: 2.	For one *believeth* that he may
		√	√		√		15:13.	with all joy and peace in *believing,*
		√	√			1Co.	1:21.	to save them *that believe.*
√		√			√		3: 5.	ministers by whom ye *believed,*
		√					9:17.	a dispensation (of the gospel) *is committed* unto me. (lit. I *am intrusted* with a dispensation)
	√			√			11:18.	and I partly *believe* it.
	√		√				13: 7.	*believeth* all things, hopeth all
		√		√			14:22.	not to them *that believe,* but
		√		√				— but for them *which believe.*
√	√	√	√		√		15: 2.	unless ye *have believed* in vain.
		√	√		√		11.	so we preach, and so ye *believed.*
		√	√	√	√	2Co.	4:13.	I *believed,* and therefore have I spoken;
		√	√	√	√			we also *believe,* and therefore speak;
		√				Gal.	2: 7.	*was committed* unto me, (lit. I *was intrusted with* the gospel)
			√	√			16.	even we *have believed* in Jesus Christ,
	√		√	√	√		3: 6.	as Abraham *believed* God,
		√	√	√			22.	might be given to them *that believe.*
√		√	√		√	Eph.	1:13.	in whom also *after that* ye *believed,*
	√		√				19.	to us-ward *who believe,*
	√	√	√	√	√	Phi.	1:29.	not only *to believe* on him,
√	√	√	√			1Th.	1: 7.	ensamples to all *that believe*
		√					2: 4.	*to be put in trust with* the gospel,
		√					10.	among you *that believe:*
		√					13.	also in you *that believe.*
		√	√				4:14.	For if we *believe* that Jesus died and
		√	√	√		2Th.	1:10.	admired in all them *that believe*
		√	√					— our testimony among you *was believed*
√		√		√	√		2:11.	that they should *believe* a lie:
√				√			12.	*who believed* not the truth,

FIGURE 7. (cont'd)

C	M	Eth	P	L	Ex		
		✓				1Ti.	1:11. which *was committed* to my trust. (lit. *with* which I *was intrusted*)
✓		✓	✓	✓	✓		16. should hereafter *believe* on him
							3:16. *believed on* in the world,
✓		✓	✓		✓	2Ti.	1:12. I know whom I *have believed,*
		✓				Tit.	1: 3. which *is committed* unto me (lit. *with* which I *have been instrusted*)
✓		✓	✓		✓		3: 8. that they *which have believed*
✓		✓	✓	✓	✓	Heb.	4: 3. we *which have believed* do enter
		✓	✓	✓	✓		11: 6. must *believe* that he is, and
	✓		✓	✓		Jas.	2:19. Thou *believest* that there is one God;
			✓	✓			— the devils also *believe,* and tremble.
		✓	✓				23. Abraham *believed* God,
	✓	✓	✓	✓	✓	1Pet.	1: 8. yet *believing,* ye rejoice
			✓		✓		21. *Who* by him *do believe* in God,
✓	✓	✓	✓	✓	✓		2: 6. and he *that believeth* on him
✓	✓	✓	✓	✓	✓		7. Unto you therefore *which believe*
✓	✓	✓	✓		✓	1Joh.	3:23. That we *should believe* on the
	✓			✓	✓		4: 1. Beloved, *believe* not every spirit,
	✓		✓	✓	✓		16. we have known and *believed*
				✓			5: 1. *Whosoever believeth* that Jesus
				✓			5. he *that believeth* that Jesus is
		✓	✓				10. He *that believeth* on the Son
		✓	✓	✓			— he *that believeth* not God
		✓	✓	✓			— because he *believeth* not the
		✓	✓				13. unto you *that believe* on the name
		✓	✓				— that ye *may believe* on the name
✓	✓	✓	✓	✓		Jude	5. destroyed them *that believed* not.

πίστις, pistis.

C	M	Eth	P	L	Ex		
	✓	✓	✓	✓		Mat.	8:10. I have not found so great *faith,*
		✓					9: 2. Jesus seeing their *faith*
		✓					22. thy *faith* hath made thee whole.
✓	✓	✓	✓				29. According to your *faith* be it
✓	✓	✓		✓			15:28. O woman, great (is) thy *faith:*
✓	✓	✓	✓	✓			17:20. If ye have *faith* as a grain of
✓	✓	✓	✓	✓			21:21. If ye have *faith,* and doubt not,
		✓					23:23. judgment, mercy, and [2]*faith:*
			✓			Mar.	2: 5. When Jesus saw their *faith,*
✓				✓			4:40. how is it that ye have no *faith?*

[1]indicates that there is no article before *π.* in the Greek, though one is inserted in the English;
[2]that there is an article in the Greek, though omitted in the English. When a pronoun, pers. or poss., or an adj. accompanies *πίστις,* the article is mostly blended with it in the rendering.

C	M	Eth	P	L	Ex			
			✓				5:34.	Daughter, thy *faith* hath made
			✓				10:52.	thy *faith* hath made thee whole.
✓	✓		✓	✓			11:22.	Have *faith* in God.
			✓			Lu.	5:20.	when he saw their *faith,*
	✓	✓	✓				7: 9.	I have not found so great *faith,*
	✓		✓				50.	Thy *faith* hath saved thee;
✓			✓	✓			8:25.	Where is your *faith?*
			✓				48.	thy *faith* hath made thee whole;
✓	✓		✓				17: 5.	Increase our *faith.*
	✓		✓				6.	If ye had *faith* as a grain of
			✓				19.	thy *faith* hath made thee whole.
✓							18: 8.	shall he find [2]*faith* on the earth?
			✓				42.	thy *faith* hath saved thee.
✓	✓		✓				22:32.	that thy *faith* fail not:
✓		✓	✓	✓	✓	Acts	3:16.	through [2]*faith* in his name
✓		✓	✓	✓	✓		—	yea, the *faith* which is by him
✓	✓						6: 5.	a man full of *faith*
✓		✓					7.	of the priests were obedient to the *faith.*
	✓						8.	Stephen, full of *faith* and power,
	✓						11:24.	full of the Holy Ghost and of *faith:*
✓	✓	✓					13: 8.	to turn away the deputy from the *faith.*
✓			✓				14: 9.	that he had *faith* to be healed,
✓	✓		✓				22.	to continue in the *faith,*
✓					✓		27.	how he had opened the door of *faith*
✓		✓	✓	✓	✓		15: 9.	purifying their hearts by [2]*faith.*
✓	✓	✓					16: 5.	established in the *faith,*
			✓	✓			17:31.	he hath given *assurance* unto all
			✓				20:21.	and *faith* toward our Lord Jesus
✓							24:24.	concerning the *faith* in Christ.
✓		✓	✓	✓	✓		26:18.	sanctified by *faith* that is in me.
✓		✓	✓	✓	✓	Ro.	1: 5.	for obedience to the [1]*faith* (lit. of *faith*)
✓	✓						8.	that your *faith* is spoken of
✓	✓		✓				12.	by the mutual *faith* both of you and
✓		✓	✓	✓	✓		17.	revealed from *faith*
✓		✓	✓	✓	✓			to *faith:*
		✓	✓	✓	✓		—	The just shall live by *faith.*
✓		✓		✓			3: 3.	make the *faith* of God without effect?
✓		✓	✓	✓	✓		22.	(which is) by *faith* of Jesus Christ
✓		✓			✓		25.	a propitiation through [2]*faith*
			✓	✓	✓		26.	of him which believeth (lit. of *faith*) in Jesus.
		✓		✓	✓		27.	but by the law of *faith.*
		✓	✓	✓	✓		28.	a man is justified by *faith*
		✓	✓	✓	✓		30.	justify the circumcision by *faith,*
		✓	✓		✓			and uncircumcision through [2]*faith.*
		✓	✓		✓		31.	make void the law through [2]*faith?*
		✓	✓	✓	✓		4: 5.	his *faith* is counted for righteousness.
		✓	✓	✓	✓		9.	for we say that [2]*faith* was reckoned
		✓	✓	✓	✓		11.	a seal of the righteousness of the *faith*
✓		✓	✓	✓	✓		12.	walk in the steps of that *faith* of our

FIGURE 7. (cont'd)

C	M	Eth	P	L	Ex	Book	Ref.	Text
		√	√	√	√		13.	through the righteousness of *faith.*
		√	√	√	√		14.	[2]*faith* is made void, and the promise
		√	√	√	√		16.	Therefore (it is) of *faith,*
		√	√	√	√		—	which is of the [1]*faith* of Abraham;
√	√	√	√	√	√		19.	being not weak in [2]*faith,*
√	√	√	√	√	√		20.	but was strong in [2]*faith,*
			√	√	√		5: 1.	being justified by *faith,*
			√		√		2.	we have access by [2]*faith* into
√		√	√	√	√		9:30.	righteousness which is of *faith.*
√		√	√	√	√		32.	Because (they sought it) not by *faith,*
		√	√	√	√		10: 6.	righteousness which is of *faith*
		√	√		√		8.	that is, the word of [2]*faith,*
√		√	√	√	√		17.	So then [2]*faith* (cometh) by hearing,
√	√		√	√	√		11:20.	and thou standest by [2]*faith.*
√	√		√		√		12: 3.	to every man the measure of *faith.*
√	√		√	√	√		6.	the proportion of [2]*faith;*
√	√						14: 1.	Him that is weak in the *faith*
√							22.	Hast thou *faith?*
	√		√				23.	because (he eateth) not of *faith:*
	√		√					for whatsoever (is) not of *faith* is
√	√	√	√	√	√		16:26.	to all nations for the obedience of *faith:*
		√			√	1Co.	2: 5.	That your *faith* should not stand in
			√		√		12: 9.	To another *faith* by the same
	√			√	√		13: 2.	though I have all *faith,*
			√	√	√		13.	And now abideth *faith,* hope,
		√	√	√	√		15:14.	and your *faith* (is) also vain.
		√	√	√	√		17.	your *faith* (is) vain;
√	√						16:13.	stand fast in the *faith,*
						2Co.	1:24.	have dominion over your *faith,*
√	√						—	for by [2]*faith* ye stand.
	√	√	√		√		4:13.	having the same spirit of [2]*faith,*
√			√		√		5: 7.	For we walk by *faith,*
√	√						8: 7.	(in) *faith,* and utterance, and knowledge,
	√	√					10:15.	when your *faith* is increased,
√	√				√		13: 5.	whether ye be in the *faith;*
√						Gal.	1:23.	now preacheth the *faith* which
			√	√			2:16.	but by the [1]*faith* of Jesus Christ,
			√	√			—	justified by the [1]*faith* of Christ,
√			√	√	√		20.	I live by the [1]*faith* of the Son
√		√	√				3: 2.	or by the hearing of *faith?*
√	√	√		√	√		5.	or by the hearing of *faith?*
√		√	√	√	√		7.	they which are of *faith,*
√		√	√	√	√		8.	justify the heathen through *faith,*
√		√	√		√		9.	they which be of *faith* are blessed
√		√	√				11.	The just shall live by *faith.*
		√	√	√			12.	the law is not of *faith:*
		√	√	√	√		14.	promise of the Spirit through [2]*faith.*
√			√	√			22.	the promise by *faith* of Jesus Christ

C	M	Eth	P	L	Ex		
✓	✓		✓	✓	✓		23. But before [2]*faith* came,
✓			✓	✓	✓		— shut up unto the *faith*
✓		✓	✓	✓	✓		24. that we might be justified by *faith.*
✓		✓	✓		✓		25. But after that [2]*faith* is come,
✓		✓	✓	✓	✓		26. children of God by [2]*faith* in Christ
✓			✓	✓	✓		5: 5. the hope of righteousness by *faith.*
✓			✓	✓	✓		6. but *faith* which worketh by love.
✓			✓		✓		22. gentleness, goodness, *faith,*
✓							6:10. who are of the household of [2]*faith.*
✓		✓	✓		✓	Eph.	1:15. after I heard of your *faith* in the Lord
			✓		✓		2: 8. are ye saved through [2]*faith;*
			✓		✓		3:12. with confidence by the *faith* of him.
			✓		✓		17. dwell in your hearts by [2]*faith;*
✓	✓				✓		4: 5. One Lord, one *faith,* one baptism,
	✓		✓		✓		13. in the unity of the *faith,*
✓	✓		✓				6:16. taking the shield of [2]*faith,*
✓					✓		23. and love with *faith,*
✓	✓		✓			Phi.	1:25. your furtherance and joy of [2]*faith;*
✓	✓		✓				27. for the *faith* (*τῇ πίστει*) of the gospel;
			✓				2:17. sacrifice and service of your *faith,*
✓			✓		✓		3: 9. which is through the [1]*faith* of Christ,
✓			✓		✓		— which is of God by [2]*faith:*
✓			✓			Col.	1: 4. Since we heard of your *faith* in Christ
✓	✓		✓		✓		23. If ye continue in the *faith* grounded
✓	✓						2: 5. and the stedfastness of your *faith* in
✓					✓		7. and stablished in the *faith,*
✓			✓	✓	✓		12. through the *faith* of the operation of God,
✓		✓	✓		✓	1Th.	1: 3. your work of *faith,* and labour of love,
✓							8. your *faith* to God-ward is spread abroad;
✓	✓	✓	✓				3: 2. to comfort you concerning your *faith:*
✓	✓						5. I sent to know your *faith,*
✓							6. good tidings of your *faith* and charity,
✓			✓				7. our affliction and distress by your *faith:*
✓	✓						10. which is lacking in your *faith?*
✓			✓				5: 8. the breastplate of *faith* and love;
✓	✓					2Th.	1: 3. your *faith* groweth exceedingly,
✓	✓						4. for your patience and *faith* in all
			✓		✓		11. and the work of *faith* with power:
✓		✓	✓		✓		2:13. and *belief* of the truth:
✓		✓	✓		✓		3: 2. for all (men) have not [2]*faith.*
✓						1Ti.	1: 2. (my) own son in the [1]*faith:*
✓	✓		✓				4. godly edifying which is in *faith:*
	✓		✓				5. and (of) *faith* unfeigned:
✓			✓		✓		14. with *faith* and love which is in
✓	✓		✓		✓		19. Holding *faith,* and a good conscience;
✓	✓						— concerning [2]*faith* have made shipwreck:
✓		✓	✓		✓		2: 7. of the Gentiles in *faith* and verity.
✓			✓				15. if they continue in *faith*

FIGURE 7. (cont'd)

C	M	Eth	P	L	Ex			
√							3: 9.	Holding the mystery of the *faith* in a
√	√						13.	great boldness in the [1]*faith* which is
√	√	√					4: 1.	some shall depart from the *faith,*
√		√	√				6.	in the words of [2]*faith* and of good
√					√		12.	in spirit, in *faith,* in purity.
√	√				√		5: 8.	he hath denied the *faith,* and is
√	√						12.	they have cast off their first *faith.*
√	√						6:10.	they have erred from the *faith,*
√	√						11.	godliness, *faith,* love, patience,
√	√		√				12.	Fight the good fight of [2]*faith,*
√	√						21.	have erred concerning the *faith.*
√						2Ti.	1: 5.	the unfeigned *faith* that is in thee,
√		√			√		13.	in *faith* and love which is in Christ
√	√				√		2:18.	and overthrow the *faith* of some.
√	√						22.	follow righteousness, *faith,*
√	√	√		√			3: 8.	reprobate concerning the *faith.*
			√	√			10.	[2]*faith,* longsuffering, charity,
√		√	√				15.	through *faith* which is in Christ
√			√				4: 7.	I have kept the *faith:*
√	√	√	√		√	Tit.	1: 1.	according to the [1]*faith* of God's elect,
√				√	√		4.	(mine) own son after the common *faith:*
√	√						13.	may be sound in the *faith;*
√	√						2: 2.	sound in [2]*faith,* in charity, in patience.
√	√						10.	but shewing all good *fidelity;*
√							3:15.	that love us in the [1]*faith.*
√			√			Philem.	5.	of thy love and *faith,*
√		√					6.	the communication of thy *faith*
√		√			√	Heb.	4: 2.	not being mixed with [2]*faith* in them
√			√		√		6: 1.	and of *faith* toward God,
√	√		√				12.	who through *faith* and patience
√	√	√	√	√			10:22.	in full assurance of *faith,*
	√	√	√	√			38.	the just shall live by *faith:*
√		√	√	√			39.	but of them that believe (lit. of *faith*) to the saving of
			√	√			11: 1.	Now *faith* is the substance of things
		√		√	√		3.	Through *faith* we understand that
		√	√	√	√		4.	By *faith* Abel offered unto God a more excellent
		√	√	√	√		5.	By *faith* Enoch was translated
		√	√				6.	But without *faith* (it is) impossible to
		√	√	√	√		7.	By *faith* Noah, being warned of God
			√				—	righteousness which is by *faith.*
		√	√	√	√		8.	By *faith* Abraham, when he was
		√	√	√	√		9.	By *faith* he sojourned in the land
		√	√	√	√		11.	Through *faith* also Sarah herself
		√	√	√	√		13.	These all died in *faith,* not having
		√	√	√	√		17.	By *faith* Abraham, when he was tried,
		√	√	√	√		20.	By *faith* Isaac blessed Jacob and Esau
		√	√	√	√		21.	By *faith* Jacob, when he was a dying,

C	M	Eth	P	L	Ex			
		✓	✓	✓	✓			22. By *faith* Joseph, when he died,
		✓	✓	✓	✓			23. By *faith* Moses, when he was born,
		✓	✓	✓	✓			24. By *faith* Moses, when he was come to
		✓	✓	✓	✓			27. By *faith* he forsook Egypt,
		✓	✓	✓	✓			28. Through *faith* he kept the passover,
		✓	✓	✓	✓			29. By *faith* they passed through the Red sea
		✓	✓	✓	✓			30. By *faith* the walls of Jericho fell
		✓	✓	✓	✓			31. By *faith* the harlot Rahab
		✓	✓	✓	✓			33. Who through *faith* subdued kingdoms,
			✓	✓				39. a good report through [2]*faith,*
	✓	✓	✓	✓	✓		12:	2. and finisher of (our) *faith;*
	✓		✓				13:	7. whose *faith* follow,
	✓		✓			Jas.	1:	3. the trying of your *faith* worketh
✓	✓		✓					6. But let him ask in *faith,*
✓							2:	1. brethren, have not the *faith* of our Lord
✓	✓		✓		✓			5. rich in *faith,* and heirs of the kingdom
	✓		✓					14. though a man say he hath *faith,* and have not works?
	✓		✓					can [2]*faith* save him?
	✓		✓					17. Even so [2]*faith,* if it hath not works,
	✓		✓					18. Thou hast *faith,* and I have works: shew
	✓		✓					me thy *faith* without thy works, and I
	✓		✓					will shew thee my *faith* by my works.
	✓		✓					20. that [2]*faith* without works is dead?
	✓	✓	✓	✓				22. Seest thou how [2]*faith* wrought, with his
	✓	✓	✓	✓				works, and by works was [2]*faith*
	✓	✓	✓	✓				24. and not by *faith* only.
	✓	✓	✓	✓				26. so [2]*faith* without works is dead
		✓	✓				5:15.	the prayer of [2]*faith* shall save
			✓	✓	✓	1Pet.	1:	5. through *faith* unto salvation
	✓		✓		✓			7. That the trial of your *faith,*
			✓		✓			9. Receiving the end of your *faith,*
			✓		✓			21. that your *faith* and hope might
✓	✓		✓				5:	9. stedfast in the *faith,*
	✓				✓	2Pet.	1:	1. obtained like precious *faith* with us
✓	✓		✓					5. add to your *faith* virtue;
			✓		✓	1Joh.	5:	4. that overcometh the world, (even) our *faith.*
✓	✓		✓			Jude		3. contend for the *faith* which was once
✓	✓	✓		✓				20. on your most holy *faith,*
✓	✓	✓				Rev.	2:13.	and hast not denied my *faith,*
✓		✓						19. thy works, and charity, and service, and *faith,*
✓		✓		✓			13:10.	the patience and the *faith* of the saints.
✓			✓				14:12.	and the *faith* of Jesus

The ethical, pathetic, and logical arguments (*pisteis*) have been explained earlier. Therefore, before examples of the various categories are given, it might be useful to relate the first three categories to the analysis of rhetoric given earlier in Chaper II. The notion of conversion or adhesion is investigated because of the continual emphasis of both Greek rhetoric and theology on the free act of the believer in assenting to the verbal message. A passage is marked conversion (or adhesion) if there is an explicit or implicit reference in the citation to the turn to the Christian message or the adherence to a previous turn. The concept of adhesion is adopted from Nock;[16] in effect, adhesion is continuous conversion. Conversion implies a change, therefore a dynamism, in the attitude of the believer. It consequently implies a rejection of a previous dogma, and adhesion implies the sustained rejection of the previous dogma.[17]

The second category is marked measure of certainty. This category had to be examined for obvious reasons. From the lengthy analyses of the concept of *pistis* in both Chapters II and III, it is manifest that the word *pistis* all through Greek history in antiquity maintained an epistemological level of certainty below that of *epistēmē* (and sometimes *gnōsis*). The epistemological status of *pistis* was largely accountable for its degraded position in the Platonic and allied systems of thought. And, I have suggested, it is also responsible for the negative view taken of the Greek concept by some theologians. In any case, it is worth examining whether the epistemological status of *pistis* is retained in the New Testament because in rhetoric, through the Sophists, Plato, Aristotle, and later rhetoricians, *pistis* manifests its inferior rank to *epistēmē:* there is always some room for doubt in a *pistis* conviction.

The last column in the categories, marked extrinsic, has already been briefly explained earlier when the ethical, pathetic, and logical appeals were compared to the Aristotelian classifications.

SOME EXAMPLES OF THE CATEGORIES

To understand the classifications, the reader must continually keep in mind the underlying motivation behind the *faith* or *act of believing* in the incident or exposition or exhortation. Take the first example given in Matthew 8:13, "and as thou hast *believed.*" I have classified this as having a measure of certainty, as having an ethical argument, as having a pathetic argument and also a logical argument. In this case, the phrase "*as* thou hast believed" already indicates a measure of certainty; however, that alone would not be evidence enough to classify the passage as indicating a degree of certainty. Yet, in the pericope, Jesus had said of the centurion's faith, "nowhere, even in Israel, have I found such faith." This implies less faith in others and is consequently evidence for an indication of a degree of faith.

The motivations in this incident are also fairly distinct. The desire for the cure of his son is the reason for the centurion's approaching Jesus; consequently, there is in part a pathetic appeal. He also believes because of the authority of Jesus, whom he recognizes as having power in his command, "You need only say the word and the boy will be cured." This explains the classification under the ethical appeal (the authority appeal). Finally, the logical appeal is involved because it is only because he had heard of the miracles and signs of Jesus and of the power of His word that the centurion comes to Jesus. The few verses just before this pericope begins emphasize this as do the concluding verses of the preceding chapter. A faith based on evidence of this sort is logical: The centurion generalizes to future signs. There is some logical motivation to his faith.

This example illustrates the necessity of considering the whole pericope, indeed even the preceding one. It also, with the exception of the logical appeal, is quite clearcut.

Another passage by way of general illustration may further clarify the classification scheme. A passage from Luke (8:12) can illustrate the two categories that the preceding passage did not. In explaining the parable of the sower to the apostles, Jesus says:

> The seed is the word of God. Those along the footpath are the men who hear it, and then the devil comes and carries off the word from their hearts for fear they should believe and be saved.

Here there is a strong indication of a conversion possibility (rejected). And the rejection is brought about by an extrinsic agency, the devil. By contrast in the next verse, the rejection comes from the hearers of the word themselves, "choked by cares and wealth and the pleasures of life." The first passage thus illustrates the *extrinsic pistis* and the conversion (negative) category.

A positive instance of the extrinsic motivation or cause can be seen in Romans (3:22–23):

> it [God's justice] is God's way of righting wrong, effective through faith in Christ for all who have such faith—all, without distinction. For all alike have sinned, and are deprived of the divine splendour, and all are justified by God's free grace alone, through his act of liberation in the person of Christ Jesus.

This passage is also categorized as embodying an ethical argument because it comes immediately after a section that has used Scriptural authority to establish the principle repeated in the verse under consideration, "all, without distinction. For all all alike have sinned." Citations from the Psalms and Isaiah in verses 10 through 18 are thus the *authority* of the statement. But the use of the Scriptural authority as a premise from which to infer the desired conclusion is a logical argument. And, finally, the expectation of justification is a pathetic appeal. Thus, the passage is coded for extrinsic, ethical, pathetic, and logical appeals.

Conversion or Adhesion. An interesting and fairly obvious example of the conjoining of conversion with some other appeals can be seen in Jesus' injunctions to the 11 at the end of Mark's gospel. After upbraiding them for their incredulity Jesus says:

> Go forth to every part of the world, and proclaim the Good News to the whole creation. Those who believe it are baptised will find salvation; those who do not believe will be condemned [16:145–16].

The reception of the good news and the turn to the new religion are explicit in this passage (note also the promise and threat—the pathetic argument).

Besides instances of positive and negative conversion, there are also many cases of adhesion, or persistent conversion. A fine example can be seen in Romans 4:18–20:

> When hope seemed hopeless, his faith was such that he became "father of many nations," in agreement with the words which

> had been spoken to him: "Thus shall your descendants be." Without any weakening of faith he contemplated his own body (for he was about a hundred years old) and the deadness of Sarah's womb, and never doubted God's promise in unbelief, but strong in faith, gave honour to God.

The phrase "without any weakening of faith" is a fine illustration of the concept of adhesion. In this case, despite a testing, Abraham's faith remains strong: he adheres to his former position. The passage also illustrates the use of Scripture to establish the meaning of the phrase "counted unto him as righteousness," which appears in the verse following the quotation. Consequently, I have also classified this passage as embodying an ethical (authority) appeal and a logical appeal. The framing of the entire chapter is structured by the argument of the third chapter, quoted earlier, about the justification through God's grace alone and by the summarizing of this same notion at the beginning of the next chapter (5:1) as well as by the repetition of the same motif at 4:2–3, 4–5, 8, and indeed the justification through God's grace alone is a motif of the entire chapter. Therefore, the passage is also coded as containing the extrinsic (outside agency) cause. And because the motivation is for the hope of righteousness, the passage is also coded for the pathetic appeal. Finally, the phrases "weakening of faith" and "strong in faith" are explicit indications of degrees of faith, so the citation is also coded for measure of certainty. Thus, the passage incorporates all six of the categories.

Measure of Certainty. The preceding example from Romans 4:19 is a superb illustration of this category, as is also this passage from Matthew 8:10: "nowhere, even in Israel, have I found such faith." To this could also be added the sequel to the passage from the parable to the sower, which we looked at earlier. In the next verse, Luke, quoting Jesus, refers to those who receive "the word with joy when they hear it, but have no root; they are believers for awhile, but in the time of testing they desert," and then he refers to those "who hear, but their further growth is choked by cares and wealth and the pleasures of life" (8:13–14).

There are many passages like this one that speak of a growth or an increase in faith or of weak faith or strong faith, and the like.

All these are coded for measure of certainty. Some examples follow: "him that is weak in faith" (Rom. 14:1), "when your faith is increased" (2 Cor. 10:15), "your furtherance and joy of faith" (Phil. 1:25), "your faith groweth exceedingly" (2 Thess. 1:3), "they have erred from the faith" (1 Tim. 6:21), and so on. I have here used the translation followed in the concordance and reproduced in the table.

Extrinsic Motivation or Cause. In the general discussion of this section as well as in some of the specific sections devoted to other categories, different types of specimens of extrinsic motivation have already been examined. The negative example of the devil's taking the faith away (Luke 8:12), the positive example of God and Abraham (Rom 3:22–23), and the repetition of this theme all through Romans, Chapter 4—all these illustrate the concept. Here is an additional sample, in which the verb *pisteusasin* (literally, "having believed") is translated "put our trust in":

> God gave them no less a gift than he gave us when we *put our trust in* the Lord Jesus Christ; how then could I possibly stand in God's way? **Acts 1:17**].

Here Peter is speaking of the gift of faith to the Gentiles and to the Jews. Peter repeats the same message in Acts 15:7–9:

> "My friends," he said, "in the early days, as you yourselves know, God made his choice among you and ordained that from my lips the Gentiles should hear and believe the message of the Gospel. And God, who can read men's minds, showed his approval of them by giving the Holy Spirit to them, as he did to us. He made no difference between them and us; for he purified their hearts by faith."

This is possibly as unambiguous an illustration of the nature of the extrinsic category as can be found. God "ordained . . . that the Gentiles should . . . believe," and "he purified their hearts by faith."

Ethical Appeals. The example of the centurion who believed in the authority of Jesus, "You need only say the word and the boy will be cured" (Matt. 8:8) illustrates the ethical appeal as well as some other appeals. And the example of Abraham, given by Paul (Rom. 4:18–19), also exemplifies the faith in the word of God:

> When hope seemed hopeless, his faith was such that he became "father of many nations," in agreement with the words which had been spoken to him: "Thus shall your descendants be." Without any weakening of faith he contemplated his own body. . . .

Faith based on a belief in Scripture is the most frequent type of ethical appeal in the New Testament. But there are other modes in which the ethical appeal can be seen. Thus, Jesus can assert the authority of His own statements or the authority that He has from the Father. Here is an example of a combination of the two:

> In very truth, anyone who gives heed to what I say and *puts his trust in* him who sent me has hold of eternal life, and does not come up for judgement, but has already passed from death to life. In truth, in very truth I tell you, a time is coming, indeed it is already here, when the dead shall hear the voice of the Son of God [John 5:24–25].

The Greek verb for "puts his trust in" is *pisteuōn*.

As in the centurion example (Matt. 8:8), the example from Paul (Rom. 4:18–19), and the example from John (5:24–25), many of the ethical arguments tend to be related to situations that emphasize the *verbal* nature of the message, a characteristic of both Greek rhetoric and Christian faith. The emphasis on the verbal is also seen in a passage like the following (John 4:50):

> Then Jesus said, "Return home; your son will live." The man believed what Jesus said [literally "the word of Jesus"] and started for home.

In many instances, the ethical appeal, either of Scripture or of Jesus' own authority, is used in a passage talking about a denial of faith: "But if you believe not what he [Moses] wrote, how are you to believe what I say?" (John 5:47)

Another critical use of the ethical appeal has to do with the relation of the verbal message to the possibility of faith. Paul points this out in Romans 10:11, "So faith comes from what is heard, and what is heard comes by the preaching of Christ."

Pathetic Appeal. The second of the rhetorical intrinsic appeals, the pathetic or emotional or audience-interest appeal, differs from writer to writer. Miracles and signs are frequently promised in the Synoptics, everlasting life in John, and justification in Paul though these are not at all exclusive appeals in any of these authors.

The incident in Mark 9:17–27, involving a father whose son was possessed by a spirit, focuses on the father's plea to Jesus:

> "But if it is at all possible for you, take pity upon us and help us." "If it is possible!" said Jesus. "Everything is possible to one who has faith." "I have faith," cried the boy's father; "help me where faith falls short" [Mark 9:22–24].

This passage, in addition to exhibiting an excellent example of the pathetic appeal, also illustrates the measure of certainty characteristic of faith (and of rhetoric).

A typical Johannine example of the appeal of everlasting life is the following:

> For it is my Father's will that everyone who looks upon the Son and puts his faith in him shall possess eternal life; and I will raise him up on the last day" [John 6:40]

Threats can also be used to motivate faith, as we see in James: "You have faith enough to believe that here is one God. Excellent! The devils have faith like that, and it makes them tremble" (2:19).

Paul's concern with justification matches that of John with everlasting life. We have already called attention to the theme of righteousness in the fourth chapter of Romans. And the theme recurs throughout Paul, often allied with the ethical appeal from Scripture.

Peter can combine the same two motivations, as he does in 2 Peter 2:6–9,

> For it stands written:
>
> > "I lay in Zion a choice corner-stone of great worth. The man who has faith in it will not be put to shame."
>
> The great worth of which it speaks is for you who have faith. For those who have no faith, the stone which the builders rejected has become not only the corner-stone, but also "a stone to trip over, a rock to stumble against." They fall when they disbelieve the Word. Such was their appointed lot.

This complex passage combines the pathetic argument with the appeal from Scripture (the ethical argument) with the argument from Scripture (the logical argument) with the extrinsic appeal ("Such was their appointed lot").

Logical Appeal. Unlike the pathetic appeal, which is usually quite easy to discern, the logical appeal can take forms that are not immediately what the twentieth-century reader would call "logical." These forms are frequently inferences from Scriptural interpretations, Midrashic applications of the Old Testament. Or they are reports of signs and miracles performed by Jesus or one of the apostles. Or they are a sustained attempt to generalize from examples or parables. Or they are applications made of an assumed principle. All these fit into the "logical" category of classical rhetoric. Let us look at some samples of these types.

Possibly the easiest to discern are those motivations of faith based on a perceived miracle or sign. A clear instance of this type is seen in Nathaniel's early faith in Jesus based on the fact that Jesus had told him facts that no earthly wisdom could have known (John 1:50):

> "Rabbi," said Nathaniel, "you are the Son of God; you are the king of Israel." Jesus answered, "Is this the ground of your faith, that I told you I saw you under the fig-tree? You shall see greater things than that.[11]

Examples of logical arguments that are inferences from Scripture or Scriptural interpretations have already been examined. A famous example of this Midrashic technique coupled with an inductive generalization can be seen in the famous catalog of Old Testament figures seen in Chapter XI of the Epistle to the Hebrews. This passage is enlightening for our purposes because of the interesting definition of faith given at the beginning of the chapter:

> And what is faith? Faith gives substance to our hopes, and makes us certain of realities we do not see [11:1].

The term used for faith is *pistis*. The term here translated "certain" is *elegkos* (it is a noun and is usually translated as a noun, "assurance" or "evidence" or "conviction"). The usual meaning of *elegkos* is an *argument* of disproof or refutation or else a testing or scrutiny. Spicq translates the phrase "proof of realities not visible," a translation that Williamson says must not be interpreted to mean *pistis* means proof.[18] Yet all the other translations and the usual meaning of *elegkos* all denote proof or something very similar. And *pistis* is here defined by *elegkos*. Williamson, to avoid this problem, distinguishes between the *pistis* of Philo, which is constituted by the phenomena of the world (they constitute the evidence) and the *pisitis* of Hebrews, which is not drawn form any such phenomena at all. I believe that Williamson is correct in this distinction.

Nonetheless, in two separable but different ways, *pistis* in this passage and in the entire chapter of Hebrews does act as proof in the sense of evidence from which a conclusion is drawn. It is not the phenomena of the world (as in Philo), but it is *pistis* as logical appeal, the rhetorical meaning of the term, that is being used in this passage. Let us look at the two manners. It is better to take a look at the entire chapter and to try to discern the purpose of all the references to *faith* (*pistis*) in the chapter. The references are framed by the first verse of Chapter 11 and the first verse of Chapter 12, which applies all these references to the readers of the Epistle. And the verses 2, 13–16, and 39–40 reiterate the thesis. The thesis, repeated five times, is that faith is the basis of our hopes and makes us certain of realities we do not see. In each case of the entire chapter, the faith of the person mentioned allows that person (or group) to achieve something that seemed difficult or impossible.

There is nothing novel about this interpretation. What may not be seen by Williamson, however, is that these instances are gathered up together to constitute a generalization and then applied to the readers of the Epistle in the first verse of the next chapter:

> And what of ourselves? With all these witnesses to faith around us like a cloud, we must throw off every encumbrance, every sin to which we cling, and run with resolution the race for which we are entered, our eyes fixed on Jesus, on whom faith depends from start to finish: Jesus who, for the sake of the joy that lay ahead of him, endured the cross, making light of its disgrace, and has taken his seat at the right hand of the throne of God.

The argument and analogy are not very obscure. The readers, like Jesus and like all the instances of the preceding chapter, should be able to endure present obstacles because of the hope of an eternal life that they had as a result of their faith. Because of faith the prototypes in the Old Testament could hope; faith, in other words, was the ground from which they could infer hope. Faith was the proof basis (*elegkos*) of their hope. That is the message of every example in the chapter.

Consequently, the faith is the proof basis of their hope, and so faith *is* a proof in this case though not in the same way Philo sees it. But this is true not only of each instance from the Old Testament (and Jesus and the reader, too) individually. Faith is also the basis of the reader's *pistis* in a more usual (and rhetorical and Philonic) sense of the term because the motivation for the reader's faith is the generalized example (the cloud of witnesses). The inductive generalization is the appeal of the entire chapter, which culminates in the generalization of the first verse of Chapter 12: "With all these witnesses to faith around us like a cloud, we must throw off every encumbrance." The appeal to the faith of the reader is based on the examples; this generalized appeal is not called a *pistis* here (the orator frequently does not call attention to the technical kind of appeal being made), but it is unquestionably an appeal from examples coming from the Old Testament and applied to the reader at the beginning of the twelfth chapter.

This is a different meaning of *pistis* from those in the individual examples. In the individual examples, the faith is assumed as accepted, and from it is drawn the ensuing hope; in a sense the faith is a sort of axiom that allows the drawing of the conclusion. In the inductive generalization from these examples, the appeal is to the faith of the reader in order to strengthen it. But both are *logical* uses of *pistis*.

An example of the sustained attempt to generalize from a parable, rather than from historical examples, is the continued application to faith of the parable of the sower, which we encountered earlier. Classical rhetoric considered both historical and fictional examples under the logical appeal.

I am prepared to concede that different readers will disagree with me on some of my classifications. A further dimension to the classifications would be a checking of these classifications with the major interpretations of *The Interpreter's Bible* and of the major commentaries on the works of the New Testament.[19] But I trust that the present classifications have at least enough vailidity to make my hypothesis possible.

A Summary Look at the Data

The data yielded by the classifications of Figure 7 is summarized in Figure 8. There are many interesting pieces of information hidden in the numbers in each column and row. The vertical columns give the figures for each individual book of the New Testament, and the horizontal rows give the figures for the books taken as a whole.

Before we go into some of the more arresting percentages, one important caution must be given as a backdrop against which any of the conclusions drawn from this study must be placed. And a telling example of the caution may help to explain it.

If one looked only at the summary table of Figure 8, one might be tempted to conclude that neither Matthew nor Mark gives any evidence of the notion of extrinsic motivation for faith. Luke, on the contrary, has two instances of such a concept, and both are drawn from the same pericope, the parable of the sower (Luke 8:4–15). In verse 12, Jesus says:

> Those along the footpath are the men who hear it [the word of God], and then the devil comes and carries off the word from their hearts for fear they should believe and be saved.

The devil's ability to take away the word indicates an extrinsic cause of belief (in this case, disbelief). And the notion occurs in the environment of the verb *believe*. Consequently, it is recorded for verses 12 and 13.

Yet the same parable occurs also in Matthew and Mark. And the *concept* of extrinsic motivation or cause is present in both Matthew and Mark. Matthew makes the devil responsible for sowing the darnel, the bad seed (13:38), and Mark says just as explicitly:

> Those along the footpath are people in whom the word is sown, but no sooner have they heard it than Satan comes and carries off the word which has been sown in them. It is the same with those who receive the seed on rocky ground [4:15–16].

Yet because the Greek terms for "believe" or "belief" are not used in this pericope in either Matthew or Mark, the notion of extrinsic cause of faith is not registered in the list for these two evangelists.

This oversight is a direct consequence of the use of a vocabulary list of words stemming form *pistis* or *pisteuō*. The reception of the word of God in Matthew and Mark is clearly the equivalent of what is called *believe* in Luke. And a conceptual, rather than a vocabulary, analysis would turn this fact up and correct the misapprehension that the categories of Figure 8 present for Matthew and Mark. The example illustrates rather vividly one of the major limitations of a vocabulary study.

Consequently, with this salutary case in mind, all the subsequent generalizations must be held in suspense until later *conceptual* checks of the type I have just made of Matthew and Luke for this one notion will have been performed. This is one major reason why I insist on calling these findings a hypothesis. Other limitations will also be made after the presentation of the findings.

PROVISIONAL GENERAL CONCLUSIONS FROM THE DATA

The first general conclusion to be drawn from the data parallels the study of *pistis* in Josephus. In contrast to the Old Testament and to Josephus, the New Testament has a high semantic density for the *pistis* and *pisteuō* roots. Using the Old Testament as a norm, as was suggested in the Josephus survey, for every 1 occurrence of the root in the Septuagint, there are 10 occurrences in Josephus and 16 in the New Testament (taking account of the size of the three corpora).[20] The notion of *belief* is obviously stronger in Josephus than it is in the Old Testament, and it is still stronger in the New Testament than in either of these other two. It would be interesting to compare the New Testament density to that of either Isocrates or Aristotle, particularly the late Aristotle. Other comparisons might also be worth pursuing (Philo, Plato, some early church fathers, Polybius, Akiba, and so on).

But the overwhelming meaning of *pistis* in the New Testament

		Matt	Mark	Luke	John	Acts	Rom	I Cor	II Cor	Gal	Eph	Phip	Col	T[…]
	Verbs (V)	11	15	9	99	39	21	9	2	4	2	1	0	
	Nouns (N)	8	5	11	0	16	40	7	7	22	8	5	5	
	Total V+N (T)	19	20	20	99	55	61	16	9	26	10	6	5	1[…]
Conversion	V	10	14	8	84	35	4	2	0	0	1	0	0	
or Adhesion	N	4	2	4	0	12	20	1	4	18	4	4	5	
	Subtotal	14	16	12	84	47	24	3	4	18	5	4	5	
	% of T	74	80	60	85	85	39	19	44	82	50	67	100	6[…]
Measure of	V	7	8	5	4	2	3	3	0	1	1	1	0	
Certainty	N	5	1	5	0	6	11	2	5	2	3	2	2	
	Subtotal	12	9	10	4	8	14	5	5	3	4	3	2	
	% of T	63	45	50	4	15	23	31	56	12	40	50	40	2[…]
Ethical	V	4	8	7	77	25	16	7	2	2	1	1	0	
Proof	N	8	0	1	0	7	27	3	2	11	1	0	0	
	Subtotal	12	8	8	77	32	43	10	4	13	2	1	0	
	% of T	63	40	40	78	58	70	63	44	59	20	17	0	5[…]
Pathetic	V	3	10	3	42	15	18	4	2	3	2	1	0	
Proof	N	4	4	10	0	8	35	4	2	19	6	5	3	
	Subtotal	7	14	13	42	23	53	8	4	22	8	6	3	
	% of T	37	70	65	42	42	87	58	44	85	80	100	60	4[…]
Logical	V	9	9	5	51	18	13	3	2	3	0	1	0	
Proof	N	4	2	1	0	5	28	4	0	15	0	0	1	
	Subtotal	13	11	6	51	23	41	7	2	18	0	1	1	
	% of T	68	69	30	51	42	67	44	22	69	0	17	20	
Extrinsic	V	0	1	2	17	9	7	3	2	1	2	1	0	
Proof	N	0	0	0	0	5	33	6	3	14	7	2	3	
	Subtotal	0	1	2	17	14	40	9	5	15	9	3	3	
	% of T	0	5	10	17	25	66	56	56	58	90	50	60	

FIGURE 8. Summary of the occurrences of *pisteuein* (verb) and *pistis* (noun) in the New Testament

is religious *pistis*. This is in distinct contrast to both the Old Testament and Josephus. Whereas in Josephus only 39 out of 425 occurrences are religious (9 percent), in the New Testament the rare exception is the use of *pistis* or *pisteuō* for a nonreligious use (there are only 6 out of 491—and 2 of these are in a religious context). In effect, the word has been totally baptized by immersion. This even contrasts strongly with the Old Testament, where

I Tim	II Tim	Tit	Phlm	Heb	Jas	I Pet	II Pet	I John	II John	III John	Jude	Rev	
3	1	2	0	2	3	4	0	10	0	0	1	0	247
19	8	6	2	32	16	5	2	1	0	0	2	4	244
22	9	8	2	34	19	9	2	11	0	0	3	4	491
1	1	1	0	1	0	2	0	1	0	0	1	0	169
18	7	6	2	31	3	1	1	0	0	0	2	4	165
19	8	7	2	32	3	3	1	1	0	0	3	4	334
86	89	88	100	94	16	33	50	9	0	0	100	100	68%
0	0	0	0	0	1	3	0	3	0	0	1	0	44
12	3	4	0	2	14	2	2	0	0	0	2	1	91
12	3	4	0	2	15	5	2	3	0	0	3	1	135
55	33	50	0	6	79	83	100	27	0	0	100	25	27%
2	1	1	0	2	1	3	0	6	0	0	1	0	175
3	3	1	1	25	5	0	0	0	0	0	1	3	106
5	4	2	1	27	6	3	0	6	0	0	2	3	281
28	44	25	50	79	32	33	0	55	0	0	67	75	57%
1	1	1	0	2	3	4	0	7	0	0	1	0	127
8	3	1	1	30	15	5	1	1	0	0	1	1	174
9	4	2	1	32	18	9	1	8	0	0	2	1	301
41	44	25	50	94	95	100	50	73	0	0	67	25	61%
1	0	0	0	2	2	3	0	6	0	0	1	0	133
0	2	1	0	26	4	1	0	0	0	0	1	1	96
1	2	1	0	28	6	4	0	6	0	0	2	1	229
5	22	13	0	76	32	44	0	55	0	0	67	25	47%
1	1	1	0	2	0	4	0	3	0	0	0	0	59
5	2	3	0	23	1	4	1	1	0	0	0	0	117
6	3	4	0	25	1	8	1	4	0	0	0	0	176
27	33	50	0	74	5	89	50	36	0	0	0	0	36%

the relatively few occurrences of the *pistis* derivates are religious only about half of the time.

But the major conclusion of the analysis is that the occurrences of the verb and of the noun *pistis* derivates sustain a rhetorical reading. They mean "persuade" or "persuasion" just as they meant in the contemporary Greek of the time. They incorporate the meanings that the word had in the rhetorical schools and in the political and legal environment of the Greek cities. The fact is that of the six component meanings that *pistis* had in the Greek rhetorical tradition, all six are incorporated into the Christian concept of faith. These six are the categories used in the classifications of the rhetorical situation: Faith is a free decision change (a conversion), faith embodies a measure of uncertainty, faith is a belief in the credibility of the source of the message (ethical argument), faith is a belief engendered by a promise of some good or threat of some evil (pathetic argument), faith is a belief engendered by a rational cause (logical argument), and faith can be a belief engendered by an outside cause (extrinsic argument). Across the entire New Testament, there is no doubt that the concept of faith generally carries these component meanings. The figures for all the components are convincing, some more than others. The conversion figure of 65 percent is very high as is the ethical argument figure (56 percent), and the pathetic argument figure (61 percent). So also is the 46 percent figure for the logical argument—a figure that might surprise some readers. But even the figures for the measure of certainty (27 percent) and for the extrinsic cause (34 percent) are very telling for the quite simple reason that if a complex concept is repeated in 491 occurrences of a sustained text and in almost one-third of the occurrences calls attention to two of its component facets, the facets certainly must be important aspects of the concept. Yet this is precisely what these figures do: 34 percent and 27 percent are quite close to one-third as a ratio.

Now it might be objected that any rhetorical analysis of a concept of persuasion would turn up figures like these for at least the ethical, the pathetic, and the logical arguments. I concede this if there really is a "rhetorical analysis of a *concept of persuasion.*" That is what I am trying to establish, and the counterargument assumes what I am seeking to prove: *Pistis* does mean persuasion. However, there is another aspect to this counterargument that must be pursued a bit more.

Granted that any analysis of a concept of persuasion will turn up something like these constants of persuasive techniques—they may be rhetorical universals—such an analysis would not prove the existence of a Greek influence. So that although the analysis might show that the *pistis* derivates mean persuasion, they might not prove a Greek source of the notion. This objection, in isolation, would be a valid argument. But three other critical factors disarm the objection in the present circumstances.

First, there are both the presence of the Greek language and the likelihood that a word used in a borrowing culture will have some of the basic meanings of the word in the original. Second, there is the curious nonpresence of the notion of persuasion in the Old Testament. I have insisted on this because most of the Old Testament was commposed before there was a significant Greek influence on the religious terminology of the Hebrews. The absence of the conscious notion of persuasion in the Semitic culture before the Hellenistic period, its presence suddenly in a massive way in the basic document of the new culture, and its presence in the word borrowed from the Hellenistic culture all speak strongly of a definitive influence.

Third, this influence argument is supported by the other three elements of the Greek notion, also carried over into the new religion: the measure of uncertainty, the concept of a free decision in conversion, and the extrinsic cause of belief. These three notions do not always accompany concepts of belief in other religions; in fact, they are absent in some. This further suggests the strong hypothesis that the notion of persuasion was taken from Greek thought and simply applied to the notion of religious persuasion. Contrary to what some theologians have maintained, there may well be a generic notion of persuasion (faith), and Christian faith may be a species with some very distinct elements, but these specific differentiae are compatible with the genus concept of general faith or persuasion.

All this suggests that the word *pistis* (and its derivates), as it is used in the New Testament, meant, at least partially, what the word meant in the primary contemporary meaning of the term: persuasion in a rhetorical sense. This idea is not at all revolutionary; it is just what would ordinarily have been expected. The reason why it has not been advanced before has already been given earlier (p. 24). The Platonic and philosophic and literary biases of the word in Greek thought discouraged the theologians from looking into the primary meaning of the word at the time, its rhetorical meaning in the *polis*.

Some Specific Conclusions from the Data

CONVERSION OR ADHESION

If faith means persuasion, then the most rhetorical of the components of the concept of faith has to be the insistence that faith means a persuasion to a new view of life, a conversion. This is in the nature of the rhetorical decision. And significantly it has the highest percentage of all of the categories: In 65 percent of the occurrences of both verbs and nouns, there is the clear indication that "believe" and "faith" imply a sense of conversion or adhesion. Faith certainly means a change in a person's life or, once the change has been achieved, a persistence in the change by voluntary choice. This component of the concept of faith is present in a strong measure in nearly all the larger documents of the New Testament. The only exception to this generalization is the Epistle of St. Paul to the Corinthians (19 percent of 16 occurrences), but this characteristic of faith is distinctly a Pauline feature in general. The exceptions (for this analysis) are the Epistle of St. James and the three Johannine Epistles, all of which have not enough occurrences to be significant statistically.

There are many other passages in which this meaning may be assumed, but when there is not some explicit textual clue, the passage has not been coded as embodying a conversion or adhesion motif.

Occasionally, the concept of conversion cooccurs with that of extrinsic causation of faith. Such a juxtaposition can be seen in 2 Thessalonians 2:11–12:

> Therefore God puts them under a delusion, which works upon them to believe the lie, so that they may all be brought to judgement, all who do not believe the truth but make sinfulness their deliberate choice.

Here the translators of *The New English Bible with the Apocrypha* use the phrase "make sinfulness their deliberate choice" for what is not usually translated with such an emphasis on the free choice. For example, the Revised Standard Version reads, "had pleasure in unrighteousness." But the context of the preceding verse, 2 Thessalonians 2:10, and the burden of much of the preceding chapter, as well as the distinct notion of consent in the verb *eudokeō* of the text all justify the translation. The preceding verse

(2:10) reads, "Destroyed they shall be, because they did not open their minds to love of the truth, so as to find salvation." And the preceding chapter includes this verse (1:8): "Then he [Jesus Christ] will do justice upon those who refuse to acknowledge God and upon those who will not obey the gospel of our Lord Jesus." Even the earlier translations, however, emphasize the notion of a conversion or adhesion. And it is clearly juxtaposed to the notion of an extrinsic motivation: "God put them under a delusion."

Frequently, as in Luke and John, the conversion motif, when conjoined with the extrinsic cause, is the refusal to convert (negative conversion, if it may be so called). Examples of this are Luke 8:12, 13; John 6:54, 8:24, 45, 56; 12:37–39. In Acts, however, the conjunction is usually with a positive conversion, and Paul usually makes this same sort of conjunction (Gal. 3:22, 23–26; 5:5, 6, for example). The same conjunction is made in Hebrews in the celebrated praise of faith in Chapter 11 (by my count 19 times between verses 6 and 39).

The varying occurrences of conversion as opposed to adhesion have not been separately codified in the classifications. But there are many instances of each. Adhesion, of course, implies a prior conversion (in the New Testament), but the opposite is not at all true. Frequently, there are conversions followed by lapses, and this is a frequent concern in the New Testament.

There are many other remarks that could be made about the conversion of adhesion factor of faith in the New Testament as a whole and about the separate books. But possibly the most important thing to be said here is that an emphasis on the notion of conversion or adhesion gives to the notion of faith a dynamism, a personal sense of vigor and responsibility, a sense of continual energy that sometimes the notion has not had. Some of the modern existential theologians are certainly justified in their emphasis on this facet of the notion of faith.

MEASURE OF CERTAINTY

The figures on our table for measure of certainty (or uncertainty) are generally consistent across the entire New Testament. The obvious exception to this is the Gospel of John, where only 4 occurrences out of 99 verbs were recorded. Even if one includes the Johannine Epistles and the Book of Revelation, the figure only goes to 6 percent (7 out of 110 total occurrences). Perhaps a conceptual analysis would correct this figure. Possibly the fact that John does not use any nouns at all in his 99 occurrences of the *pist-* root in the Gospel accounts partly for this because the measure of certainty notion is much more common with the nouns than with the verbs (92 as opposed to 40) despite the fact that the nouns and the verbs have an amost equal number of occurrences (244 nouns, 247 verbs). There is a semantic clustering phenomenon here that I am presently at a loss to explain.

Paul, on the contrary, is higher than average in the totals of his Epistles (excluding Hebrews). He has 85 instances of measure of certainty in 196 total occurrences of the *pistis* words, for a 43 percent ratio.

Possibly the view that faith involves a measure of certainty, which is also to say a measure of uncertainty by the same token, in a good number of the major texts concerning faith may be one of the more significant findings of the survey. The figure of 27 percent is quite surprising, in my opinion. It means that, in more than one-fourth of the occurrences of the verb and noun, the notion of a degree of certainty was coupled with the notion of believing or belief. This degree of uncertainty was, especially in some later centuries, obscured by blanket statements about the certainty of faith. It might be useful, in this regard, to recall the solution of Aquinas: The motive of faith (God's word) was quite certain, but the object of faith (the doctrine, the *mysteries* sometimes) was not at all so certain.[21] In rhetorical terms, this means that the ethical argument is stronger than the logical one, an interpretation suggested by the figures of our study.

In any case, the analytical argument of this chapter supports the semantic argument of the second chapter and the historical argument of the third chapter in that it reenforces the rhetorical sense of *pistis* in the New Testament as embodying a sense of uncertainty, a persistent element of the Greek rhetorical tradition, indeed even of the Greek philosophic tradition.

THE ETHICAL ARGUMENT

The next element in the taxonomic analysis of Figures 7 and 8 has to do with the use of the ethical argument (the argument from authority) as a motivation for belief. This argument is also high, with 56 percent of the occurrences of the words incorporating this meaning.

Generally speaking, the ethical argument derives from either the authority of Scripture or from the authority of the speaker in the pericope. Given the usual format for the apostles and disciples to spread the news of the Gospel, the use of a discussion in the synagogue of the town being visited, the use of the authority of Scripture is not surprising, particularly with Jewish audiences. But the Scriptural authority is also present in the Gospels with the frequent Midrashic interpretations given to passages from the Old Testament.

However, Jesus (and later His disciples) did not hesitate to invoke His own authority as the motivation for belief, as many passages show. Jesus' answer to Nicodemus is a typical forthright statement:

> In very truth I tell you, we speak of what we know, and testify to what we have seen, and yet you all reject our testimony. If you disbelieve me when I talk to you about things on earth, how are you to believe if I should talk about the things of heaven? [John 3:11–12]

Paul also speaks of the oracles entrusted to his care (I Cor. 9:17, Gal. 2:7, I Tim. 1:11).

Another characteristic of the ethical proof, related indeed to the argument from Scripture, is the emphasis on the word in the act of persuasion and faith. This facet, also stressed by Bultmann, as we have seen (earlier, p. 32), is more characteristic of the New Testament than of the Old (see earlier, p. 10) and is quite consistent with the emphasis on the verbal seen in the rhetorical tradition, a fact insisted on at some length in the sketch of that tradition given in Chapter III. Of course, this affirmation of the preeminence of the word reaches its highest point in John's deification of the logos: In the beginning was the Word (1:1). It is not surprising, therefore, that John has one of the highest percentages of the use of the ethical argument (75 out of 99 occurrences in the Gospel), second only to the Epistle to the Hebrews (79 percent).

THE PATHETIC APPEAL

The most frequent appeal in the New Testament is the appeal based on the promise of something to be gained by the believer.

This is called the pathetic appeal because, as was pointed out earlier, it is based on the Greek word for emotion, and frequently the pathetic appeal is an emotional appeal. Although all three of the traditional rhetorical appeals—ethical, pathetic, and logical—are strong throughout the New Testament, of the three, the pathetic appeal is most dominant (61 percent). It is also more easily broken down into large and obvious categories.

There are the recurrent motivations for faith based on the desire for miracles or signs. Then, particularly in St. Paul, this faith is grounded on the hope for justification. Finally, strongest in John, is the faith grounded on the hope for eternal life.

Of all of the writers, Paul—this may appear surprising—has a very high pathetic appeal (67 percent of all the occurrences of the verb and the noun forms). It is highest in Paul in Romans, Galatians, and Philippians. Three small books also have very high percentages for the pathetic argument: Peter's two Epistles (91 percent) and James (95 percent). James, of course, has a heavy emphasis on the threat, the negative promise: "The devils have faith like that, and it makes them tremble" (2:19).

THE LOGICAL ARGUMENT

The percentage of the logical argument is, in my opinion, quite high (46 percent). For a religious persuasion to ground nearly half of its appeals on a rational argument is perhaps somewhat surprising. The rational appeals are of two distinct types. In the Synoptics and occasionally in the appeals of the writers of the Epistles, there is the appeal to the logic of a miracle or sign reported. Credibility follows from the report of the miracle. I have already given several examples of these appeals (John 1:50, e.g.). The populace is often influenced by this appeal: "While he was in Jerusalem for Passover many gave their allegiance to him when they saw the signs that he performed" (John 2:23 *episteusan*, usually translated "believed," is the word here translated as "gave their allegiance").

The second dominant type of logical argument is the inference from Scripture. In such cases, of course, there is the combination of the logical with the ethical appeal of the Scriptural quotation. Possibly the most famous instance of this combination is the long sequence in Hebrews (11:3–12:1), which was analyzed at some length earlier. It combines the ethical appeal of Scripture, the logical appeal of inference from Scripture, and the logical appeal of a generalization drawn from a series of particulars. In addition, of course, it has a solid pathetic appeal (each of the examples from the Old Testament is an instance of a person's pursuing an objective held out to him or her by faith: "faith gives substance to our hopes"). Finally, the passages also have strong extrinsic motivation.

In addition to adducing Scriptural authority and also drawing on His own authority, Jesus Himself frequently uses the logical appeal of the fictional example, the parable.

Despite the different forms of the logical appeal, it is a persistent motif in the concept of faith in the New Testament, with the exception of a few smaller books that do not have enough occurrences of the *pistis* root to establish an adequate sample anyway. The logical appeal, judging from this analysis, is highest in Matthew, John, Paul, and the Epistle to the Hebrews.

THE EXTRINSIC MOTIVATION

The extrinsic motivation, as I term it here, might better be called the extrinsic cause. Both in traditional rhetoric and in the New Testament, the extrinsic motivation for faith was not an appeal through language to the person of whom belief was expected, but rather a coercion in the sense of a nonvoluntary response to a nonverbal stimulus.

But the involuntary response can be accompanied by a partial voluntary response, as we saw earlier, in examining the conjunction of the conversion and the extrinsic motivation in a fair number of passages.

Unlike some of the other appeals and characteristics of the concept of faith, the extrinsic motivation is not as consistent through the New Testament. It is not generally a synoptic feature of faith (but the reader should remember the caution made in this matter earlier: A conceptual, rather than a vocabulary, analysis gives a different picture of the parable of the sower of the seed in both Matthew and Mark). Nor is the extrinsic motivation strong in Acts either.

Basically, the extrinsic motivation is a Pauline feature of faith as far as the larger books of the New Testament are concerned. Of the 169 occurrences of the extrinsic motivation, 100, or 59 percent of them, are from the Pauline epistles. If one adds the Epistle to the Hebrews, 73 percent are accounted for.

Again, as with the measure of certainty and the pathetic proof, the extrinsic motivation is much more concentrated in the noun passages than in the verb passages (113 to 56).

Peter's two Epistles are also high in the extrinsic motivation (89 percent and 50 percent respectively for 1 and 2 Peter). Conversely, James is quite low (this is quite consistent with the notion that faith without works is dead).

The extrinsic motivation, however, despite its sporadic appearances, is an important aspect of the concept of faith, for it relates faith to grace. And the history of theology has been bound up with the concept of grace since the earliest centuries of Christianity.

CHAPTER V

The New Hypothesis:
Conclusions, Limitations, and Further Study

I began with a statement of the old thesis about the Christian concept of faith: It did not have its origin in the Old Testament nor did it have its origin in Greek thought. The evidence presented here sustains the first part of the old thesis, upheld by most traditional and most contemporary theologians, whether Christian or Jewish. But it runs counter to the second part of the old thesis, which is also upheld by most traditional and contemporary Christian theologians. It is the hypothesis of this book that a substantial part of the concept of faith found in the New Testament can be found in the rhetorical concept of persuasion, which was a major meaning of the noun *pistis* (faith or *persuasion*) and the verb *pisteuein* (to believe) in the Greek language at the period the New Testament was written.

The reasons why such a hypothesis has not been given serious attention before this time are outlined in the first chapter. They center on the disrepute in which rhetoric, the study of persuasion, has been held for the past century and a half in academic circles, the period in which investigations into the origins of the notion of faith have been made. They also include the low regard for the concept of *pistis* in certain important thinkers of the Greek philosophic tradition and the disinclination of theologians to consider such a lowly concept as a possible origin for the noble Christian concept.

The new hypothesis is supported by three distinct but related arguments: the semantic argument of the second chapter, the historical argument of the third chapter, and the analytical argument of the fourth chapter. The semantic argument attempts to establish the possibility of a historical influence of one concept (persuasion) on the other (faith) by showing the similarity of the two concepts: They are at least theoretically compatible. The second argument attempts to establish the probability of such an influence by erecting the social, linguistic, and educational background of the period in which the books of the New Testament were written. The Hellenistic rhetorical influence was so massive at the time that it is highly probable that the authors of the New Testament were vividly aware of the major meaning of the word *pistis* at the time, its rhetorical meaning in political and educational circles. The third argument is a verification of the second. If the authors of the New Testament were aware of the fundamental rhetorical meaning of *pistis,* such an awareness ought to be very visible in the texts in which the word and its derivates are used. The third argument (Chapter IV) is a systematic attempt to make a rhetorical analysis, by means of the categories of the contemporary meanings of the term, of the 491 occurrences of the verb and the noun. The analysis overwhelmingly supports such a rhetorical interpretation of the terms *pistis* and *pisteuein*. Thus, the hypothesis is supported by this cumulative argument.

A summary of the type of evidence offered for each stage of the argument may help to assess the validity of the conclusion.

The first argument was semantic in that it attempted to show a similarity of meaning between the two concepts of faith, as understood by Christians, and of persuasion, as understood by rhetoricians of the first century A.D. To arrive at a concept of faith that would incorporate the major components of meaning of mainstream Christianity, eight twentieth-century theologians (Barth, Bultmann, Weiser, Hatch, Baillie, O'Connor, Jacobs, and Buber), representing Evangelical, Lutheran, Presbyterian, Episcopalian, Catholic, and Jewish points of view, were chosen for a composite synthesis. A recurrent formulation, frequently employed by Barth, the Old Protestant structure of trust, assent, and knowledge, was adopted as a framework around which the fundamental tenets of Christian faith could be assembled. They include a trust in God, an assent to God's message, and the resulting knowledge obtained from the message. Around the trust notion are associated the concepts of faith as gift and of God as the object of the assent and as the source of the salvation that results from the assent. Around the central notion of assent are the notions of conversion, freedom, and justification. Because the assent is to God's word, the emphasis on the word must be a major component of faith. Finally, around the notion of knowledge hinges the concept of a proclamation of the doctrines of the faith, to which some measure of certainty is attached.

Now there are undoubtedly different emphases on various facets of this composite model of the concept of faith. But the general structure seems tenable for the Christian theologians used. Historically also there have been different emphases, Protestantism at one time emphasizing trust and Catholicism emphasizing assent, for instance.

After this model for the concept of faith was posited, the second chapter then sketched a model for the concept of persuasion. Drawing on the extant comprehensive rhetorics of the Hellenistic period, a composite model of the concept of persuasion was erected. It encompasses the usual notions of the techniques of persuasion by personal appeal, by audience appeal, and by knowledge of the subject matter. These are traditionally called the ethical argument, the pathetic argument, and the logical argument. The Greek word for argument in this context is the word *pistis,* the word translated as "faith" in Christianity.

With these two frameworks juxtaposed, it is possible to see in both a common semantic structure: The trust, assent, and knowledge of the model of faith have important similarities to the ethical, pathetic, and logical elements of the model of persuasion. These two models are then combined into a composite model for the rhetorical analysis of the texts.

Before the analysis is carried out, however, the historical question of whether the people who fabricated the faith model had any knowledge of the rhetorical mdoel must be broached. The answer to this question is the task of Chapter III.

The historical question is the most difficult section of the cumulative argument. To answer the question one must gather together much of what we now know about the Hellenization of Palestine at this period. The massive influence of the Greek language, particularly in Galilee, and the importance of the many Greek cities, 37 or more, which flourished at this time in Palestine, are looked into. The participation of the Jews as citizens in the political life of the important two largest Greek cities in Galilee and some other Greek cities of Palestine is reviewed. Then the nature of the education to citizenship of the Greek cities is examined by looking at the *ephēbia,* the training period to citizenship in the Greek city. The *ephēbia,* which nearly every one of the 350 Greek cities in the Mediterranean area established, was generally a two-year period of training in military arts, in some literature and philosophy, but especially in rhetoric, to train the future citizen to be able to participate in the political and legal life of the city. It was originally mandatory, but at this period it was only optional for some of the Greek cities.

Paralleling the ephebic training was the beginning of rabbinical education or study groups similar to the rabbinical training in Jewish centers, the capstone of a thorough education to literacy throughout all of Israel. This education system is examined in some detail. In particular, the influence of Greek rhetoric and law on the beginnings of Hebraic hermeneutics and Biblical exegesis is examined.

The general conclusion is that a person speaking or writing Greek in northern Palestine at this period would almost inevitably have encountered the rhetorical meanings of *pistis* in either the Greek or the Hebraic educational system (or from persons trained in them) and in the political life and the legal activities of the Greek cities and even of the smaller towns of the area, and such a person would normally perceive these meanings as the major contemporary meanings of the term. The details of the argument cannot be repeated here, but there is enough detail to suggest a strong probability for this supposition.

Finally, the fourth chapter analyzes the occurrences of the terms *pistis* and *pisteuein* in the New Testament. The analysis is made by means of the components of the concept of persuasion established in Chapter II: the ethical, pathetic, and logical appeals; the extrinsic appeal; and the associated notions of a free decision in conversion and a measure of certainty. These and the idea clusters built around them are examined for their presence in the occurrences of the noun and verb for "faith" and "to believe" in the New Testament.

The analysis supports the hypothesis: Judged by the contemporary criteria of persuasive discourse, as seen in Greek rhetoric, the *pistis* of the New Testament can almost always be interpreted as persuasion. There are the usual appeals (ethical, pathetic, logical, and extrinsic), and there are the additional elements of a measure of uncertainty, an emphasis on the verbal, and especially the notion of a change or turn (a conversion). Indeed, in many cases, the word "faith" translating *pistis* could just as well be translated "persuasion," and the word "believed" translating the verb could just as easily be translated "was persuaded." Very few of the 491 occurrences resist a rhetorical analysis.

The evidence for the presence of the six analyzed elements is so strong that one has to predicate the presence of each in any concept of faith derived from the New Testament. Most of the elements are sufficiently represented in all the books of the New Testament to provide a sample of occurrences from which to generalize.

The analysis thus verifies the presence of rhetorical elements in the concept of faith as it is presented in the New Testament. The analytic argument thus supports both the historical and the semantic arguments. And the absence of such rhetorical elements in the Old Testament and in other Semitic cultures argues against such a concept's being a universal semantic religious notion.

The present study labors under some important limitations. These limitations suggest other areas of investigation that might either support the hypothesis we have presented or cast doubt on its validity.

Possibly the most conspicuous limitation is the fact that this has been a vocabulary study, not a conceptual study. The study simply examines the occurrences of *pistis* and its derivates, but it does not examine the synonyms or antonyms or other words of the semantic cluster surrounding *pistis*. It is true that there was a brief look at the meaning of "faith" implied in the parable of the sower in Matthew and Mark despite the absence of the term in the texts, but this excursus was made expressly to illustrate the weakness of the vocabulary technique (see pp. 130–131).

Several investigations could support or call into question the conclusions reached by analyzing only the *pistis* derivates. In the first place, a conceptual analysis of the relevant pericopes would undoubtedly turn up additional instances of all the features of the notion of faith discussed here. The conclusions reached by the present analysis might thus be signficantly strengthened. But the conceptual analysis could call into the question some of the interpretations reached by the isolated *pistis* analysis.

Second, because the vocabulary analysis has been made only in the context of the immediate pericope or, at best, several contiguous pericopes, the conclusions of the present analysis should be checked against a full text and historical context analysis. Thus, my findings about an individual passage from 1 Corinthians should be checked against the background of the full text of the entire Epistle, as well as against what we know about the historical background of the epistle.

In addition, rhetorical analyses should be made of related words, such as conversion (*metanoia, metastrophē,* and so on), time (*kairos*), glory (*doxa*), choice (*hairesis,* and so on), and other words that took on particular meaning in the Christian dispensation. Nearly all these words had rhetorical connotations that could be relevant to an interpretation of the analysis of the concept of faith in the environment of such words.

A third limitation of this study had been the lack of consideration given *pistis* and its derivates by major commentators on the texts in which the terms occur. A colleague of mine, Dr. Charles Robert Kline, is currently at work on this enterprise.

Besides the major commentators, the major theologians, Christian and other, of the tradition should be consulted in comparative studies. Another kind of comparative study that could shed further light on the origins of the concept of faith in the Semitic tradition could be investigations into the concept of persuasion in other cultures that, like the Semitic, had no explicit term for persuasion at a given point in their history.

All the preceding limitations and suggetions have been of an anlytical nature. But there are distinct limitations to the historical presentation of the third chapter. The study of the Hellenization of Palestine in the three centuries preceding the compostion of the New Testament is far from completed. Controversial issues like the participation of the Hebrews in the active political life of the

Greek cities and the smaller towns influenced by these cities need to be resolved. We also know relatively little about the Greek educational and the Jewish educational systems of the period. My tentative generalizations about both of these issues need to be tested with further research. And, of course, our knowledge of the educational sophistication of the writers of the books of the New Testament is only embryonic.

Certain other historical investigations also seem critical. We really should have more study into the use of such concepts as persuasion and faith in Hebraic documents other than the Septuagint. Other Semitic languages could also be studied for such concepts. Further studies should also be made in the meanings of faith and persuasion in Philo, Josephus, Akiba, and other contemporary figures. A comparative study of reason (*logismos*) in 4 Maccabees may also show some interesting similarities with the notion of faith, similarities deriving from the same rhetorical tradition conjoined with the religion of the Old Testament. Finally, additional investigations could be made into the contemporary Greek authors' uses of words like "faith" and "persuasion."

All these limitations and suggestions for future study are made in the context of the educational environments of the Greeks and Hebrews of the Hellenistic period and the ensuing educational environment of the early Christian community. My hypothesis can, therefore, be partially aligned with that of Jaeger in *Early Christianity and Greek Paideia.* According to Jaeger, early Christianity, the assembly of the new city of God, can be viewed as a continuation of the old education (*paideia*) of the Greeks. He points out that the term chosen for those who belong to this assembly—the *ekklēsia*—meant also the gathering of the citizens of the Greek *polis*. The persuasion (*pistis*) of the new (*polis*) can, therefore, be viewed as derived legitimately from the persuasion (political) of the old city. My hypothesis is simply a corollary of Jaeger's thesis. Speaking of the author of the *Acts of the Apostle Philip* and of his imitation of St. Paul, Jaeger says:

> In calling Christianity the paideia of Christ, the imitator stresses the intention of the apostle to make Christianity to be a continuation of the classical paideia, which it would be logical for those who possessed the older one to accept.[1]

Jaeger finds the notion of such a Christian *paideia* implicit in many of the writings of the New Testament and of many contemporary documents. But he analyzes in detail the explicit articulation of such a conscious continuation of Greek *paideia* in Clement of Rome (pp. 13–26); Justin the Martyr (pp. 27–32); Origen and Clement of Alexandria (pp. 37–67); and Basil, Gregory of Nazianzus, and Gregory of Nyssa (pp. 75–100).

Jaeger finds the rhetorical tradition alive in such figures. I would enlarge the picture to many, many others. Just as persuasion was central to the old tradition, so, too, was persuasion central to the new tradition. The notion of *pistis* underwent a marked change at this time (it was baptized) as did the notion of *paideia,* but there is a basic continuity. Or, as Clement of Alexandria worded it, the *paideia* of the Greeks was the *propaideia* for the true *paideia* of Christianity.[2]

Notes

Chapter I

1. Henry George Liddell and Robert Scott, *A Greek-English Lexicon,* 9th ed. rev. Sir Henry Stuart Jones, Robert McKenzie (Oxford: Clarendon Press, 1968), p. 1408. Henceforth Liddell and Scott.

2. The phrasing is that of Oscar Cullmann, *The Johannine Circle,* trans. John Bowden (Philadelphia: The Westminster Press, 1976), p. 39.

3. John Frank Kermode, *The Genesis of Secrecy: On the Interpretation of Narrative* (Cambridge, Mass.: Harvard University Press, 1979). The book is dedicated to those outside, and the notion of outsiders to an interpretation is very much a part of the first chapter and of his whole analysis of the Gospel of Mark.

4. D. M. Baillie, *Faith in God and Its Christian Consummation: The Kerr Lectures for 1926* (Edinburgh: T. and T. Clark, 1927), p.5.

5. Baillie, p. 5.

6. Baillie, p. 5; he is here quoting Cheyne.

7. Baillie, pp. 9–19.

8. Baillie, pp. 18–19, 50.

9. Baillie, p. 31.

10. Baillie, p. 44.

11. William Henry Paine Hatch, *The Pauline Idea of Faith in Its Relation to Jewish and Hellenistic Religion,* Harvard Theological Studies II (Cambridge, Mass.: Harvard University Press, 1917; rpt, New York: Kraus Reprint Co., 1969), pp. 1–20.

12. Hatch, pp. 21–26.

13. Hatch, pp. 26–27.

14. Hatch, p. 27.

15. Hatch, p. 28; he gives several references in his footnotes.

16. Hatch, pp. 35, 47–48.

17. Edward D. O'Connor, C.S.C., *Faith in the Synoptic Gospels: A Problem in the Correlation of Scripture and Theology* (South Bend, Ind.: University of Notre Dame Press, 1961), p. xi.
18. O'Connor, pp. xi–xii.
19. O'Connor, p. 3.
20. O'Connor, pp. 3–18.
21. Louis Jacobs, *Faith* (London: Valentine, Mitchell, 1968), p. 4.
22. Jacobs, p. 7.
23. Jacobs, p. 5. For his last sentence, he refers to Maimonides, *Sepher Ha-Mitzwoth', Mitzwoth, Aseh,* I, Part II, pp. 3–4 and commentaries.
24. Jacobs, pp. 12–13.
25. A. Weiser, "The Old Testament Concept," in "*Pisteuō,*etc.," *Theological Dictionary of the New Testament,* ed. Gerhard Kittel, trans. and ed. in English by Geoffrey W. Bromiley (Grand Rapids, Mich.: Eerdmans, 1964–1976), VI, 182–197; also Rudolf Bultmann, "*Pisteuō,*etc.," in Kittel, pp. 174–182, 197–228, esp. 197–199.
26. Weiser, p. 182.
27. Weiser, p. 183.
28. Weiser, p. 183.
29. Weiser, pp. 186–189.
30. Weiser, pp. 190–191, 196.
31. Weiser, pp. 191–196.
32. Weiser, pp. 196–197.
33. Bultmann, pp. 197–203, and especially 205–207.
34. Bultmann, p. 197, note 149.
35. Bultmann, pp. 208–215.
36. Bultmann, p. 215.
37. I have used Edwin Hatch and Henry Redpath, *A Concordance to the Septuagint and the Other Greek Versions of the Old Testament* (*Including the Apocryphal Books*) (Graz, Austria: Akademische Druck U. Verlagsanstalt, 1954), II, for *pistis,* and so on. Consequently, when citing from this source, I follow it in using the King James translation. Ordinarily, I use *The New English Bible with the Apocrypha,* Oxford Study Edition, eds. Samuel Sandmel, M. Jack Suggs, and Arnold J. Tkacik, O.S.B. (New York: Oxford University Press, 1976).
38. Bultmann, p. 197.
39. Baillie, p. 31.
40. Hatch, p. 83.
41. Bultmann, p 179.
42. On this see Bultmann, 179–182.
43. Bultmann, p. 182.
44. Richard Reitzenstein, *Hellenistic Mystery Religions: Their Basic Ideas and Significance,* trans. John E. Steely (Pittsburgh: The Pickwick Press, 1978).
45. Dieter Lührmann, "Pistis im Judentum," *Zeitschrift für Neutestamentliche Wissenschaft,* 64:1–2 (1973): 21–23.
46. Lührmann, pp. 23–25.
47. Lührmann, pp. 29–35.

48. Lührmann, p. 36.
49. Lührmann, p. 36.
50. Lührmann, p. 38.
51. Lührmann, p. 19.
52. Gerhard Ebeling, *The Nature of Faith,* trans. Ronald Gregor Smith (Philadelphia: Muhlenberg Press, 1961), pp. 20–21. His mild criticism of Bultmann can be seen in Gerhard Ebeling, *Word and Faith,* trans. James W. Leitch (London: SCM Press, Ltd., 1960), pp. 223–224.
53. Martin Buber, *Two Types of Faith,* trans. Norman P. Goldhawk, M.A. (New York: Macmillan, 1951), p. 7.
54. Buber, p. 10.
55. Buber, p. 10.
56. Buber, p. 11.
57. Buber, pp. 9–10, 170–172, and passim.
58. Buber, pp. 10–11, 172–173, and passim.
59. Buber, pp. 170–174.
60. Buber, p. 172.
61. Buber, p. 37.
62. Buber, p. 140.
63. E.g., Buber, p. 46.
64. E.g., Buber, p. 46.
65. Bruno Snell, *The Discovery of Mind: The Greek Origins of European Thought,* trans. T. G. Rosemeyer (Oxford: Basil Blackwell, 1953), pp. 136–152, for all these figures.
66. Snell, p. 136.
67. Cited in Snell, p. 136; *Iliad,* II, 484, ff.
68. Snell, pp. 136–152.
69. Snell, pp. 139–141, for Xenophanes; and pp. 146–147, for Alcmaeon.
70. See Mario Untersteiner, *The Sophists,* trans. Kathleen Freeman (Oxford: Basil Blackwell, 1954), pp. 19 ff., for a sympathetic discussion.
71. For Plato's interpretation, see *Protagoras,* 331a ff.; *Theaetetus,* 178b ff.; *Phaedrus,* 260a–267a ff. For Aristotle's interpretation, see *Metaphsics,* 1053a31, *Rhetoric,* II,Ch. 24.
72. See W. K. C. Guthrie, *A History of Greek Philosophy* (Cambridge: Cambridge University Press, 1975), IV, 273, for a translation of "Helen." For Plato's interpretation, especially as it relates to probability and persuasion, see *Phaedrus,* 267A ff., and *Gorgias,* 452d, 454c ff., 459a ff., on knowledge [*epistēmē*] versus belief [*pistis*].
73. For the text, translation, and commentary, see G. S. Kirk and J. E. Raven, "Parmenides of Elea," *The Presocratic Philosohpers: A Critical History with a Selection of Texts* (Cambridge: Cambridge University Press, 1971), pp. 263–285.
74. Kirk and Raven, p 266.
75. For the *Gorgias* and references, see note 72.
76. Bultmann, p. 176, note 19.
77. *Republic,* 518e, trans. Benjamin Jowett.

78. Werner Jaeger, *Aristotle: Fundamentals of the History of His Development,* trans. Richard Robinson (Oxford: Clarendon Press, 1948), pp. 76–77, 85, 90.

79. A. von Harnack, *History of Dogma,* trans. from the 3d German ed. by Neil Buchanan (New York: Russell and Russell, 1958), I, 225, 260, but cf. 266.

80. Hans Jonas, *The Gnostic Religion: The Message of the Alien God and the Beginnings of Christianity,* 2d ed. (Boston: Beacon Press, 1963), p. 34.

81. Jonas, p. 32.

82. Baillie, p. 62.

83. Baillie, p. 51.

84. Hatch, p. 65.

85. Hatch, p. 65.

86. Baillie, p. 44.

87. Paul Ricoeur, *The Rule of Metaphor: Multidisciplinary Studies of the Creation of Meaning,* trans. Robert Czerny (Toronto: University of Toronto Press, 1977); Gérard Genette, "La Rhétorique restreinte," *Figures III* (Paris: Editions du Seuil, 1972), pp. 21–40.

88. Joachim Goth, *Nietzsche und die Rhetorik: Untersuchungen zur deutschen Literaturgeschichte* (Tübingen: Max Niemeyer Verlag, 1970).

89. Chaim Perelman, *The Realm of Rhetoric,* trans. William Klubeck (South Bend, Ind.: University of Notre Dame Press, 1982).

90. Most of the material for this paragraph is drawn from a chapter I wrote for *The Present State of Scholarship in Historical and Contemporary Rhetoric,* ed. Winfred Horner (Columbia, MD.: University of Missouri Press, 1983), pp. 168–171.

Chapter II

1. Karl Barth, *Church Dogmatics,* trans. G. T. Thomson (Edinburgh: T. & T. Clark, 1936), I, i, 268; see also "older dogmatics," IV, i, 758.

2. For the recurring trilogy, see ibid., I, i, 234, 268, 269, 270; IV, i, 616, 758–776.

3. Barth, I, i, 270.

4. Barth, IV, i, 758.

5. Barth, IV, i, 616.

6. See Barth, I, i, 269–70. Volume I, i was published in 1932; IV, i, in 1953. Barth goes to some pains to show how Melanchthon also emphasizes *assent* despite his famous definition of faith as nothing other than a trust in the promise of God's mercy, a definition expressly condemned by the Council of Trent (see Barth, op. cit., I, i, 268–269; IV, i, 626). Barth himself does not claim any primacy for *fiducia* (see I, i, 269).

7. William Henry Paine Hatch, *The Pauline Ideal of Faith in Relation to Jewish and Hellenistic Religion,* Harvard Theological Series II (Cambridge, Mass.: Harvard University Press, 1917; rpt. New York: Kraus Reprint Co., 1969), pp. 65.

8. Hatch, pp. 35–37.

9. D. M. Baillie, *Faith in God and Its Christian Interpretation: The Kerr Lectures for 1925* (Edinburgh: T. & T. Clark, 1927), pp. 146–149.

10. Rudolf Bultmann, "*Pisteuō,* etc.," *Theological Dictionary of the New Testament* [henceforth *TDNT*], ed. Gerhard Kittel, trans. and ed. in English by Geoffrey W. Bromiley (Grand Rapids, Mich.: Eerdmans, 1964–1976), VI, 224.

11. Barth, I, i, 245–256, 281–283, 514–533; see Jerome Hamer, O.P., *Karl Barth,* trans. Dominic M. Maruca (Westminster: Md.: Newman Press, 1962), pp. 45–50, 63; also Hans Urs von Balthasar, *The Theology of Karl Barth,* trans. John Drury (New York: Holt, Rinehart and Winston, 1971), p. 94.

12. Edward D. O'Connor, C.S.C., *Faith in the Synoptic Gospels: A Problem in the Correlation of Scripture and Theology* (South Bend, Ind.: University of Notre Dame Press, 1961), pp. xi–xii, 111–113.

13. Hatch, pp. 35, 47–48, 65.

14. Baillie, pp. 51, 121–149.

15. Barth, IV, i, 766–767, 769, 771, 776. The commentators on Barth also emphasize this; see Balthasar, op. cit., pp. 100, 132; see also Henri Bouillard, *Karl Barth: Parole de dieu et existence humaine, deuxième partie—La Réponse de l'homme* (Aubier: Editions Montaigne, 1957), II, 25–27, 31, 35.

16. O'Connor, pp. 25, 150–151.

17. Bultmann, VI, 208, 211, 217, and passim.

18. Bultmann, VI, 225.

19. Barth, I, i, 235, 243; IV, i, 766, 767, 769, 776.

20. See A. Weiser, "The Old Testament Concept," in "*Pisteuō,* etc.," *Theological Dictionary of the New Testament,* ed. Gerhard Kittel, trans. and ed. in English by Geoffrey W. Bromiley (Grand Rapids, Mich.: Eerdmans, 1964–1976), VI, 188–189, 197; see also Bultmann, VI, 217, 219; Barth, IV, i, 620; O'Connor. pp. 104–105.

21. Bultmann, VI, 203, 204, 214, 226, 227.

22. Bultmann, VI, 204.

23. Barth, IV, i, 771–775.

24. Hans Conzelmann, *The Theology of St. Luke,* trans. Geoffrey Buswell (London: Faber & Faber, 1960), pp. 225–231; J. Behm, "*Metanoeō,* etc.," in Kittel, *TDNT,* IV, 974–980, 989–1022; E. Würthwein does the section on pp. 980–989 within Behm's article in *TDNT;* M. Buber, *Two Types of Faith,* trans. Norman P. Goldhawk, M.A. (London: Macmillan, 1951), pp. 9–10, 26–27, 93–94, 156–158.

25. See Hatch, pp. 51–52.

26. Baillie, pp. 189–222.

27. Weiser, VI, 186, 188.

28. O'Connor, pp. 44, 64–71, 92, 106–107, 143, 145.

29. Barth, IV, i, 758 ff.

30. Bultmann, VI, 209–210.

31. Barth, IV, i, 758.

32. Barth, I, i, 262–269.

33. Barth, IV, i, 765.

34. Bultmann cites Rom. 10:9 several times in this section as well as 1 Cor. 15:11, Rom 4:24, 1 Thess. 4:14, Col. 2:12, and Acts 2:22–24; 3:13–15; 10:37–41; 13:26–37, as instances of kerygma; see VI, 203, 204, 208, 209, and passim.

35. Bultmann, VI, 212, 218.
36. Bultmann, VI, 221, 227.
37. O'Connor, pp. 38, 142.
38. O'Connor, pp. 94–95.
39. Baillie, pp. 143–144. The first word that is italicized, *absolute,* is his; I have italicized the last sentence.
40. Hamer, p. 77 (his italics).
41. Barth, I, i, 530–532; IV, i, 762.
42. Hamer, pp. 77.
43. Thomas Aquinas, *Summa Theologica,* trans. Fathers of the English Dominican Province, rev. Daniel J. Sullivan; Great Books of the Western World, No. 20 (Chicago: Encyclopaedia Britannica, 1952), II–II, Q. 4, Art. 8. The inferiority of faith to science and understanding and wisdom is, however, only true relatively, that is, in regard to human beings.
44. For the references to St. Augustine, see G. L. Keyes, *Christian Faith and the Interpretation of History* (Lincoln, Neb.: University of Nebraska Press, 1966), pp. 56–62.
45. Hatch, pp. 33–35.
46. Barth, I, i, 136.
47. See Bouillard, II, 31, for example.
48. See earlier, pp. 11–12.
49. Liddell and Scott, p. 1408.
50. Liddell and Scott, p. 1408. The other two meanings are "that which is intrusted" and "political protection."
51. Hesiod, *Theognis,* quoted by William Smith, ed., "Peitho," *Dictionary of Greek and Roman Biography and Mythology* (New York: AMS Press, 1967), III, 175.
52. Aeschylus, *Agamemnon,* lines 385–388, cited with this English translation in Mario Untersteiner, *The Sophists,* trans. Kathleen Freeman (Oxford: Basil Blackwell, 1954), pp. 107–108. All the translations consulted emphasize the demeaning of Peitho. One of the more explicit was:

To force the plot
  That her dam, Death, hath hatched,
Temptation [Peitho] cometh, that foul
  witch unmatched,

a translation by G. M. Cookson in *Aeschylus, Sophocles, Euripides, Aristophanes,* Great Books of the Western World, ed. Robert Maynard Hutchins (Chicago: Encyclopaedia Britannica, 1952), V, 56.
53. M. P. Voigt, "Peitho," *Paulys Real-Encyclopädie des klassischen Altertums Wissenschaft,* ed. Georg Wissowa and Wilhelm Kroll (Stuttgart: J. B. Metzlehrsche Verlagsbuchhandlung, 1938), XIX, 194 ff.
54. On unfavorable attitudes to women in the Greek family, see Philip E. Slater, "The Greek Family in History and Myth," *Arethusa,* 7:1 (1974): 9–44, esp. 10–18, 28–29. Slater, however, presents an ambivalent attitude toward women in Greek society. So also does Sarah B. Pomeroy in her bibliographic survey of the

topic in "Selected Bibliography on Women in Antiquity," *Arethusa,* 6:1 (1973): 125–157, esp 140–143. All of Volume 6 is devoted to this issue.

55. Untersteiner, p. 108.

56. Voigt, p. 205.

57. Voigt, pp. 203–205.

58. See Voigt, p. 211, for references.

59. Democritus, Gorgias, Plato, Aristotle, Polybius, Plutarch, and Herodian are mentioned by Voigt, p. 211.

60. The term Alcmaeon used, *tekmairesthai,* is translated as either conjecture or inference (*erschliessen,* in Hermann Diels, *Die Fragmente der Vorsokratiker, Griechisch und Deutsch,* ed. Walther Kranz [Zurich: Weidman, 1968], I, 24 B 1, p. 214). It is the word that Aristotle used in dialectic and rhetoric for a premise of high probability (see *Rhetoric,* 1359a 9–11). For a careful study of its meaning in the *Rhetoric,* as opposed to its meaning in the *Prior Analytics* (24a22 ff., for example), see William Grimaldi, *Studies in the Philosophy of Aristotle's Rhetoric,* Einzelschriften, Heft 25, *Hermes: Zeitschrift für klassische Philologie* (Wiesbaden: Franz Steiner Verlag, 1972).

61. Isocrates, "On the Peace," 8, in *Isocrates,* trans. George Norlin (Cambridge, Mass: Harvard University Press, 1954), Vol. II.

62. Isocrates, "Antidosis," 271 (same ed. and trans. as in note 61). For further references, see "Antidosis," 268, 269; "Against the Sophists," 1–3; "Panathenaicus," 26–28: "Helen," 67. Two of the key words throughout these passages are those we have become accustomed to: science (*epistēmē*) versus conjecture (doxa).

63. Isocrates, "Antidosis," 275.

64. Henry I. Marrou, *A History of Education in Antiquity,* trans. George Lamb (London: Sheed & Ward, 1956), p. 194.

65. Marrou, p. 285.

66. Marrou, p. 287.

67. For example, "Kallimachus," 25, 30, 46; "Trapeziticus," 11, 19; "Archidamus," 20; "Helen," 20, all in the Norlin Loeb edition.

68. For example, "Helen," 22; "Trapeziticus," 44; "Antidosis," 125, in the Norlin Loeb edition.

69. For example, "Panegyricus," 110; "Busiris," 37; "Antidosis," 256, 278, 280; "Nicocles," 8; "Panegyricus," 54. The qualifier, of course, may give a negative connotation. x3

70. René Antoine Gauthier, O.P., and Jolif Jean Yves, O.P., *Aristote: L'Ethique à Nicomaque* (Louvain: Publications Universitaires de Louvain, 1959), II, 467; Takatura Ando, *Aristotle's Theory of Practical Cognition* (The Hague: Martinus Nijhoff, 1971), p. 175. See Plato, *Theaetetus,* 187a–189e, for his later view of opinion.

71. Gauthier and Yves, II, 467–470. Aristotle's final respect for Isocrates was not achieved immediately.

72. Ando, p. 174.

73. Werner Jaeger, *Aristotle: Fundamentals of the History of His Development,* trans. Richard Robinson (Oxford: Clarendon Press, 1948), pp. 85, 292 (general); pp. 233 ff., for ethics; pp. 270 ff., for politics.

74. See note 73.

75. See *Metaphysics,* XI, 7, 1064al6 ff.; H. H. Joachim, *Aristotle: Nichomachean Ethics* (Oxford: Clarendon Press, 1951), pp. 2–4, 14–19.

76. *Rhetoric,* 1354a34–1354b15, 1357al–8, 1358bl–3, 1377b21 ff., and 1391b8–20.

77. Hans von Arnim, *Leben und Werke des Dio von Prusa, mit einer Einleitung: Sophistik, Rhetorik, Philosophik, in ihrem Kampf um die Jugenbildung* (Berlin: Weidmann, 1898), p. 84.

78. Eduard Zeller, *A History of Eclecticism in Greek Philosophy,* trans. S. F. Alleyne (London: Longmans, Green, and Co., 1883), pp. 4–6.

79. Ibid., p. 5.

80. A. A. Long, *Hellenistic Philosophy: Stoics, Epicureans, Sceptics* (London: Gerald Duckworth and Company, Limited, 1974), p. 106.

81. R. E. Witt, "Albinus and the History of Middle Platonism," *Transactions of the Cambridge Philological Society,* VII (Cambridge: Cambridge University Press, 1937), p. 15.

82. Long, op. cit., p. 97.

83. Eduard Zeller, *The Stoics, Epicureans, and Sceptics,* trans. Rev. Oswald J. Reichel (London: Longmans, Green, and Co., 1892), p. 555. Zeller refers to Sextus Empiricus, *Adversus Mathematicos,* I, 173, 176, 181, 183, 184.

84. Zeller, *Stoics,* p. 534. He is quoting Sextus Empiricus again (VII, 158).

85. Plutarch, *The Lives of the Noble Greeks and Romans,* the Dryden translation, Great Books of the Western World, No. 14 (Chicago: Encyclopaedia Britannica, 1952), p. 705.

86. Von Arnim, pp. 84, 100–102.

87. George Kennedy, *The Art of Rhetoric in the Roman World World. 300 B.C.–A.D. 300* (Princeton, N.J.: Princeton University Press, 1972), p. 54.

88. George Watson, *The Stoic Theory of Knowledge* (Belfast: The Queen's University, 1966), p. 54.

89. In speaking of the Stoics, Witt uses the term *epistēmē tou eu legein,* a juxtaposition that seems strange, suggesting a certainty of the probable or a science of the probable (see Witt, p. 15). The words used in this expression for "probable" literally mean "good speaking."

90. Watson, p. 64.

91. J. M. Rist, *Stoic Philosophy* (London: Cambridge University Press, 1969), p. 169.

92. Watson, p. 64.

93. Kennedy, p. 328.

94. Von Arnim, p. 79.

95. P. H. de Lacy, "Epicureanism and the Epicurean School," *The Encyclopedia of Philosophy,* ed. Paul Edwards (New York: Macmillan, 1967), III, 2–3.

96. See Von Arnim, pp. 73–76; Kennedy, pp. 300–301.

97. For a treatment of this movement, see Paul Moraux, *Der Aristotelismus bei den Griechen von Andronikos bis Alexander von Aphrodisias*. Erster Band: *Die Renaissance des Aristotelismus im I. Jh. v. Chr.* (Berlin, New York: Walter de Gruyter, 1973).

98. See Moraux especially for Areios Didymos, pp. 316P–350; for Xenarchos of Seleucia, pp. 208–210; for Boethos of Sidon (also a Stoic), pp. 178–179.

99. See Moraux pp. 403–418, esp. p. 406, fn. 288.

100. For instance, at the end of Areios Didymos' ethics, there is a dance of the virtues led by *phronēsis,* see Moraux, p. 333; see also pp. 330, 385–386, and 392–393.

101. Kennedy, p 272.

102. See von Arnim, p. 83.

103. Kennedy, p. 322; for primary sources, see p. 323.

104. Bultmann, VI, 179–182.

105. Bultmann, VI, 181.

106. Richard Reitzenstein, *Hellenistic Mystery Religions: Their Basic Ideas and Significance,* trans. John E. Steely (Pittsburgh: Pickwick Press, 1978), pp. 488–495.

107. The quotation and the material of this paragraph are from Kennedy, pp. 432–433.

108. Leonardi Spengel, ed., *Rhetores Graeci,* 3 volumes (Leipzig: B. G. Teubner, 1883; rpt. Frankfurt am Main: Minerva, 1966). The other edition of Greek rhetorics, by Christian Walz, *Rhetores Graeci,* 9 volumes (Stuttgart: J. G. Cottai, 1832–1836), covers much of the same ground as Spengel. However, it includes more of the rhetorics of the second through the fourth centuries A.D. I have chosen to follow Spengel because he includes some of the major comprehensive rhetorics that Walz omits, because his selections are more closely aligned with the Hellenistic period, and because he has an index. I do not believe that I am omitting any significant Greek rhetorician among the comprehensive rhetoricians (as I have defined them).

109. See Anaximenes, I, 192–204, in Spengel.

110. Rufus, I, 469, and Anonymous, I, 445–453, in Spengel, op. cit.

111. Aristotle, *The "Art" of Rhetoric,* trans. John Henry Freese, Loeb Classical Library (Cambridge, Mass.: Harvard University Press, 1925).

112. Aristotle's own summary of these basic arguments is presented in Bk. I, Ch. 2, 1355b25–1356a23. An excellent discussion of the meanings of these *pisteis* can be seen in William M. A. Grimaldi, S.J., *Aristotle, Rhetoric I: A Commentary* *New York: Fordham University Press, 1980), in the Appendix, "The Role of the *Pisteis* in Aristotle's Methodology," pp. 349–356. A classic earlier discussion was "*Pisteis,*" in Edward Meredith Cope, *An Introduction to Aristotle's Rhetoric with Analysis Notes and Appendices* (London: Macmillan, 1867; rpt. Dubuque, Iowa: Wm C. Brown, Reprint Library, n.d.), pp. 355–362. An application of Aristotle's concept of *pistis* as faith in some Christian, Jewish, and Moslem theologians can be seen in Harry Austryn Wolfson, "The Double Faith Theory in Clement, Saadia, Averroes and St. Thomas, and Its Origin in Aristotle and the Stoics." *Jewish Quarterly Review,* 33(1942–43): 213–264. For an analysis and a sample that is analyzed by the Aristotelian methodology, see James L. Kinneavy, *A Theory of Discourse* (New York: W. W. Norton, 1980), pp. 225–229.

113. See Aristotle, Bk. II, Ch. 1. For a discussion, see Kinneavy, pp. 238–241; for an analyzed example of the use of the ethical argument in a political speech, see Kinneavy, pp. 256–258.

114. Quintilian, *Institutiones Oratoriae,* trans. H. E. Butler, Loeb Classical Library (Cambridge, Mass.: Harvard University Press, 1921), III, 8, 12.

115. See Aristotle, *Rhetoric,* Bk. II, Chs. 2–17. For a discussion of these chapters, see Kinneavy, pp. 241–245; for an analyzed example, see Kinneavy, 258–260.

116. See Aristotle, *Rhetoric,* Bk. II, Ch. 20, for induction. For a discussion and exemplification, see Kinneavy, pp. 249–250, 260–263.

117. For enthymemes and maxims, see Aristotle, *Rhetoric,* Bk. II, Chs. 22, 24–26. For discussion and exemplification, see Kinneavy, pp. 250–255, 260–263.

118. On topics, see Aristotle, *Rhetoric,* Bk. II, Chs. 19, 23, 24. For discussion and exemplification, see Kinneavy, pp. 245–250, 260–263.

119. See Bultmann, VI, 175. It is worthy of note that the Latin *fides* derives from the Greek *pith-* root also; that is, its original meaning was "persuasion."

120. I have departed from the Oxford translation, *The New English Bible with the Apocrypha,* because it translates *epeisthēsan* "convinced." The revised Standard Version translates it "persuaded," making the literal point I am interested in.

121. For the notion of ethnoscience, see Kinneavy, pp. 127–129. The validity of the basic distinctions of scientific, rhetorical, and poetic is discussed at great length in the second chapter, pp. 48–72.

122. Bertram, in Bultmann, "Peithō," *Theological Dictionary of The New Testament,* ed. Gerhard Kittel, trans. and ed. in English by Geoffrey W. Bromiley (Grand Rapids, Mich.: Eerdmans, 1964–1976), V, 1.

123. See Jack R. Lundbom, *Jeremiah: A Study in Ancient Hebrew Rhetoric,* Society of Biblical Literature and Scholars Press, Dissertation Series, No. 18 (Missoula, Mont.: The Society of Biblical Literature, 1975); also Yehoshua Gitay, *Prophecy and Persuasion: A Study of Isaiah 40–48,* No. 14, in Forum Theologiae Linguisticae (Bonn: Linguistica Biblica, 1981).

124. Edwin Hatch and Henry Redpath, *A Concordance to the Septuagint and the Other Greek Versions of the Old Testament (Including the Apocryphal Books) (Graz, Austria: Akademische Druck V. Verlagsanstalt, 1954, II, 1114–1115.*

125. Ralph D. Winter, ed. *The New Englishman's Greek Concordance* (South Pasadena, Calif.: William Carey Library, 1972), Numbers 543, 544, 545, 3981, 3982.

126. Luke 16:31; Acts 13:43, 17:4, 18:4, 19:8, 19:26, 28:23, 28:24,; Rom. 14:14, 2 Cor. 5:;11, 2 Tim. 1:12.

Chapter III

1. Emil Schürer, *The History of the Jewish People in the Age of Jesus Christ (175 B.C.–A.D. 135),* a new English version rev. and ed. Geza Vermes, Fergus Millar, and Matthew Black; original trans. by John Macpherson (Edinburgh: T. & T. Clark, 1979), II, 52.

2. Schürer, II, 62, 70–71.

3. Schürer, II, 56. He uses the Greek terms in the last sentence.

4. Abraham Negev, ed., *Archaeological Encyclopedia of the Holy Land* (Englewood, N.J.: SBS Publishing, 1980), p. 284.

5. Michael Avi–Jonah, "Sepphoris," *The Encyclopedia of Archaeological Excavations in the Holy Land* (Englewood Cliffs, N.J.: Prentice–Hall, 1976), IV, 1053.

6. Negev, p. 53.

7. Negev, p. 314; Schürer, II, 45 (the first reference is to Gerasa and the second to Gadara).

8. See Chapter II, note 85.

9. These details are drawn from Martin Hengel, *Judaism and Hellenism: Studies in Their Encounter in Palestine During the Early Hellenistic Period,* trans. John Bowden (Philadelphia: Fortress Press, 1974), I, 83–85; and Schürer, II, 49–50.

10. Emil Schürer, *The Literature of the Jewish People in the Time of Jesus,* trans. Peter Christie and Sophia Taylor, ed. and intro. by Nathan Glazer (New York: Schocken, 1972), pp. 156–381. Henceforth references to this book will be listed as Schürer, *Literature,* and references to Schürer's history (see note 1 earlier) will be simply Schürer.

11. Schürer, *Literature,* p. 204, for Eupolemus; p. 222, for Justus of Tiberias.

12. Schürer, II, 49–50.

13. Erwin R. Goodenough, *By Light, Light: The Mystic Gospel of Hellenistic Judaism* (New Haven, Conn.: Yale University Press, 1935), p. 7.

14. Victor Tcherikover, *Hellenistic Civilization and the Jews,* trans. S. Applebaum (Philadelphia: Jewish Publication Society of America, 1959), p. 116.

15. Tcherikover, pp. 212, 250–252.

16. A. H. M. Jones, *The Greek City from Alexander to Justinian* (Oxford: Clarendon Press, 1940), p. 291.

17. Tcherikover, pp. 20–21, but cf. also p. 344.

18. Schürer, II, 74.

19. J. N. Sevenster, *Do You Know Greek? How Much Greek Could the First Christians Have Known?* trans. J. de Bruin (Leiden: E. J. Brill, 1968), pp. 142, 185, 189.

20. Gustaf Dalman, *Jesus-Jeshua: Studies in the Gospels,* trans. Paul P. Levertoff (London: Society for the Promotion of Christian Knowledge, 1929), pp. 3–4.

21. Saul Lieberman, *Greek in Jewish Palestine* (New York: Jewish Theological Seminary of America, 1942), p. 30.

22. Lieberman, p. 2

23. Sevenster, p. 16, citing Alfred Wikenhauser, *Einleitung in das Neue Testament* (Freiburg: Herder, 1953), pp. 346–347, and F. W. Grosheide, *De Brief aan de Hebrieen en de Brief van Jakobus* (Kampen: J. H. Kok, 1955), p. 326.

24. See Harold W. Hoehner, *Herod Antipas* (Cambridge: Cambridge University Press, 1972), p. 62; Sevenster, p. 10.

25. Sevenster, p. 10.

26. Sevenster, p. 10.

27. Sevenster, p. 9.

28. Sevenster, p. 2.

29. Dalman, p. 5.

30. Sevenster, pp. 25–28, 189.

31. Dalman, pp. 5–6; Sevenster, pp. 33–35. See Schürer, II, pp. 20–21, note 68, for a bibliography on the topic.

32. Schürer, II, 20–26, 74.

33. Schürer, II, 80. In fn. 23, he calls attention to the criticism of Sevenster's thesis by D. M. Lewis, in the latter's review of *Do You Know Greek?* in the *Journal of Theological Studies* 20 (1969): 583–588.

34. See Dalman, p. 5.

35. Oscar Cullman, *Peter: Disciple, Apostle, Martyr—A Historical and Theological Study,* 2d rev. ed. (London: SCM Press, 1962), p. 19.

36. Werner Foerster, "Iēsous," *Theological Dictionary of the New Testament,* ed. Gerhard Kittel, trans. and ed. in English by Geoffrey W. Bromiley (Grand Rapids, Mich.: Eerdmans, 1964–1976), III, 285, 289.

37. Dalman, p. 6.

38. Edwyn Bevan, *Jerusalem Under the High Priests: Five Lectures on the Period Between Nehemiah and the New Testament* (London: Edward Arnold, 1918), p. 33.

39. Tcherikover, pp. 21, 36.

40. C. J. Dancy, *A Commentary on 1 Maccabees* (Oxford: Basil Blackwell, 1954), p. 45; Schürer, for instance, devotes almost 100 pages to a discussion of the Greek cities (II, 85–184) in his history of the Jews at this period.

41. A. H. M. Jones, *The Greek City from Alexander to Justinian* (Oxford: At the Clarendon Press, 1940), p. 5.

42. Mikhail Ivanovich Rostovtseff, *The Social and Economic History of the Hellenistic World,* 2d ed. rev. P. M. Fraser (Oxford: Clarendon Press, 1957), II, 859.

43. Dancy, p. 46.

44. Dancy, p. 46.

45. Michael Avi-Jonah, *The Holy Land from the Persian to the Arab Conquest (536 B.C. to A.D. 640); A Historical Geography* (Grand Rapids, Mich.: Baker Book House, 1966), pp. 215–216. See also J. Klausner, "Chapter IX: Judah Aristobulus and Jannaeus Alexander," in Abraham Schalit, ed., *The World History of the Jewish People.* Vol. VI: *The Hellenistic Age—Political Histroy of Jewish Palestine from 332 B.C.E. to 67 B.C.E.* (New Brunswick, N.J.: Rutgers University Press, 1972), pp. 236–237.

46. Jones, p. 257.

47. Tcherikover, p. 265.

48. Jones, p. 257.

49. For a more thorough quick survey of the history of the Greek cities in Palestine, see Schürer, II, 87–97.

50. Jones, p. v.

51. Tcherikover, p. 22; see also Rostovtseff, I, 528, and Schürer, II, 67–97, 182–183.

52. See on this matter Schürer, II, 86, 188–198; and Avi-Jonah, pp. 127–180, for the extent of the cities' territories. There were even subdivisions within these cities with special privileges, such as exemption from special taxes or from special regulations, a point that was to have particular signficance for the Jews and reli-

gious regulations under the Seleucids. On these special distinctions, see Schürer, pp. 93–97.

53. Rostovtseff, I, 512.

54. Josephus, *Wars of the Jews,* in *Josephus, Complete Works,* trans. William Wiston (Grand Rapids, Mich.: Kregel Publications, 1960), Bk. II, Ch. xviii, Sections 1, 3, and 5 for Caesarea, Scythopolis, and Ascalon, and Bk. VII Ch. viii, Section 7 for Damascus.

55. Tcherikover, p. 22.

56. See Schürer, II, 85–184, list on p. vii; Tcherikover, pp. 91 ff.; Jones, bibliographic list, pp. 565–569, also pp. 546–547.

57. Schürer, II, 175.

58. Schürer, II, 176.

59. Josephus, *The Antiquities of the Jews* (same ed. and tr. as in note 54), XIV, v, 4.

60. Josephus, *Antiquities,* XVII, x, 9.

61. Josephus, *Antiquities,* XVIII, ii, 1. I am here following the English translation in Schürer, II, 173.

62. Hoehner, p. 85.

63. E. Mary Smallwood, *The Jews Under Roman Rule* (Leiden: E. J. Brill, 1976), p. 118; the basis for this is probably Josephus, *Antiquities* XVIII, ii, 1, on which see Schürer, II, 174, fn. 485.

64. Josephus, *Antiquities,* XVIII, ii, 3.

65. Negev, "Sepphoris," *Archaeological Encyclopedia,* p. 284, possibly basing his opinion on Josephus, *Wars of the Jews,* III, ii, 4.

66. Negev, "Sepphoris," p. 284.

67. Smallwood, p. 118.

68. Schürer, II, 174. The passage lists a number of categories of people who can be certain of being Israelites, among them, says Rabbi Jose in the text, "Everyone who was signed up as a witness in the registry office of pedigrees in Yoshanah near Sepphoris" (from Philip Blackman, *Mishnayoth, In Six Volumes,* Volume III: *Order Nashim* [London: Mishna Press, 1953], III, 477). Schürer states that both interpretations of this text recognize that the members of the old government of Sepphoris would have been "pure-blooded Israelites."

69. Michael Avi-Jonah, "Sepphoris," *Encyclopedia Judaica* (Jerusalem: Macmillan, 1971–1972), XIV, 1178.

70. Schürer, II, 179.

71. Schürer, II, 179–180.

72. Josephus, *Life* (same ed. and tr. as in note 54), Section 12.

73. Josephus, *Life,* Section 27.

74. Josephus, *Life,* Section 9; on the handling of the audience by Jesus, see Sections 27–28.

75. Josephus, *Life,* Section 9.

76. Josephus, *Antiquities,* XX, viii, 7; *Wars of the Jews,* II.

77. Josephus, *Antiquities,* XX, ix, 9.

78. Schürer, II, 117, fn. 169.

79. Dalman, pp. 75–76.

80. Schürer, II, 181.

81. Moses Hadas, ed. and trans., *The Third and Fourth Book of The Maccabees* (New York: Harper & Brothers, 1953), p. 111; see Josephus, *Antiquities,* XI, iii, 1.

82. Schürer, II, 110, 183; see Josephus, *Wars of the Jews,* IV, iii, 2, and viii, 1.

83. Schürer, II, 112–113, 183.

84. See later for discussion of Jewish membership in the *gymnasium.*

85. Hengel, I 68.

86. See Tcherikover, p. 350.

87. See Hengel, I, 67; Sir William Woodthorpe Tarn, *Hellenistic Civilization,* 3d ed., rev. by the author and G. T. Griffith (New York: World, 1961), p. 222; Josephus, *Antiquities,* XII, iii, 2; XVI, ii, 3.

88. Josephus, *Antiquities,* XII, iii, 1 (Asia here means Asia Minor).

89. Schürer, II, 183, 427.

90. Rostovtseff. II, 689.

91. Schürer, II 427.

92. Louis H. Feldman, "The Orthodoxy of the Jews in Hellenistic Egypt," *Jewish Social Studies,* 23 (1960): 223.

93. Tarn, p. 221.

94. Harry Austryn Wolfson, *Philo: Foundations of Religious Philosophy in Judaism, Christianity, and Islam* (Cambridge, Mass.: Harvard University Press, 1962), I, 79–80.

95. Dora Askowith, *The Toleration of the Jews Under Julius Caesar and Augustus* (New York: Columbia University Press, 1915), pp. 1–10, 160–174; Tarn, pp. 220–221; Harold Arthur Harris, *Greek Athletics and the Jews,* ed. I. M. Barton and A. J. Brothers (Cardiff: Univ. of Wales Press, 1976), pp. 99–100; cf. Schürer, II, 93–97.

96. Askowith, pp. 164–165, and pp. 194–195 for the Seleucid exemptions; see note 52 earlier.

97. Isocrates, "Panegyricus," 51 (see Ch. II, note 61, for full bibliographic data).

98. Hengel, I, 65.

99. Hengel, I, 65.

100. See earlier, notes 39, 40, 41.

101. R. Merkelbach, "Die griechische Wortschatz und die Christen," *Zeitschrift für Papyrologie und Epigraphik, 18:2 (1975): 109.*

102. Merkelbach, p. 109.

103. Feldman, p. 224.

104. Jean Delorme, *Gymnasion: Etude sur les monuments consacrés à l'education en Grèce, des origines à l'empire romain* (Paris: Editions de Boccard, 1960), p. 3.

105. Jones, pp. 225–226.

106. Hengel, I, 66.

107. Delorme, p. 3.

108. See Delorme, p. 320, p. 456; Jones, pp. 220, 225.

109. Delorme, pp. 320–323, 353–358; see also Rostovtseff, I, 324; II, 1059–1064.

110. Aristotle, *The Athenian Constitution,* trans. Sir Frederic G. Kenyon, in *Aristotle,* Volume 2, Great Books of the Western World, No. 9, ed. Robert Maynard Hutchins (Chicago: Encylopaedia Britannica, 1952), Chapter 42; Pausanias, *Description of Greece,* trans. W. H. S. Jones, in Loeb Classical Library (Cambridge, Mass.: Harvard University Press, 1954), VI, 27, 5.

111. Pausanias, VI, 27, 5.

112. Tcherikover, pp. 163, 311 ff., 327, 350, 467, 511, 515.

113. Jones, p. 220.

114. E. Mary Smallwood, p. 321.

115. Solomon Zeitlin, *The Second Book of the Maccabees,* ed. with intro. and commmentary, trans. Sidney Tedesche (New York: Harper & Brothers, 1954), pp. 131–132.

116. Delorme, Table de Concordance [for Figures 61 to 64], end of book. He considers only an explicit mention of a *gymnasium* or a *palaestra* in historical records; he does not, for example, assume that a gymnasiarch implied a *gymnasium* (see p. 5).

117. Henri I. Marrou, *A History of Education in Antiquity,* tr. George Lamb (London: Sheed and Wards, 1956), p 110.

118. Chrysis Pélékidis, *Histoire de l'éphébie des origines à 31 avant Jésus* (Paris: Editions E. de Boccard, 1962), Ch. IV, pp. 211–256.

119. Marrou, p. 106. With regard to new laws, a second version substitutes "and those that the people enact by common consent" for "those that the wisdom of the rulers may enact."

120. See Pélékidis, p. 266.

121. Marrou, p. 105.

122. Delorme, pp. 479–480.

123. Delorme, pp. 479–480.

124. Henri I. Marrou, *Histoire de l'éducation dans l'antiquité,* 6th ed., rev. and enlarged (Paris: Editions du Seuil, 1965), p. 281. Usually, I use the English translation of Marrou cited earlier, note 117.

125. See Pélékidis, p. 267.

126. See Charles Henry Oldfather, "The Greek Literary Texts from Greco-Roman Egypt: A Study in the History of Civilization," *University of Wisconsin Studies in the Social Sciences and History,* 9 (1923): 80 ff.

127. H. L. Pinner, *The World of Books in Classical Antiquity* (Leiden: A. W. Sijthoff, 1948), p. 43.

128. Marrou, pp. 267, 287.

129. See Tcherikover, p. 105, for Kanawat and Gerasa; Schürer, II, 47, for Ptolemaïs; II, 54, fn. 1, for Jericho; II, 48, for Philadelphia and Scythopolis (a *pancratium* for both boxing and wrestling in each); Hengel, I, 70, for Damascus, Ptolemaïs, Philadelphia, Petra, Tyre, and Sidon; see note 135 later for Jerusalem.

130. Hengel, I, 66, 71; Marrou, p. 110.

131. See Hengel, I, 68, for references.

132. Hengel, I, 68; II, 48, fn. 84.

133. Hengel, II, 48, fn. 84.

134. Hengel, II, 48, fn. 84.

135. See 2 Maccabees 4:12, in Solomon Zeitlin, ed., *The Second Book of the Maccabees,* trans. Sidney Tedesche (New York: Harper & Brothers, 1954). See also 4 Maccabees 4:20, in Moses Hadas, trans. and ed., *The Third and Fourth Books of the Maccabees* (New York: Harper & Brothers, 1953). See also the discussion in Zeitlin, pp. 9–20.

136. Josephus, *Antiquities,* IV, viii, 12.

137. Nathan Drazin, *History of Jewish Education from 515 B.C.E. to 220 C.E.,* No. 29 of the Johns Hopkins Studies in Education (Baltimore, Md.: The Johns Hopkins Press, 1940), p. 37; Schürer, II, 309.

138. Abram Simon, "The Biblical Era," *Jewish Education: Historical Survey* (Philadelphia: Jewish Chataqua Society, 1912), p. 37, quoting Welhausen.

139. Drazin, p. 37. See also Birger Gerhardsson, *Memory and Manuscript: Oral Tradition and Written Transmission in Rabbinic Judaism and Early Christianity* (Lund: C. W. K. Gleerup, 1961), p. 59.

140. Schürer, II, 419.

141. Schürer, II, 419.

142. Schürer, II, 419.

143. Gerhardsson, p. 59.

144. Drazin, pp. 87–93; Schürer, II, 419–420; Dalman, pp. 31–37.

145. Gerhardsson, pp. 62–63, 124–126; Drazin, p. 141; William Boyd; *The History of Western Education,* 6th ed. (London: Adam & Charles Black, 1959), p. 64.

146. Gerhardsson, pp. 45, 124–126.

147. Gerhardsson, p. 124.

148. Gerhardsson, p. 89.

149. W. K. C. Guthrie, *A History of Greek Philosophy,* Volume III: *The Fifth-Century Enlightenment (Cambridge: Cambridge University Press, 1969), pp. 55–261.*

150. Henry A. Fischel, ed., *Essays in Greco-Roman and Related Talmudic Literature* (New York: KTAV Publishing House, 1977), p. xiv. Boaz Cohen, in the introduction to his two–volume study, *Jewish and Roman Law: A Comparative Study* (New York: Jewish Theological Seminary of America, 1966), instances David Daube, J. Dauvillier, Elias J. Bickerman, J. Derrett, and Nörr as five important authors who have made important studies relating Hellenistic law to the New Testament (p. xvi). His own name must, of course, also be added to this eminent list; and there are others who must now be added.

151. See note 150 for Cohen.

152. Cohen, pp. 38–41, for Aristotle and Hermagoras, and pp. 41–47 for Cicero and Roman law.

153. Cohen, p. 36 (my italics).

154. Cohen, pp. 56–57. (I have transliterated the Greek and the Hebrew; I also omitted some footnote references.)

155. See earlier p. 53 and later p. 103–106.

156. David Daube, "Rabbinic Methods of Interpretation and Hellenistic Rhe-

toric," *Hebrew Union College Annual,* 22 (1949): 240. He gives three other articles of his in his footnote. All these articles and later work of his on the topic are listed in his full bibliography, "Publications of David Daube," *Journal of Jewish Studies,* 25 (1974): 7–15. The entire issue is entitled *Studies in Jewish History in Honour of David Daube.*

157. See L. Jacobs, "Hermeneutics," *Encyclopedia Judaica,* VIII, 367.

158. Saul Lieberman, *Hellenism in Jewish Palestine* (New York: Jewish Theological Seminary of America, 1954), pp. 61, 79.

159. Lieberman, *Hellenism,* p. 78.

160. Karl Heinrich Rengstorf, "Didaskō, etc." *Theological Dictionary of the New Testament,* ed. Gerhard Kittel, trans. ed. in English by Geoffrey W. Bromiley (Grand Rapids, Mich.: Eerdmans, 1964–1976), II, p. 142.

161. Rengstorf, p. 142. I omitted some footnote numbers from the quotation.

162. Krister Stendahl, *The School of St. Matthew and Its Use of the Old Testament* (Lund: C. W. K. Gleerup, 1954), pp. 35, 191–194, 207.

163. R. Alan Culpepper, *The Johannine School: An Evaluation of the Johannine School Hypothesis Based on an Investigation of the Nature of Ancient Schools,* Society of Biblical Literature Dissertation Series, No. 26 (Missoula, Mont.: Scholars Press, 1974), pp. 1–38, 261–290. For the Hellenistic bent of the Johannine circle, see Oscar Cullmann, *The Johannine Circle,* trans. John Bowden (Philadelphia: Westminster Press, 1976), pp. 43–49.

164. Martin Dibelius, *From Tradition to Gospel,* trans. Bertam L. Wolff (Greenwood, S.C.: Attic Press, 1971).

165. Rudolf Bultmann, *History of the Synoptic Tradition,* trans. John Marsh (New York: Harper & Row), 1968.

166. This is a composite listing of their categories.

167. Dibelius, pp. 14–15.

168. On diatribe, see Arthur Marmorstein, "The Background of the Haggadah," *Hebrew Union College Annual,* 6 (1929): 141–204; Edmund Stein, "Die homiletische Peroratio im Midrasch," *HUCA,* 8–9 (1931–1932): 353–371. On the figure of the sage, see David Daube, *The New Testament and Rabbinic Judaism* (London: Athlone, 1956), pp. 86 ff.; Henry A Fischel, "Story and History: Observations on Greco-Roman Rhetoric and Pharisaism," in Fischel, *Essays,* pp. 443–472; Hans Dieter Betz, *Der Apostel Paul und die sokratische Tradition.* Beiträge zur historischen Theologie, ed. Gerhard Ebeling, No. 45 (Tübingen: Siebeck, 1972). On aretologies, see Betz, preceding citation; Howard Clark Kee, *Aretologies, Hellenistic "Lives" and the Sources of Mark* (Berkeley, Calif.: Center for Hermeneutical Studies in Hellenistic and Modern Culture, 1975); H. Koester, "One Jesus and Four Primitive Gospels," in J. M. Robinson, ed., *Trajectories Through Early Christianity* (Philadelphia: Fortress Press, 1971), pp. 187–193. On martyrologies and Hellenistic romances, see Howard Clark Kee, *Community of the New Age* (Philadelphia: Westminster Press, 1977), pp. 18–19, 21–22. Kee's book surveys all these genres in the introduction.

169. Philadelphia: Fortress Press, 1979.

170. Betz, p. xiv.

171. Betz, pp. 14–15.

172. Betz, pp. 16–23.
173. Betz, pp. 18–23, and commentary on Galatians 2:15 to 4:31.
174. See Betz's note, p. 23.
175. On sorites, see Henry A. Fischel, "The Uses of Sorites (*climax, gradatio*) in the Tannaitic Period," *HUCA*, 44 (1973): 119–151.
176. On *topoi*, see E. E. Halévi, "Greek Topoi in Aggadic Literature [translation]," *Tarbiz*, 40 (1970): 293–300.
177. See L. Goppelt, *Typos: die typologische Deutung des Alten Testaments im Neuen* (Darmstadt: Wissenschaftliche Buchgesellschaft, 1969).
178. E. Earle Ellis, "How the New Testament Uses the Old," in I. Howard Marshall, ed., *New Testament Interpretation: Essays on Principles and Methods* (Grand Rapids, Mich.: Eerdmans, 1977), p. 215.
179. Dalman, p. 34.
180. Schürer, II, 423–463.
181. See note 156 earlier.
182. Elie Bikerman, "La Chaine de la tradition pharisienne," in Fischel, *Essays*, pp. 132–137.
183. Quoted in Lieberman, *Hellenism*, p. 104.
184. Schürer, II, 78, fn. 265, quoting Saul Lieberman.
185. Sevenster, p. 44.
186. Baillie, p. 44.
187. Schürer, *Literature*, p. 321.
188. Wolfson uses the term "religious philosophy" in the subtitle to his work on Philo.
189. Samuel Sandmel, *The First Christian Century in Judaism and Christianity* (New York: Oxford University Press, 1960), p. 113.
190. J. B. Carpzov, *Sacrae exercitationes in St. Pauli epistolam ad Hebraeos ex Philone Alexandrino* (Amsterdam: 1750). This work was unavailable to me.
191. C. Spicq, O.P., *L'Epître aux Hebreux* (Paris: Librairie Lecoffre, 1952), I, 37–91, esp. 76–85.
192. Ronald Williamson, *Philo and the Epistle to the Hebrews* (Leiden: E. J. Brill, 1970), esp. pp. 308–372.
193. Williamson, pp. 5–6.
194. Spicq, I, 79.
195. Spicq, I, 79.
196. Spicq, I, 79–80.
197. Spicq, I, 80–81.
198. Williamson, p. 333.
199. Williamson, p. 352.
200. Williamson, p. 353.
201. Williamson, p. 362. He clearly supports the concepts of confidence in the divine power, especially in trials, as well as the assurance of providence, as his assent to Spicq's second point illustrates.
202. Adolf Schlatter, *Der Glaube im Neuen Testament*, 5th ed. (Stuttgart: Colwer Verlag, 1963), pp. 582–585.
203. Schlatter, pp. 561–573, 575–581.

204. Hans Schreckenberg, *Bibliographie zu Flavius Josephus,* Vol. 1 of *Arbeiten zur Literatur und Geschichte des Hellenistischen Judentums* (Leiden: E. J. Brill, 1978). I was not able to use the work of Abraham Schalit, ed., *Zur Josephus-Forschung* (Darmstadt: Wissenschaftliche Buchgesellschaft, 1973).

205. Josephus, *Antiquities,* X, 114. From now on, all references to Josephus will be from Flavius Josephus, *Josephus,* trans. H. St. J. Thackeray, Loeb Classical Library (London: W. Heinemann, 1926).

206. Weiser, Artur, "Pisteuō." *TDNT,* VI, 183.

207. *Antiquities,* XV, 87.

208. Schlatter, p. 583. He also adduces Josephus, *Life,* 22, for the same comparison.

209. *Antiquities,* II, 274.

210. *Antiquities,* III, 27.

211. *Antiquities,* X, 267–268.

212. For example, for religious uses: *Antiquities,* I, 231; VIII, 110; XII, 304; XIV, 455; XVIII, 211 (this last in a pagan religious context). For examples of uses in a secular sense: *Antiquities,* VI, 289; VII, 178; X, 28; XIV, 265; XVI, 82, 107, 121, 205, 217; *Wars,* IV, 337.

213. As in *Antiquities,* VI, 263; VIII, 72.

214. For example, see Josephus, *Life,* 84; *Antiquities,* XVIII, 194; XVII, 246; *Wars,* V, 121.

215. See earlier Chapter II, pp. 46–47.

216. For example, for pledge, sworn assurances, or oaths: *Wars,* III, 535; IV, 417; V, 320; VI, 345; for oaths, *Antiquities,* II, 153; VI, 69, 326; X, 63; for word, *Wars,* II, 639.

217. *Against Apion,* I, 38, 72.

218. *Antiquities,* XIV, 28.

219. *Antiquities,* X, 28.

220. *Antiquities,* II, 272; for other verbal religious contexts, see *Antiquities,* III, 317; X, 178; XI, 96.

221. See earlier, pp. 9–71 Chap. II, notes 75 and 76.

222. See notes 72 through 77.

223. See *Life,* 30, 31.

224. *Antiquities,* IX, 86.

225. Schlatter, citing *Antiquities,* IX, 12; X, 39.

226. See earlier, pp. 17–20.

227. See note 208 earlier.

228. *Antiquities,* III, 309.

229. See, for example, *Against Apion,* I, 14; *Antiquities,* X, 188; XVI, 400; XVIII, 142; XIX, 247; *Wars,* 438.

Chapter IV

1. G. Bertram, "Peithō, etc.," in *Theological Dictionary of the New Testament,* ed. Gerhard Kittel, trans. and ed. in English by Geoffrey W. Bromiley

(Grand Rapids, Mich.: Eerdmans, 1964–1976), V, 1. The rest of the article is by Rudolf Bultmann.

2. Edwin Hatch and Henry A. Redpath, assisted by other scholars, *A Concordance to the Septuagint and the Other Greek Versions of the Old Testament (including the Apocryphal Ones)* (Graz, Austria: Akademische Druck U. Verlagsanstalt, 1954), I, 1114–1115.

3. See J. Stegenga, *The Greek-English Analytical Concordance of the Greek-English New Testament* (Jackson, Miss.: Hellenes-English Biblical Foundation, 1963), pp. 614–615.

4. Stegenga, pp. 615–619.

5. See, for example, Acts 18:19; 19:8–9, 26, 28; Luke 16:31.

6. Jack R. Lundbom, *Jeremiah: A Study in Ancient Hebrew Rhetoric,* Dissertation Series, No. 16, Society of Biblical Literature and Scholars Press (Missoula, Mont.: Scholars Press, University of Montana, 1975), p. 2.

7. Lundbom, pp. 1–2.

8. Yegoshua Gitay, *Prophecy and Persuasion: A Study of Isaiah 40–48,* in Forum Theologiae Linguisticae, No. 14, ed. Erhardt Güttgemans (Bonn: Linguistica Biblica, 1981), pp. 7–8, 16–26.

9. Gitay, p. 27.

10. Gitay, pp. 34–39, 58.

11. Martin Dibelius, *From Tradition to Gospel,* trans. Bertram L. Wolff (Greenwood, S.C.: Attic Press, 1971).

12. Gitay, pp. 7–26.

13. Gitay, p. 36.

14. On some limitations of this approach, see James L. Kinneavy, *A Theory of Discourse* (New York: W. W. Norton, 1980), pp. 242–243, 248–249, 252–253, 253–255.

15. George V. Wigram, *The Englishman's Greek Concordance of the New Testament,* Ninth edition (Grand Rapids, Mich.: Zondervan Publishing House, reprinting 1903 ed., 1971), pp. 622–630.

16. Arthur Darby Nock, *Conversion: The Old and the New in Religion from Alexander the Great to Augustine of Hippo* (Oxford: Clarendon Press, 1933), p. 7.

17. See Kinneavy, pp. 102–104, 141–146, for a more general application of these concepts.

18. Ronald Williamson, *Philo and the Epistle to the Hebrews, Arbeiten zur Literatur und Geschichte des Hellenistischen Judentums,* No. 4, ed. K. H. Rengstorf et al. (Leiden: E. J. Brill), p. 348.

19. Dr. Charles Robert Kline, a colleague of mine, is currently at work on this. He did check my classifications for each of the 491 occurrences and disagreed with me in very few cases. In fact, the correlation was higher than 90 percent.

20. These figures were arrived at by a rough estimate of the number of words in the three texts, estimating the number of average words per line, lines per page, and pages per text.

21. St. Thomas Aquinas, *Summa Theologiae,* trans. Fathers of the Dominican Province, rev. Daniel J. Sullivan, Great Books of the Western World, No. 20, ed.

by Robert Maynard Hutchins (Chicago: Encyclopaedia Britannica, 1952), II–III, Question 1, Article 3, pp. 381–382.

Chapter V

1. Werner Jaeger, *Early Christianity and Greek Paideia* (Cambridge, Mass.: Belknap Press, 1961), p. 7.
2. Jaeger, pp. 61–62

Bibliography

Aeschylus, Sophocles, Euripides, Aristophanes. Trans. G. M. Cookson, Richard C. Jebb, Edward P. Coleridge, Benjamin Bickley Rogers, respectively. Great Books of the Western World, No. 5. Ed. Robert Maynard Hutchins. Chicago: Encyclopaedia Britannica, 1952. Cookson only translated Aeschylus.

Ando, Takatura. *Aristotle's Theory of Practical Cognition.* The Hague: Mattinus Nijhoff, 1971.

Aquinas, Thomas. *Summa Theologica.* Trans. Fathers of the English Dominican Province; rev. by Daniel J. Sullivan. Great Books of the Western World, No. 20. Ed. Robert Maynard Hutchins. Chicago: Encyclopaedia Britannica, 1952. II.

Aristotle. *The "Art" of Rhetoric.* Trans. John Henry Freese. Loeb Classical Library. Cambridge, Mass.: Harvard University Press, 1925.

———. "The Athenian Constitution." *Aristotle: II.* Trans. Sir Frederic G. Kenyon. Great Books of the Western World, No. 9, Ed. Robert Maynard Hutchins. Chicago: Encyclopaedia Britannica, 1952. II.

———. "Metaphysics." *Aristotle: I.* Trans. W. D. Ross. Great Books of the Western World, No. 9. Ed. Robert Maynard Hutchins. Chicago: Encyclopaedia Britannica, 1952. I.

———. "Nichomachean Ethics." *Aristotle: II.* Trans. W. D. Ross. Great Books of the Western World, No. 9. Ed. Robert Maynard Hutchins. Chicago: Encyclopaedia Britannica, 1952. II.

———. "Rhetoric." *Aristotle: II.* Trans. W. Rhys Roberts. Great Books of the Western World, No. 9. Ed. Robert Maynard Hutchins. Chicago: Encyclopaedia Britannica, 1952. II.

Arnim, Hans von. *Leben und Werke des Dio von Prusa, mit einer Einleitung: Sophistik, Rhetorik, Philosophik, in ihrem Kampf um die Jugenbildung.* Berlin: Weidmann, 1898.

Askowith, Dora. *The Toleration of the Jews Under Julius Caesar and Augustus.* New York: Columbia University Press, 1915.

Avi-Jonah, Michael. *The Holy Land from the Persian to the Arab Conquest (536 B.C. to A.D. 640); A Historical Geography.* Grand Rapids, Mich.: Baker Book House, 1966.

———. "Sepphoris." *Encyclopedia Judaica.* Jerusalem: Macmillan, 1971–1972. XIV.

Baillie, D. M. *Faith in God and Its Christian Consummation: The Kerr Lectures for 1926.* Edinburgh: T. & T. Clark, 1927.

Barth, Karl. *Church Dogmatics.* Trans. G. T. Thomson. Edinburgh: T. & T. Clark, 1936. I, IV.

Behm, J. "Metanoeō, etc." In *Theological Dictionary of the New Testament* [henceforth *TDNT*]. Ed. Gerhard Kittel. Trans. and ed. in English by Geoffrey W. Bromiley. Grand Rapids, Mich.: William B. Eerdmans, 1964–1976. IV, 974–980, 989–1002.

Betz, Hans Dieter. *Der Apostel Paul und die sokratische Tradition.* Beiträge zur historischen Theologie. Ed. Gerhard Ebeling, No. 45. Tübingen: Siebeck, 1972.

———. *Galatians: A Commentary on Paul's Letter to the Churches in Galatia.* Philadelphia: Fortress Press, 1979.

Bevan, Edwyn. *Jerusalem Under the High Priests: Five Lectures on the Period Between Nehemiah and the New Testament. London: Edward Arnold, 1918.*

Bikerman, Elie. "La Chaine de la tradition pharisienne." In *Essays in Greco-Roman and Related Talmudic Literature.* Ed. Henry A. Fischel. New York: KATV Publishing House, 1977. Pp. 127–137.

Boyd, William. *The History of Western Education.* 6th ed. London: Adam & Charles Black, 1959.

Bouillard, Henri. *Karl Barth: Parole de dieu et existence humaine. Deuxième partie—La Réponse de l'homme.* Aubier: Editions Montaigne, 1957. II.

Blackman, Philip, F.C.S. *Mishnayoth, In Six Volumes.* Volume III: *Order Nashim.* London: Mishna Press, Ltd., 1959.

Buber, Martin. *Two Types of Faith.* Trans. Norman P. Goldhawk, M.A. London: Macmillan, 1951.

Bultmann, Rudolf. *History of the Synoptic Tradition* Trans. John Marsh. New York: Harper & Row, 1968.

———. "Peithō." In Kittel, *TDNT.* VI.

———. "Pisteuō, etc." *TDNT.* VI.

Carpzov, J. B. *Sacrae exercitationes in St. Pauli epistolam ad Hebraeos ex Philone Alexandrino.* Amsterdam: Vveygandiana, 1750. (This work was unavailable to me.)

Chroust, Anton-Hermann. *Aristotle: New Light on His Life and on Some of His Lost Works.* London: Routledge and Kegan Paul, 1973. I, II.

Cohen, Boaz. *Jewish and Roman Law: A Comparative Study.* New York: Jewish Theological Seminary of America, 1966. I.

Conzelmann, Hans. *The Theology of St. Luke.* Trans. Geoffrey Buswell. London: Faber & Faber, 1960.

Culpepper, R. Alan. *The Johannine School: An Evaluation of the Johannine School Hypothesis Based on an Investigation of the Nature of Ancient Schools.* Society of Biblical Literature Dissertation Series, No. 26. Missoula, Mont.: Scholars Press, 1974.

Dalman, Gustaf. *Jesus-Jeshua: Studies in the Gospels.* Trans. Paul P. Levertoff. London: Society for the Promotion of Christian Knowledge, 1929.

Dancy, C. J., M.A. *A Commentary on 1 Maccabees.* Oxford: Basil Blackwell, 1954.

Daube, David. *The New Testament and Rabbinic Judaism.* London: Athlone, 1956.

———. "Rabbinic Methods of Interpretation and Hellenistic Rhetoric." *Hebrew Union College Annual* [henceforth *HUCA*], 22 (1940): 239–264.

Delorme, Jean. *Gymnasion: Etude sur les monuments consacrés à l'éducation en Grèce, des origines à l'empire romain.* No. 196 of Bibliothèque des Ecoles Françaises d'Athènes et de Rome. Paris: Editions E. de Boccard, 1960.

Dibelius, Martin. *From Tradition to Gospel.* Trans. Bertram L. Wolff. Greenwood, S.C.: Attic Press, 1971.

Diels, Hermann. *Die Fragmente der Vorsokratiker.* Ed. Walther Kranz. Zurich: Weidman, 1968.

Drazin, Nathan. *History of Jewish Education from 515 B.C.E. to 220 C.E..* The Johns Hopkins Studies in Education, No. 29. Baltimore: Johns Hopkins University Press, 1940.

Ebeling, Gerhard. *The Nature of Faith.* Trans. Ronald Gregor Smith. Philadelphia: Muhlenberg Press, 1961.

———. *Word and Faith.* Trans. James W. Leitch. London: SCM Press, Ltd., 1960.

Ellis, E. Earle. "How the New Testament Uses the Old." In *New Testament Interpretation: Essays on Principles and Methods.* Ed. I. Howard Marshall. Grand Rapids, Mich.: William B. Eerdmans, 1977. Pp. 199–219.

Feldman, Louis H. "The Orthodoxy of the Jews in Hellenistic Egypt." *Jewish Social Studies,* 23 (1960): 215–237.

Fischel, Henry A. "Story and History: Observations on Greco-Roman Rhetoric and Pharisaism." In *Essays in Greco-Roman and Related Talmudic Literature.* Ed. Henry A. Fischel. New York: KTAV Publishing House, 1977. Pp. 443–472.

Foerster, Werner. "Iēsous." *TDNT,* III. 284–293.

Gauthier, René Antoine, O.P., and Jolif Jean Yves, O.P. *Aristote: L'Ethique à Nicomaque.* Louvain: Publications Universitaires de Louvain, 1959. II.

Gerhardsson, Birger. *Memory and Manuscript: Oral Tradition and Written Transmission in Rabbinic Judaism and Early Christianity.* Lund: C. W. K. Gleerup, 1961.

Gitay, Yehoshua. *Prophecy and Persuasion: A Study of Isaiah 40–48.* Forum Theologiae Linguisticae, No. 14. Ed. Erhardt Güttemans. Bonn: Linguistica Biblica, 1981.

Goodenough, Erwin R. *By Light, Light: The Mystic Gospel of Hellenistic Judaism.* New Haven, Conn.: Yale University Press, 1935.

Goppelt, L. *Typos: Die typologische Deutung des Alten Testaments im Neuen.* Darmstadt: Wissenschaftliche Buchgesellschaft, 1969.

Goth, Joachim. *Nietzsche und die Rhetorik: Untersuchungen zur deutschen Literaturgeschichte.* Tübingen: Max Niemeyer Verlag, 1970.

Grimaldi, William M. A., S.J. *Aristotle—Rhetoric I: A Commentary.* New York: Fordham University Press, 1980.

———. *Studies in the Philosophy of Aristotle's Rhetoric.* Einzelschriften, Heft 25, *Hermes: Zeitschrift für klassische Philologie.* Wiesbaden: Franz Steiner Verlag, 1972.

Guthrie, W. K. C. *A History of Greek Philosophy.* Cambridge: Cambridge University Press, 1975. IV.

Hadas, Moses, ed. and trans. *The Third and Fourth Book of the Maccabees.* New York: Harper & Brothers, 1953.

Halévi, E. E. "Greek Topoi in Aggadic Literature [translation]." *Tarbiz,* 40 (1970): 293–300.

Hamer, Jerome, O.P. *Karl Barth.* Trans. Dominic Maruca. Westminster, Md.: Newman Press, 1962.

Hammond World Atlas. Maplewood, N.J.: Hammond, 1926.

Harnack, Carl J. A. von. *History of Dogma.* Trans. from the 3d German ed. by Neil Buchanan. New York: Russell & Russell, 1958. I.

Hatch, Edwin, and Henry Redpath. *A Concordance to the Septuagint and the Other Greek Versions of the Old Testament (Including the Apocryphal Books).* Graz, Austria: Akademische Druck U. Verlagsanstalt, 1954. II.

Hatch, William Henry Paine. *The Pauline Idea of Faith in Its Relation to Jewish and Hellenistic Religion.* Harvard Theological Studies II. Cambridge, Mass.: Harvard University Press, 1917. Rpt., New York: Kraus Reprint Co., 1969.

Hengel, Martin. *Judaism and Hellenism: Studies in Their Encounter in Palestine During the Early Hellenistic Period.* Trans. John Bowden. Philadelphia: Fortress Press, 1974. I, II.

Hoehner, Harold. *Herod Antipas.* Cambridge: Cambridge University Press, 1972.

Isocrates. *Isocrates.* Trans. George Norlin. The Loeb Classical Library. Cambridge, Mass.: Harvard University Press, 1954. I, II, III.

Jacobs, L. "Hermeneutics." *Encyclopedia Judaica.* Jerusalem: *Encylopedia Judaica,* 1971. VIII.

Jacobs, Louis. *Faith.* London: Valentine, Mitchell, 1968.

Jaeger, Werner. *Aristotle: Fundamentals of the History of His Development.* Trans. Richard Robinson. Oxford: Clarendon Press, 1948.

———. *Early Christianity and Greek Paideia.* Cambridge, Mass.: Belknap Press of Harvard University Press, 1961.

Jonas, Hans. *The Gnostic Religion: The Message of the Alien God and the Beginnings of Christianity.* 2d ed. Boston: Beacon Press, 1963.

Jones, A. H. M. *The Greek City from Alexander to Justinian.* Oxford: Clarendon Press, 1940.

Josephus, Flavius. *Josephus.* Trans. H. St. J. Thackeray, I–IV; H. St. J. Thackeray and Ralph Marcus, V; Ralph Marcus, VI–VII; Ralph Marcus and Allen

Wikgren, VIII; L. H. Feldman, IX. The Loeb Classical Library. London: W. Heinemann, 1926.

———. *Josephus, Complete Works.* Trans. William Wiston. Grand Rapids, Mich.: Kregel Publications, 1960.

Kee, Howard Clark. *Aretologies, Hellenistic "Lives," and the Sources of Mark.* Berkeley, Calif.: The Center for Hermeneutical Studies in Hellenistic and Modern Culture, 1975.

———. *Community of the New Age.* Philadelphia: Westminster Press, 1977.

Kennedy, George. *The Art of Rhetoric in the Roman World.* Princeton, N.J.: Princeton University Press, 1972.

Kermode, John Frank. *The Genesis of Secrecy: On the Interpretation of Narrative.* Cambridge, Mass.: Harvard University Press, 1979.

Keyes, G. L. *Christian Faith and the Interpretation of History.* Lincoln, Neb.: University of Nebraska Press, 1966.

Kinneavy, James L. "Contemporary Rhetoric." In Winifred Horner, ed. *The Present State of Scholarship in Historical and Contemporary Rhetoric.* Columbia, Mo.: University of Missouri Press, 1983. pp. 167–213.

———. *A Theory of Discourse.* New York: W. W. Norton, 1980.

Kirk, G. S., and J. E. Raven. *The Presocratic Philosophers: A Critical History with a Selection of Texts.* Cambridge: Cambridge University Press, 1971.

Kittel, Gerhard, ed. *Theological Dictionary of the New Testament.* Ed. and trans. in English, Geoffrey W. Bromiley. Grand Rapids, Mich.: William B. Eerdmans, 1964–1976. I, IV, VI.

Klausner, J. "Chapter IX: Judah Aristobulus and Jannaeus Alexander." In Abraham Schalit, ed. *The World History of the Jewish People.* Volume VI: *The Hellenistic Age—Political History of Jewish Palestine from 332 B.C.E. to 67 B.C.E.*. New Brunswick, N.J.: Rutgers University Press, 1972. VI, 222–241.

Koester, Helmut. "One Jesus and Four Primitive Gospels." In J. M. Robinson, ed. *Trajectories Through Early Christianity.* Philadelphia: Fortress Press, 1971.

Lacy, P. H. de. "Epicureanism and the Epicurean School." In Paul Edwards, ed. *The Encyclopedia of Philosophy.* New York: Macmillan, 1967. III.

Lewis, D. M. "Review of J. N. Sevenster, *Do You Know Greek? How Much Greek Could the First Christians Have Known?*" *Journal of Theological Studies,* 20 (1969): 583–588.

Liddell, Henry George, and Robert Scott. *A Greek-English Lexicon.* 9th ed. rev. Henry Stuart Jones, Robert McKenzie. Oxford: Clarendon Press, 1968.

Lieberman, Saul. *Greek in Jewish Palestine.* New York: Jewish Theological Seminary of America, 1942.

———. *Hellenism in Jewish Palestine.* New York: Jewish Theological Seminary of America, 1950.

Long, A. A. *Hellenistic Philosophy: Stoics, Epicureans, Skeptics,* London: Gerald Duckworth and Company, Limited 1974.

Lührmann, Dieter. "Pistis im Judentum." *Zeitschrift für Neutestamentliche Wissenschaft,* 64:1–2 (1973): 19–38.

Lundbom, Jack R. *Jeremiah: A Study in Ancient Hebrew Rhetoric.* Society of

Biblical Literature and Scholars Press, Dissertation Series, No. 18. Missoula, Mont.: Society of Biblical Literature, 1975.

Marmorstein, Arthur. "The Background of the Haggadah." *Hebrew Union College Annual,* 6 (1929): 141–204.

Marrou, Henri I. *Histoire de l'éducation dans l'antiquité.* 6th ed., rev. and enlarged. Paris: Editions du Seuil, 1965.

———. *A History of Education in Antiquity.* Trans. George Lamb. London: Sheed and Ward, 1956.

Merkelbach, R. "Die griechische Wortschatz und die Christen." *Zeitschrift für Papyrologie und Epigraphik,* 18:2 (1975): 101–149.

Moraux, Paul. *Der Aristotelismus bei den Griechen von Andronikos bis Alexander von Aphrodisias.* Erster Band: *Die Renaissance des Aristotelismus im I. J. v. Chr.* Berlin, New York: Walter de Gruyter, 1973.

Negev, Abraham, ed. *Archaeological Encyclopedia of the Holy Land.* Englewood, N.J.: SBS Publishing, 1980.

———. "Sepphoris." In ibid.

The New English Bible with the Apocrypha. Ed. Samuel Sandmel. Oxford Study Edition. New York: Oxford University Press, 1976.

O'Connor, Edward D., C.S.C. *Faith in the Synoptic Gospels: A Problem in the Correlation of Scripture and Theology.* South Bend, Ind.: University of Notre Dame Press, 1961.

Oldfather, Charles Henry. "The Greek Literary Texts from Greco-Roman Egypt: A Study in the History of Civilization." *University of Wisconsin Studies in the Social Sciences and History.* 9 (1923): 1–104.

Pausanias. *Description of Greece,* Trans. W. H. S. Jones. The Loeb Classical Library. Cambridge, Mass.: Harvard University Press, 1954. VI.

Pélékidis, Chrysis. *Histoire de l'éphébie attique des origines à 31 avant Jésus.* Paris: Editions E. de Boccard, 1962.

Perelman, Chaim. *The Realm of Rhetoric.* Trans. William Kluback. South Bend, Ind.: University of Notre Dame Press, 1982.

Pinner, H. L. *The World of Books in Classical Antiquity.* Leiden: A. W. Sijthoff, 1948.

Plato. *Plato.* The Dialogues trans. Benjamin Jowett; "The Seventh Letter," trans. J. Harward. Great Books of the Western World, No. 7. Ed. Robert Maynard Hutchins. Chicago: Encyclopaedia Britannica, 1952.

Plutarch. *The Lives of the Noble Greeks and Romans.* The Dryden Translation. Great Books of the Western World, No. 14. Chicago: Encyclopaedia Britannica, 1952.

Pomeroy, Susan. "Selected Bibliography on Women in Antiquity." *Arethusa,* 6:1 (1973): 125–157.

Quintilian. *Institutiones Oratoriae.* Trans. H. E. Butler. The Loeb Classical Library. Cambridge, Mass.: Harvard University Press, 1921. III.

Ricoeur, Paul. *The Rule of Metaphor: Multidisciplinary Studies of the Creation of Meaning.* Trans. Robert Czerny. Toronto: University of Toronto Press, 1977.

Reitzenstein, Richard. *Hellenistic Mystery Religions: Their Basic Ideas and Significance.* Trans. John E. Steely. Pittsburgh: Pickwick Press, 1978.

Rengstorf, Karl Heinrich, ed. *A Complete Concordance to Flavius Josephus*. Leiden: E. J. Brill, 1973.

———. "Didaskō, etc." *TDNT*. II.

Sandmel, Samuel. *The First Christian Century in Judaism and Christianity*. New York: Oxford University Press, 1960.

Schalit, Abraham, ed. *Zur Josephus-Forschung*. Darmstadt: Wissenschaftliche Buchgesellschaft, 1973.

Schlatter, Adolf. *Der Glaube im Neuen Testament*. 5th ed. Stuttgart: Colwer Verlag, 1963.

Schrekenberg, Hans. *Arbeiten zur Literatur und Geschichte des hellenistischen Judentums*. Volume I: *Bibliographie zu Flavius Josephus*. Leiden: E. J. Brill, 1978.

Schürer, Emil. *The History of the Jewish People in the Age of Jesus (175 B.C. to A.D. 135)*. A new English version rev. and ed. Geza Vermes, Fergus Millar, and Matthew Black; original trans. John MacPherson. Edinburgh: T. & T. Clark, 1979. I, II.

———. *The Literature of the Jewish People in the Time of Jesus*. Trans. Peter Christie and Sophia Taylor, ed. and intro. by Nathan Galzer. New York: Schocken, 1972.

Sevenster, J. N. *Do You Know Greek? How Much Greek Could the First Christians Have Known?* Trans. J. de Bruin. Leiden: E. J. Brill, 1968.

Simon, Abram. "The Biblical Era." *Jewish Education: Historical Survey*. Philadelphia: Jewish Chataqua Society, 1912.

Slater, Philip E. "The Greek Family in History and Myth." *Arethusa*, 7:1 (1974): 9–44.

Smallwood, E. Mary. *The Jews Under Roman Rule*. Leiden: E. J. Brill, 1976.

Smith, William, ed. "Peithō." *Dictionary of Greek and Roman Biography*. New York: AMS Press, 1967. III.

Snell, Bruno. *The Discovery of the Mind: The Greek Origins of European Thought*. Trans. T. G. Rosemeyer. Oxford: Basil Blackwell, 1953.

Spengel, Leonardi, ed. *Rhetores Graeci*. 3 vols. Leipzig: B. G. Teubner, 1883; reprinted Frankfurt am Main: Minerva, 1966. I, II, III.

Spicq, C., O.P. *L'Epître aux Hebreux*. Paris: Librairie Lecoffre, 1952. I.

Stegenga, J. *The Greek-English Analytical Concordance of the Greek-English New Testament*. Jackson, Miss.: Hellenes–English Biblical Foundation, 1963.

Stein, Edmund. "Die homiletische Peroratio im Midrasch." *HUCA*, 8–9 (1931–1932): 353–371.

Stendhal, Krister. *The School of St. Matthew and Its Use of the Old Testament*. Lund: C. W. K. Gleerup, 1954.

Tarn, Sir William Woodthorpe. *Hellenistic Civilization*. 3d ed., rev. by the author and G. T. Griffith. New York: World, 1961.

Tcherikover, Victor. *Hellenistic Civilization and the Jews*. Trans. S. Applebaum. Philadelphia: Jewish Publication Society of America, 1959.

Untersteiner, Mario. *The Sophists*. Trans. Kathleen Freeman. Oxford: Basil Blackwell, 1954.

Voigt, W.P. "Peithō." *Paulys Real-Encyclopädie des klassischen Altertums Wissen-*

schaft. Ed. Georg Wissowa and Wilhelm Kroll. Stuttgart: J. B. Metzlehrsche Verlagsbuchhandlung, 1938. XIX.

Watson, George. *The Stoic Theory of Knowledge.* Belfast: The Queen's University, 1966.

Weiser, Artur. "The Old Testament Concept." In "Pisteuō, etc." *TDNT.* VI.

Wigram, George V. *The Englishman's Greek Concordance of the New Testament.* Ninth edition. Grand Rapids, Mich.: Zondervan Publishing House, 1971. (This is a reprint of the 1903 edition.)

Williamson, Ronald. *Philo and the Epistle to the Hebrews.* Leiden: E. J. Brill, 1970.

Witt, R. E. "Albinus and the History of Middle Platonism." *Transactions of the Cambridge Philological Society,* Volume VII. Cambridge: Cambridge University Press, 1937.

Wolfson, Harry Austryn. *Philo: Foundations of Religious Philosophy in Judaism, Christianity, and Islam.* Cambridge, Mass.: Harvard University Press, 1962. I.

Wolfson, Harry Austryn. "The Double Faith Theory in Clement, Saadia, Averroes and St. Thomas, and its Origin in Aristotle and the Stoics." *Jewish Quarterly Review,* 33 (1942–1943): 213–264.

Würthwein, E. "*Metanoeō,* etc." In Kittel, *TDNT,* IV, 980–989.

Zeitlin, Solomon. *The Second Book of the Maccabees, Edited with Introduction and Commentary.* Trans. Sidney Tedesche. New York: Harper & Brothers, 1954.

Zeller, Eduard. *The Stoics, Epicureans, and Sceptics.* Trans. Rev. Oswald J. Reichel. London: Longmans, Green, and Co., 1892.

Index